GW00838331

Anything Dale Ralph Davis touches t
say that about the Scriptures since 1
thus I should say that Davis reveals to
there. His commentary on Luke is clas
insightful exposition along with theolc
commentaries, I find it quite easy to set them aside, but Davis's
exposition of Luke is so winsome, wise, and illuminating that I
found it hard to put down. His pastoral application with stories
and illustrations is nothing short of brilliant. Read the exposition,
meditate and pray on what you read, and encounter Jesus Christ.

Thomas R. Schreiner
James Buchanan Harrison Professor of New Testament Interpretation
Associate Dean, The Southern Baptist Theological Seminary,
Louisville, Kentucky

Many colorful words describe this book. To name just ten: practical,
scholarly, whimsical, logical, shrewd, humorous, insightful,
creative, thoughtful, gripping. But best of all it is true to the text
and intent of Luke's Gospel and its focal point, Jesus Christ.
Davis wonderfully combines a scholar's skills and wisdom with
a storyteller's knack and a pastoral heart. The reader will learn
Luke's Gospel afresh, see details from fresh angles, and be better
equipped to grasp its message, grow in faith, and share this good
news with others.

Robert W. Yarbrough
Professor of New Testament, Covenant Theological Seminary,
St. Louis, Missouri, USA

Brimming with insightful exegesis, theological depth, vivid illustration and pastoral application, these two volumes are vintage
Dale Ralph Davis. Whether you use them in personal devotion, or
a small group, or as a preacher seeking to teach your congregation,
this engaging journey through Luke's gospel will be a very useful
and edifying guide.

Reuben Hunter
Pastor, Trinity West Church, West London

A remarkable, crisply written, practical expository commentary.
As always, Dale Ralph Davis does what any skilled chef does. With
due diligence, Davis raids the exegetical pantry stocked with Bible
dictionaries, Bible translations, exegetical-critical commentaries,
theological wordbooks, scholarly articles, and other written works
on Luke. Using the ingredients gathered, he insightfully engages

the text of Scripture with a solid understanding of the original language and the perspective of an Old Testament Scholar. Then, in his characteristically plain-spoken and often witty style of writing, Ralph serves up a straightforward, theocentric, finger-on-the Text, applicable, engaging, and incredibly tasty two-volume commentary on the Gospel of Luke. Davis not only informs your mind (helpful technical footnotes are included on the bottom of the pages); he feeds your soul, fills your heart, and moves you to praise and thank God for the one who came to seek and to save the lost (Luke 19:10).

Steve Jussely
Senior Pastor, Lakeland Presbyterian Church (PCA),
Flowood, Mississippi,
Former Adjunct Professor of Homiletics,
Reformed Theological Seminary

Written with Dale Ralph Davis' usual clarity, humour and warmth, these volumes will not only serve as a sure guide to help readers understand Luke's Gospel but will strengthen them in their faith in the Jesus about whom Luke writes. Peter Orr
Lecturer in New Testament,
Moore Theological College, Sydney

Dr Davis is one of the most hospitable commentators you'll ever know. His books, like his preaching, have an unusual ability to combine theological precision with a warm and pleasant style. You'll be glad you opened the cover and settled in. You won't find the drudgery and technicality that are common in other commentators. But you will find helpful and engaging footnotes. You also won't find even a hint of the dry, doubting, soul-sucking unbelief that resides in many academic commentaries. But here is a scholar (he is a ninja in the original languages) and a convicted pastor and a winsome believer. In Dr Davis' Luke exposition, your eye is drawn to authorial intent and your heart is drawn to the matchlessness of Christ. Dr Davis continually reminds me to preach with the agenda of the text at the forefront and the wise pastor's effort to speak to the people where they are and bring them into the world of the text. This masterful Old Testament preacher knows his way around the New Testament as well! Austin T Duncan
Professor of Pastoral Ministries, Director of D.Min Studies, Director,
The MacArthur Center for Expository Preaching,
The Master's Seminary, Los Angeles, California

LUKE

The Year of the Lord's Favor

Dale Ralph Davis

CHRISTIAN
FOCUS

Dale Ralph Davis lives in Tennessee with his wife. He was formerly Minister in Residence of First Presbyterian Church, Columbia, South Carolina. Prior to that he was pastor of Woodland Presbyterian Church, Hattiesburg, Mississippi and Professor of Old Testament at Reformed Theological Seminary, Jackson, Mississippi.

Copyright © 2021 Dale Ralph Davis

ISBN 978-1-5271-0638-3

10 9 8 7 6 5 4 3 2 1

Printed in 2021
by
Christian Focus Publications Ltd.,
Geanies House, Fearn, Ross-shire,
IV20 1TW, Scotland, U.K.

www.christianfocus.com

Cover design by Moose77

Printed and bound by
Bell & Bain, Glasgow

Contents

Abbreviations

AB	Anchor Bible
ABD	*Anchor Bible Dictionary*
AV	Authorized Version
BECNT	Baker Exegetical Commentary on the New Testament
BST	The Bible Speaks Today
CSB	Christian Standard Bible
DJG	*Dictionary of Jesus and the Gospels*
EBC	*Expositor's Bible Commentary*
EGGN	Exegetical Guide to the Greek New Testament
ESV	English Standard Version
HCSB	Holman Christian Standard Bible
ICC	International Critical Commentary
ISBE	*International Standard Bible Encyclopedia*
KJV	King James Version
LXX	The Septuagint
NAC	New American Commentary
NASB	New American Standard Bible (updated ed.)
NDB	*New Bible Dictionary*
NCB	New Century Bible
NET	New English Translation
NICNT	New International Commentary on the New Testament

NICOT	New International Commentary on the Old Testament
NIDB	*New Interpreter's Dictionary of the Bible*
NIDNTTE	*New International Dictionary of New Testament Theology and Exegesis*
NIGTC	New International Greek Testament Commentary
NIV	New International Version
NKJV	New King James Version
PNTC	Pillar New Testament Commentary
RSV	Revised Standard Version
TDNT	*Theological Dictionary of the New Testament*
TEV	Today's English Version
TNTC	Tyndale New Testament Commentaries
TOTC	Tyndale Old Testament Commentaries
TWOT	*Theological Wordbook of the Old Testament*
ZECNT	Zondervan Exegetical Commentary on the New Testament
ZIBBC	*Zondervan Illustrated Bible Backgrounds Commentary*

Preface

I have a personality disorder that has controlled my life. I am always driven to pull for the underdog. Which explains why I have spent most of my academic and pastoral days preaching, teaching, and writing on what we usually call the Old Testament. It has always been, it seems, the 'under-testament,' shamefully neglected in the church. One dreams, then, of redressing that wrong. Still, one dare not ignore the New Testament. One dare not want to right a wrong by committing another wrong; hence I've probably spent forty per cent of my time in NT studies, though, for myself, I tend to find the New Testament more difficult than the Old Testament. One day, while in a New Testament orbit, I had noticed that the 'Focus on the Bible' series seemed to have no 'Luke' volume. One should not be curious about such things, but, upon inquiry, I was told I could submit one if I liked. Which nicely occupied four years.

I should alert you to certain matters. This commentary is exegetically based but is cast in an expository form and is not allergic to application (though I do not major on this last). I try at least to keep a proper balance between 'forest' and 'trees.' Translations of biblical texts are my own unless noted otherwise. And I've provided no 'proper' introduction to Luke (see the first chapter). As our forebears might say, there are 'sundry and divers' places where a reader can find that material.

This book is the work of an unprofitable servant (17:10) but is nevertheless dedicated to the One who came to seek and to save the lost (19:10)—even though He had to come into a Presbyterian manse to find him.

DALE RALPH DAVIS

June 2020

9

A Working Outline for Luke

[The commentary does not religiously follow this outline; it is provided as a 'reader's map' for Luke's gospel]

Preface, 1:1-4

I. **A New Chapter in World History, 1:5-4:13**
Remnant church, 1:5-2:52
Faithful forerunner, 3:1-20
Triumphant Savior, 3:21-4:13

II. **The Year of the Lord's Favor, 4:14-9:50**
An introduction to Jesus' ministry, 4:14-5:16
Negative, 4:14-30
Positive, 4:31-5:16
Jesus and His critics, 5:17-6:11
An introduction to Jesus' teaching, 6:12-49
Jesus and His friends, 7:1-50 (centurion, widow, John, sinner)
The problem of the word of God, 8:1-21
Jesus and His triumphs, 8:22-56
An introduction to Jesus' discipleship, 9:1-50

III. **The Turn in the Road (or: The Shadow of the Cross), 9:51-19:10**
Preparing the Lord's way, 9:51-10:24
A critique of Judaism, 10:25-37
Proper devotion, 10:38-11:13

I

Always Read the Preface
(Luke 1:1-4)

Let's pretend that my four older brothers decided to compile a cookbook of their favorite recipes and dishes. Let's say it's about 200 pages and organized into the customary gastronomical categories (desserts, meats, casseroles, appetizers, etc.). If you simply browsed through, you might be struck with the absence of any recipes using or dealing with chicken. You may find this frustrating and even maddening after a while. However, had you taken time to read the preface, you would not be perplexed. In the preface my brothers would have explained all. They don't eat chicken; they don't care for chicken. It goes back to their childhood. Our father, a pastor, would periodically come home from making a pastoral call on one of his farming parishioners. The farmer had given my father a live chicken; it was placed in a burlap bag and imprisoned in the trunk (boot) of his car for transit. When he arrived home, he would take his axe to the chicken's neck and then my brothers were enlisted in the nauseating job of defeathering the creature and preparing it for its skillet debut. This smelly process served to bring about a certain alienation from all things 'chicken'. Today one would say they suffer from 'chicken intolerance'. Now if they compiled a cookbook, I am sure they would have included a chicken-absence-explanation in the preface—but you would need to read the preface or you would be baffled and irritated by the chicken omission.

It's the same with a gospel—like Luke's. Don't skip the preface. It's there you find some clue of *what* the gospel is about, *why* he wanted to write it, and *how* he went about the task. It may save you some frustration and help you to know what to expect. I know it's usual even in a shorter commentary like this to include a few pages on author, date, background, and so on. But that's been done so often that I tend to think it unnecessary.[1] We can touch on some of those things as needed. But Luke has written his own introduction to his gospel and I'd much rather pay attention to that.

Perhaps most importantly Luke tells us there is a **fascination** at the heart of his 'gospel project'. He says that 'many have taken in hand to compile a narrative of the events that have reached fulfillment among us' (v. 1). Part of the fascination comes from expectancy—these matters did not merely occur, happen, or get accomplished (cf. NASB, ESV); rather they have 'reached fulfillment'.[2] Such matters, he implies, were the grist of (what we call) 'Old Testament' prophecies—promises and predictions—and they have now come to pass. To see that generates a certain excitement. Nor is this fascination peculiar to Luke. *Many*, he says, have attempted to write up accounts of these things. Does the 'many' include other 'gospel' writers, like, for example, Mark? Perhaps. But it must include quite a number of folks who wrote accounts of one sort or another. Can we envision a Christian writing up a 'gospel tract' rehearsing three or four of Jesus' miracles in order to explain Jesus to non-Christian neighbors? Perhaps. 'Many' were drawn into this task apparently by sheer interest and preoccupation with Jesus' story.

Then Luke tells us that he himself was bitten by this bug: 'it seemed good to me also to write' (v. 3). There were the 'many'; there was Luke himself—such an *eagerness* all around to pass on the gospel record. I think we can easily miss this

---

1. See the treatment in D. A. Carson and Douglas J. Moo, *An Introduction to the New Testament*, 2nd ed. (Grand Rapids: Zondervan, 2005), pp. 198-224, who argue for authorship by Luke the physician, a Gentile, and propose a date in the mid-to-late 60s (A.D.). Robert J. Cara prefers to date Luke in the A.D. 50s or early 60s! See his discussion in Michael J. Kruger, ed., *A Biblical-Theological Introduction to the New Testament* (Wheaton, IL: Crossway, 2016), pp. 93-113, especially pp. 94-96.

2. For discussion, see J. A. Fitzmyer, *The Gospel According to Luke I-IX*, AB (Garden City, NY: Doubleday, 1981), p. 293.

note of fascination in Luke's preface. The whole story gave early believers itchy pens. And it wasn't simply that ancient prophecy was being fulfilled; it was, above all, *Jesus Himself* who so attracted them. He whetted their appetite, He stirred their interest; they somehow couldn't get over Him, couldn't get enough of Him!

Barbara Tuchman tells of once speaking with a young member of a college history department. He was bogged down in his doctoral thesis; it was about an early missionary in the Congo who had never been 'done' before. 'I just don't like him,' he said. Sad when one can't muster enthusiasm for the task of obtaining one's academic union card. All of which led Tuchman to say, '[I]t is this quality of *being in love with your subject* that is indispensable for writing good history.'[3] Luke's gospel then should be 'good,' for he's clearly in love with his subject, along with many others at the time. They were captivated by Jesus; they simply couldn't leave His story alone. And where is our fascination?

Secondly, Luke says there's a **passion** that marks this gospel story (vv. 2-3a). It's a passion for accuracy—and not merely on Luke's part but on the part of the 'many' others who had sketched accounts. They passed on their story 'just as' the original eyewitnesses of the gospel events had 'handed them on'.[4] There was a concern for exactness; they refused to fudge or pad or exaggerate what came to them from the eyewitnesses. And Luke himself followed suit. His work was characterized by the most painstaking and thorough research: 'it seemed (good) to me also, having followed all things carefully from the beginning...' (v. 3a). One can imagine, among other things, that when Luke was with Paul in Jerusalem (Acts 21:15), and perhaps in Israel during Paul's two-year confinement in Caesarea (Acts 24:27), that he could well have interviewed any number of original eyewitnesses and confirmed their testimonies.

Sometimes we don't always appreciate the care artists and others take in producing their work. Norman Rockwell

3. Barbara W. Tuchman, *Practicing History* (New York: Alfred A. Knopf, 1981), p. 14 (emphasis mine).

4. The eyewitnesses were those who 'became servants of the word'. I identify these primarily with the apostles.

produced a cover, called *The Shiner*, for 'The Saturday Evening Post.' It shows a girl about ten with red braids and a black eye, sitting outside the school principal's office. She's perhaps had a fight with a boy? Rockwell's model was Mary Whalen, the daughter of his lawyer. But how to paint a 'black eye,' which can sometimes show a variety of colors. He checked a local hospital for eye-injured patients—there were none. He told a newspaper reporter he would accept a black eye in any of its advanced stages of discoloration. Several hundred people, including many prisoners, responded. He finally used as his model a two-and-a-half-year-old boy who had fallen down a flight of stairs and come up with two shiners. Rockwell painted the bruise on little Tommy Forsberg's eye on to 'Mary Whalen's' face.[5] All that trouble and care just to get it right. And Luke is saying that he and his predecessors took the utmost care to be exact and accurate in their writing.[6] It was a passion.

Some might object that since Luke and others had an *agenda* (to win people to Jesus) they obviously must have 'souped up' the truth in order to make their account more convincing. But they dared not do that. There were gobs of eyewitnesses around in the first century and not all eyewitnesses were pro-Jesus. In the first century there were many eyewitnesses who were hostile to Jesus and opposed to the apostles. If the early Christians, whether in written accounts or in oral witness, had exaggerated or twisted the truth, they would've been exposed by the 'anti-Jesus' coalition. They *had* to be careful with their claims. So, it is simply not true that evangelism compromises historicity; rather, evangelism demands accuracy. And since such care was taken for truth, you need to face its claims.

Finally, Luke tells us his **intention** in writing his gospel: 'to write an orderly account for you, most excellent Theophilus, in order that you can know the certainty of the matters of which you've been instructed' (vv. 3b-4).

I take Theophilus to be the real name of an individual, who was likely already a Christian but needed additional

---

5. Deborah Solomon, *American Mirror: The Life and Art of Norman Rockwell* (New York: Farrar, Straus and Giroux, 2013), p. 280.

6. I am not denying the God-breathed or 'inspired' character of Luke's gospel; but inspiration does not negate perspiration.

instruction. He may have been reasonably wealthy—some think he covered Luke's publishing costs (cf. also Acts 1:1). Luke designed to write 'an orderly account' for him. This phrase translates an adverb (*kathechēs*), only used in Luke and Acts in the New Testament. Luke uses it in Acts 11:4, where the NASB translates it 'in orderly sequence'. That is likely the idea here. It need not imply a strict or slavishly chronological report but certainly a connected, coherent, and generally sequential account that one could readily follow. Luke is hot after *readability*, and that is important. Luke knows that both veracity *and* packaging matter. Truth (vv. 1-3a) is vital but one can damage truth if it is not presented attractively. I remember once reading of a US congressman or senator who was debating before his peers the viability of a proposal and closed his argument by asking, 'But can it be did?' He may have been on the right side of the issue, but his grammatical monstrosity sullied his point. Luke believed truth was worthy of his best presentation.

Of course, Luke's goal was to use both accuracy and readability as the means to bring assurance and stability to the faith of Theophilus (v. 4). A Christian's assurance may come and go and be affected by all sorts of matters, but it will never begin to exist unless built on the firm foundation of a true gospel.

2

A Funny Thing Happened in Church
(Luke 1:5-25)

Luke begins his gospel story with a sketch of the remnant church. He introduces us to the likes of Zechariah and Elizabeth, Mary and Joseph, Simeon and Anna—folks we might call 'Old Testament' believers, who are clinging to Yahweh and waiting for His kingdom. And, as Luke the historian carefully notes, it all happened 'in the days of Herod, king of Judea' (v. 5a).[1] Then Luke makes his move. It's as if he says: As for what is historical, it took place in Herod's reign, but as for what is *significant*, it has to do with an obscure priest named Zechariah who's squirreled away in the hill country of Judah. He seems to delight in the strange focus of the gospel story; it has its backdrop in secular history, but primary attention falls on the remnant church, the servants God has kept and who call on His name. This will prove typical of Luke: to make some prominent ruler provide the background and then focus on someone who at first glance would seem utterly inconsequential.

Luke's manner reminds me of my high school Algebra teacher. Mr McCamley [M'-CAME-lee] had a kind of relaxed way about him. As he looked at a certain student, he would begin describing the specific items in the algebra problem

---

1. This is Herod 'the Great,' who ruled 37–4 B.C. 'Judea' here means 'Palestine at large' (cf. 4:44; 23:5), including Judea proper, Samaria, Galilee, and part of Perea.

under review, which often caused a bit of tension in the
student he was addressing, because said student assumed
that momentarily he/she would be asked some particular
question dealing with the vagaries of the problem. But this
almost never happened. Even with his eyes locked on the
worried student, he would say something like, 'So how
would you handle that, Mr. _____'—calling the name of
another student three rows over and four seats back. One had
to be ready; the stress was not usually on the obvious. And
that is Luke's pattern: Herod is necessary for chronology, but
the real story of the kingdom picks up with this priest and his
barren wife in the backwater of Judah.

Perhaps the best way to get at this passage is by
highlighting the testimony Luke provides. First, he gives us **an
encouraging—and sobering—picture of the people of God**
(vv. 5-7). Luke begins with the huge fact that matters most:
'they [Zechariah and Elizabeth] were both righteous before
God' (v. 6a). That refers to their standing in God's sight—
they are 'justified'. Then Luke details how that right standing
plays out: they were 'going along in all the commandments
of the Lord blamelessly' (v. 6b). Verse 6b is not the cause of
their right standing (v. 6a) but the fruit or result of it. Their
right standing (6a) led them to right living (6b).

Here is a marvelous thing. You barely step out of the Old
Testament and here, already, you run into the people of God.
They are still here—extant in the world. Israel has come
through the Babylonian exile, through Persian domination,
through the ravages of Antiochus Epiphanes, and now
they are under the thumb of the Romans, but Yahweh still
has a faithful people. Well, look at them. There they are—
Zechariah and Elizabeth. What glorious stubbornness on
God's part to preserve through thick and thin a people who
hold on to His word!

Yet there's a sad note: this couple has no child. Elizabeth
is barren. Nor is there much hope; they are both up in years.
The positive and the negative are side-by-side: they were both
righteous before God (6a) and they had no child (7). Isn't this
sort of combination frequently 'normal'? That is, there are
those who are true servants of the Lord and yet some trial,
some disappointment, that may be life-long, hangs over their

lives. 'Righteous before God' yet 'they had no child'. A very huge fact and a very deep sadness are pressed together. This leads into another observation: Luke underscores **the circumstances in which God delights to work** (e.g., vv. 7, 18). With Elizabeth's barrenness and what follows, Luke suggests that God does His most impressive works in a context of impossibility. Verse 7 resurrects a familiar Old Testament motif. Elizabeth is only the next-to-last candidate for Most Unlikely Mother of the Year.

Sarah is the first exhibit of this biblical pattern (Gen. 18). Everyone knew 90-year-old, post-menopausal Sarah couldn't have a son (Isaac), except that she did (Gen. 21) because promise trumped genetics. Then Rebekah, Isaac's wife, was barren for the first twenty years of their marriage until their twins, Esau and Jacob, were born (Gen. 25). Rachel was childless until at long last Joseph was born (Gen. 30). In Judges 13 we meet the wife of Manoah; she was barren, but, as God promised, gave birth to Samson. One might include Ruth, who had no children by a first marriage—would her marriage to Boaz (Ruth 4) prove otherwise? Obed is proof of it. Hannah obviously had a horrid emotional roller-coaster over her barrenness (1 Sam. 1) until Yahweh gave her Samuel. Nor should we forget the unnamed woman from Shunem in 2 Kings 4—and her unnamed son. All of which backs up what we see in Luke 1—God tends to begin His finest works in the face of human hopelessness and human weakness.

Third, Luke shows us **what a high regard God holds toward the prayers of His people** (vv. 8-17). 'Your prayer has been heard' (v. 13). How often in future days the angel's words must've haunted Zechariah—in a good way. The prayer in question was his prayer for a child, as the next lines of verse 13 show: 'and your wife Elizabeth will bear you a son and you will call his name John.' It was a prayer that Zechariah had probably long ceased to pray.

But we are getting ahead of ourselves. The angel had appeared to Zechariah during a premier moment in his life (vv. 8-10). There were far more priests available than strictly needed; in fact, each 'division' of priests served one week twice a year; so they cast lots to determine who would perform specific functions—like placing the incense on the hot coals of the altar of incense in the Holy Place of the temple. The incense symbolized the ascent of Israel's prayers—note the people were praying out in the court (v. 10). This day the lot happened to fall on Zechariah to burn incense. In all his time of service this had probably never happened. Not likely it would ever happen again. A once-in-a-lifetime opportunity, a never-to-be-repeated privilege, a red-letter day and likely the high point of his priestly career. I suppose Zechariah was already keyed up over his holy duty and the angel on the right side of the altar of incense probably scared the daylights out of him (vv. 11-12).

The angel fleshes out the significance of this soon-to-be-born son. He speaks of (1) the joy he will bring (v. 14)—and not merely for Zechariah and Elizabeth; (2) the equipping he will have (v. 15); and (3) the difference he will make (vv. 16-17). This last indicates that the answer to Zechariah's personal prayer will pack benefits for all Israel. The child will 'turn many of the sons of Israel to the Lord their God' (v. 16); they may be 'covenant people' but they need to be 'converted'. Verse 17b merely reinforces this point.[2] So answered prayer will both gladden a couple and transform a people, even though it was a prayer that had perhaps long ceased to be prayed (cf. v. 18). But it was on record in heaven, where the Lord treasures the verbs and nouns and adverbs of His people—and does not despise the prayer of the destitute (Ps. 102:17), an encouragement we may particularly need on a bleak Thursday afternoon.

Finally, Luke illustrates **how God may turn His rebukes into assurance** (vv. 18-23). It was embarrassment in excelsis. Folks worried about Zechariah's time lapse in the temple (v. 21). What had happened? And when he came out, he had to play charades to 'explain', but he remained mute (v. 22). Zechariah couldn't even pronounce the priestly benediction (cf. Num. 6:24-26).

---

2. The third line of v. 17 ('to turn the hearts of fathers to/upon children') alludes to Malachi 4:6. It's not likely that it refers to some sort of family harmony or reconciliation. Douglas Stuart points out that the Hebrew preposition 'al can have the sense of 'in addition to' or 'as well as'—so the text points to the turning back of both fathers and children to God—an extensive affair ('Malachi,' in T. E. McComiskey, ed., The Minor Prophets, 3 vols. [Grand Rapids: Baker, 1998], 3:1395). Interestingly, J. C. Ryle long ago took this view of this text in Luke (Expository Thoughts on the Gospels: St. Luke, 2 vols. [New York: Baker & Taylor, 1858], 1:16).

So the angel's words proved true. Zechariah had so much as said, 'I hear you, but what about the facts of life?' (see v. 18). Gabriel answered and did not play pussyfoot with him: 'You did not believe my words,' he said, and hence 'you will be silent and unable to speak until the day when these things take place' (v. 20). And, sure enough, he stood in front of those people totally dumb (v. 22). Gabriel's words were a rebuke and yet, in a way, an assurance as well.

Sometimes a negative is also a positive. In the mid-1930s, fifteen-year-old Pete Reiser went to a baseball tryout camp run by the St. Louis Cardinals. The kids the scouts were interested in were asked to come back the next day. Pete Reiser wasn't asked back; he was 'cut'. He went home discouraged. In a couple of days, a big Buick pulled up in front of the Reiser home. It was the head scout of the Cardinals wanting to talk about signing up Pete with the Cards. But, Pete's father asked, why had they cut him from the tryouts? They'd done that, the scout explained, because they didn't want any scouts from other teams to see him — or those scouts would've gone after him. They had 'cut' him in order to take him 'off the market' and keep him for the Cardinals.[3]

Now it's something like that here for Zechariah, for just as Gabriel had said Zechariah would be mute and he already was at benediction time, so just as surely Zechariah could depend on Gabriel's *other word* (v. 13) coming to pass. If the mute-threat is true, so is the child-promise! So Zechariah's silence becomes a kind of back-handed assurance. And is that not characteristic of the gracious ways of our God, whose severity is laced with kindness and whose rebukes turn into encouragements? It's one of the funny things that happens in church.

---

3. Donald Honig, *Baseball when the Grass Was Real* (New York: Coward, McCann & Geoghegan, 1975), pp. 287-88.

3

Hail to the Blessed Virgin
(Luke 1:26-38)

Gabriel is kept busy. In the sixth month (i.e., of Elizabeth's pregnancy, vv. 24, 26) he pays Mary a visit. Have you ever noticed how the Virgin Mary rarely gets a passing notice among many Protestants except when they use the Apostles' Creed? Quite in contrast to Roman Catholicism which holds to her (1) immaculate conception, i.e., that she was free from original sin (finalized in 1854), (2) perpetual virginity (contrary to the natural implication of Matthew 1:25), (3) assumption, body and soul, into heavenly glory (finalized in 1950), and (4) her role as intercessor and mediatrix. These Roman dogmas do not have New Testament support and yet—perhaps partly in reaction?—that should not lead us to relegate Mary to the attic of Christian history. J. C. Ryle was right:

> [N]o woman was ever so highly honored as the mother of our Lord. It is evident that one woman only out of the countless millions of the human race, could be the means whereby God could be 'manifest in the flesh,' and the Virgin Mary had the mighty privilege of being that one.[1]

So we turn to Luke's testimony as he introduces us to the Virgin Mary.

---

1. J. C. Ryle, *Expository Thoughts on the Gospels: St. Luke*, 2 vols. (New York: Baker & Taylor, 1858), 1:23.

First off, we see what **a humble setting** Luke depicts (vv. 26-28). Note as well how unabashedly supernatural the Bible is! Gabriel is sent 'from God to ... Nazareth.' No trick really to negotiate that. Supernatural but not mythological, for the account is riddled with concrete people and actual places—this is not in the orbit of Peter Pan and Never-neverland. But note the places and people. Galilee. One might say Gabriel is not sent to the more orthodox Judea but to this mini-crossroads of trade and contact with the world. And yet for all that he comes to Nazareth, a town never mentioned in the Old Testament or Josephus or early Jewish literature. Its population may've tallied 400-500 people.[2] Hence it was relatively obscure and perhaps with not the best reputation (John 1:46). And he is sent to an unknown girl, probably between thirteen and eighteen, betrothed to a man named Joseph.[3] We can simply note it: here is neither place nor people who 'cut' it.

So as He brings His Son into the world God begins with a place that's small and people who are obscure. Which is really a pattern of His (1 Cor. 1:26-29). Which in turn is why God is so refreshing. He is never chained to the boring tedium of human expectations nor imprisoned in the box of social correctness.

Then we notice that through Gabriel's announcement Luke provides us with **a kingdom perspective** (vv. 30-33).

---

2. L. F. DeVries, NIDB, 4:240-41; J. F. Strange, ABD, 4:1050-51. Some would boost Nazareth's population up toward 2,000. Sepphoris, four miles northwest of Nazareth, was the prominent town in the area. However, Nazareth's proximity to Sepphoris and to the Egypt-Damascus trade route show it was not exactly 'Hicksville' (DJG, 1st ed., p. 36).

3. One can't resist Luther's quip on translating Gabriel's greeting: 'When the angel greets Mary, he says: "Greetings to you, Mary, full of grace, the Lord is with you." Up to this point, this has simply been translated from the simple Latin; but tell me, is that good German? Since when does a German speak like that—being "full of grace"? One would have to think about a keg "full of" beer or a purse "full of" money. So I translated it: "You gracious one". This way a German can at last think about what the angel meant by his greeting. Yet the papists rant about me corrupting the angelic greeting—and I still have not used the most satisfactory German translation. What if I had used the most satisfactory German and translated the salutation: "God says hello, Mary dear" (for that is what the angel was intending to say and what he would have said if he had been German!).' Cited in N. R. Needham, *2,000 Years of Christ's Power*, 4 vols. (Fearn, Ross-shire: Christian Focus Publications, 2016), 3:116.

Gabriel ties the coming Jesus-child to an old promise to David and his royal line:

> He shall be great
> and shall be called the Son of the Most High,
> and the Lord God will give to him the throne of his father David,
> and he shall reign over the house of Jacob forever
> and of his kingdom there will be no end (vv. 32-33).[4]

So this coming child is connected to the promise at the heart of the 'Davidic covenant'. Yahweh had told David, 'Your throne shall be established forever' (2 Sam. 7:16), and 'his [David's] line shall endure forever, his throne as long as the sun before me' (Ps. 89:36). Micah 4:7 and Daniel 7:14 also speak of the unendingness of this regime. So Gabriel repeats God's promise to Mary: *David's descendant upon David's throne ruling over Jacob's people.* How would Mary understand his ruling 'over the house of Jacob'? Doubtless as hope for believing Israel. God does not let go of Israel. Sometimes it's common for expositors to stumble all over themselves claiming that, of course, this kingdom is not an earthly, temporal matter but a spiritual kingdom, and so on. Really? Should we quit praying Matthew 6:10 ('Your kingdom come—your will be done *on earth* as it is in heaven') and stop singing Revelation 5:9-10 ('and you made them a kingdom, even priests to our God, and they shall reign *on earth*')?

But you sense the real dilemma, don't you? This was an *old* promise. At the moment in Israel there was no reigning king, no Davidic king—hadn't been one for near 600 years. This people had been under Babylon, then Persia, then Syria, now Rome. The odds seemed to be that it wouldn't happen. Is that the way with the promise? Had it expired? Had the sell-by date come and gone? Gabriel implies that those hundreds of years don't matter—the kingdom promise of 2 Samuel 7 and Daniel 7 was still 'on the books'. He implies that God doesn't write 'Oops!' after His promises.

Next, we notice how the angel gave Mary **a restrained explanation** (vv. 34-35). She clearly understood Gabriel's

---

4. Note how verse 27 has already noted that Joseph was 'of the house of David'.

announcement to refer to something that was to happen
presently and not some time down the road. So Mary asked
about the biology of all this. Her query arose because she
knew the facts of life. She was having no sexual relations
with a husband, so how will this conception occur? Notice
the restraint in Gabriel's answer:

> The Holy Spirit will come upon you,
> and the power of the Most High will overshadow you
> —therefore also the child to be born will be called holy,
> the Son of God (v. 35).

This conception would be a supernatural deed; normal human
agency would not be involved. The powerful presence of God
would bring it about, but there are no details, no precise
explanation of the 'how'. Sometimes God draws a veil of
mystery over His work, and we are to be content with that.

One of my friends, Michael Philliber, passed on a story of
a newly-ordained preacher and his young wife. They vowed
to be more considerate of one another: she promised not to
be so critical of his sleep-inducing sermons and he promised
to respect her privacy by not looking through her dresser
drawers. They were true to their words, and the marriage
went smoothly. However, after fifty years their children threw
a huge party for their parents; they received many gifts; they
were putting them away that evening and the preacher noticed
his wife left one dresser drawer slightly open. Try as he might,
he couldn't resist looking and found three eggs in it—and
$10,000 in cash. Puzzled, he asked his wife about this. 'Oh,' she
said, 'you remember years ago when we promised to be more
considerate of each other, and I promised to stop criticizing
your boring sermons? Well, instead every time you preached
a real snoozer, I put an egg into that drawer.' The preacher
was rather pleased: 'Fifty years of sermons,' he said, 'and only
three eggs. But what about all the money?' The wife responded
quietly, 'Every time I got a dozen eggs, I sold them.'

Sometimes it's better not to know. And sometimes
God puts us in that position. Here, for example, there are
no intricate details about the virginal conception of Jesus.
This is rather typical: with the living God we often meet

conundrums—the mystery of Jesus' conception, the mystery of the cross, the mysteries of Christian experience, the perplexity of unanswered prayer, or the quandaries behind suffering. Some of God's mysteries may be intentional. It may be that He does not want to feed our curiosity but to lead us to worship. It is not that He wants you to be ignorant of things but to be content that He is competent. He may not want you to speculate but to adore.

Gabriel goes on to provide what we might call **a typical encouragement** (vv. 36-37). Without skipping a beat he brings up the case of Mary's relative, Elizabeth. 'She herself has conceived a son in her old age.' Everyone had dubbed her 'barren'—but she's in her sixth month of pregnancy now! Then Gabriel takes us beyond Elizabeth and back to Genesis, for verse 37 is a reference to, or paraphrase of, Genesis 18:14 ('Is anything too wonderful for Yahweh?'). The 'wonderful' in that text really means 'supernatural'. So it's as if, after mentioning old Elizabeth's fertility, Gabriel takes Mary back to post-menopausal (Gen. 18:11b) Sarah, who conceived Isaac, not because she was able but because Yahweh had promised.[5] My concern here is simply to point out how typical this is of the God of the Bible. Again and again we catch Him, as it were, stooping down and saying to His servants, 'Here, let me see if I can give you something to help you believe this.' He seems to have a holy anxiety to sustain our faith through every encouragement He can bring to bear. He did that with Mary, telling her of Elizabeth and reminding her of Sarah. Unusual births are one of God's fortes.

Finally, we see that Mary provides us with **a model response**. She calls herself 'the slave girl of the Lord' and says, 'Let it happen to me as you have said' (v. 38).

We are often too familiar with these 'Advent' texts, and familiarity may tend to deaden appreciation. But Mary had to count the cost. In one sense, was this privilege or punishment for her?

---

5. Cf. Oosterzee: 'The laws of nature are not chains which the Divine Legislator has laid upon Himself; they are threads which He holds in His hand, and which He shortens or lengthens at will' (cited in F. Godet, *A Commentary on the Gospel of St. Luke*, 2nd ed., 2 vols. [Edinburgh: T. & T. Clark, 1870], 1:95).

How would it seem to her? She was jeopardizing (for all she knew) all her security with Joseph. What would he say? What would he do? Someone may say, 'Why, just tell him the truth!' Right. Fine. And what sane man would swallow that explanation?

Jewish betrothal was a step far more serious than 'engagement' in our western culture. The marriage, of course, was not consummated during betrothal, but betrothal was considered as binding as marriage and any violation of the relation was considered adultery. Mary's pregnancy would suggest she'd been adulterous. At this time the death penalty for adultery was seldom carried out. But does that really matter?[6] For all Mary knew, she would be deserted and despised—wrongly so, but that wouldn't change what would likely happen. So far as she could tell, she was being asked to risk everything that gives stability to life.[7] She submits: she calls herself 'the slave girl of the Lord'.

In that benediction in Hebrews 13:20-21, there is that part that asks that God may 'do in us what pleases him' (TEV). I have always found that a bit scary—who knows what all it is that may please Him? Who knows what God may take us through? It was Thomas Hog (d. 1692) who said that submission is preferable to consolation, for consolation pleases us, but submission pleases God.[8] God must've been pleased with this premier disciple, 'the slave girl of the Lord,' the blessed Virgin indeed.

---

6. It is possible that in John 8:41 when the Jews say, 'We were not born of fornication,' they were casting a slur on Jesus' own birth, as if to say, 'We are not bastards, but we understand there were questionable circumstances regarding your birth.'

7. Matthew 1:18-21 gives us a glimpse of the turmoil and upheaval Mary's pregnancy caused for Joseph.

8. See D. Beaton, *Some Noted Ministers of the Northern Highlands* (Glasgow: Free Presbyterian Publications, 1985), p. 4.

4

A Visit to the Country

(Luke 1:39-56)

We are curious creatures and want to know all kinds of trivia that the Bible refuses to tell us. Mary's journey was likely some seventy miles from Nazareth to Elizabeth's home somewhere in Judah. Mary was likely still a teenager. Surely her family wouldn't allow her to go alone, would they, amid all the possible hazards and dangers? Did some relative accompany her? Or did she hook up with a caravan going south? What town or locale in Judah was her exact destination? Apparently, none of this really matters; Luke doesn't satisfy us. Two speeches (vv. 41-45 and 46-56) dominate the passage and from these we can divine that the women did not talk about what lovely hot pads Elizabeth had hanging by her oven.

We can't help noticing, right at the first, that there is **an urgency for fellowship** (vv. 39-40) on Mary's part. Mary let no grass grow under her feet but went off immediately ('in a hurry') toward Judah. Gabriel's words in verse 36 were likely all Mary knew about Elizabeth, but that was motivation enough. Older Elizabeth being pregnant (given her 'Sarah-situation') was something momentous indeed, and surely with her Mary could count on some understanding. Mary surely thought it would be profitable, consoling, and steadying for her to confer with Elizabeth. How could Mary try to broach her secret in her own home? 'Dad and Mum,

I'm going to be pregnant, but don't worry, because an angel appeared to me and said ....'[1] No, not now, not yet.

Let us push the 'pause' button long enough to observe the significant age difference between Mary (in her mid-teens?) and Elizabeth (perhaps four times Mary's age)—and that is no barrier. Much church thinking and practice today go against this. Churches often seem to think we have to separate people into blobs of similar ages, similar backgrounds, similar social status—as if the church were a collection of homogenized cliques. I was recently preaching in a solidly 'evangelical' church but noted in their bulletin that its church school classes were divided into categories, e.g., college and college age, medical students, young professionals, young married couples, parents of elementary and high school students, parents of older children, 'empty-nesters'—you get the picture. Some of our best fellowship occurs when we defy such attempted categorization.

Secondly, we meet here such **a thrill over redemption** (vv. 41-44). Let us not forget that there is a good bit that Elizabeth already knows. Though Zechariah could not talk, he could write (v. 63) and he surely had jotted down for Elizabeth a summary of what had happened in verses 13-17. Moreover, she was 'filled with the Holy Spirit' (v. 41b) and that doubtless accounts for what she knows as well. Elizabeth meets Mary's greeting with a pronouncement of blessing ('How blessed you are among women! And how blessed the fruit of your womb!' [v. 42b]), a sense of wonder ('How could this happen to me that the mother of my Lord should come to me?' [v. 43]),[2] and a report of joy (v. 44). We readers had already been told of this last item (v. 41). Pre-natal John got a kick out of Mary's arrival and, hence, so did Elizabeth! Luke wants us to catch the sheer joy of the scene. There is a certain

---

1. Cf. Norval Geldenhuys, *Commentary on the Gospel of Luke*, NICNT (Grand Rapids: Eerdmans, 1951), p. 82: 'In her own environment she would naturally not yet be able to discuss with anyone the sacred experiences that had befallen her. In Elizabeth, however, she would find an understanding person.'

2. I don't think we need to tone down Elizabeth's use of 'Lord' here (in 'the mother of my Lord'). Already in verse 16 we heard that John would turn many 'to the Lord their God', and in the next line we're told John 'will go before him' (v. 17a). The 'him' must be 'the Lord' of verse 16. Luke likely wants us to surmise that, yes, Jesus is 'the Lord'; he doesn't shy away from deity-claims.

ecstasy simply in Elizabeth's confession, 'the mother of my Lord,' and bursting excitement in fetal John's antics. That's as it should be. If the age of redemption is going to mean deliverance from enemies (vv. 71, 74a), life without fear (v. 74b), and decisive forgiveness of sins (v. 77), how can one remain calm (cf. Isa. 49:13; 52:9)? The situation is something like that in 5:33-35. The question was—Why don't Jesus' disciples fast? Jesus' answer was that there would be a time when they would fast (5:35), but right now the bridegroom was with them and it is ludicrous to fast at wedding time. Can you imagine a wedding reception with guests ready to nibble at the repast and a bass voice comes booming over the sound system, 'Now, let us fast!' At a wedding? Ridiculous. Might it be healthy to do so? Perhaps. But it's not *appropriate*.

Luke's point here is that you should catch some of the thrill over the Redeemer and the redemption that is coming, over the deliverance and security and pardon it will involve. If that doesn't stir you, there's something wrong. It is, after all, only this joyous gospel that keeps some of us above the sludge line.

Finally, Luke sets before us **a canticle of praise** (vv. 46-56), Mary's 'Magnificat.' What does Mary offer praise for? You can use the following sketch to trace it all in your biblical text; she gives praise for …

(1)   The privileges God gives, vv. 47-49
(2)   The pattern God follows, vv. 50-53
(3)   The promise God keeps, vv. 54-55

She moves from *particular mercies* God has granted her (vv. 47-49) to the *general tendencies* of God's ways (i.e., He has shown specific mercies to me but these are but a particular example of the way He has always acted in redemptive history; vv. 50-53) to the *unforgotten covenant* that God is now on the verge of fulfilling in Jesus (vv. 54-55).

Mary's praise 'paltrifies' our dull attempts at exposition, but two general observations are in order. First, Mary's praise rests upon the foundation of God's sure and indefectible word. As she says, He has 'helped his servant Israel by remembering mercy, *even as he spoke to our fathers*' (vv. 54-55a). What God is about to do through Mary's son is in faithful fulfillment of

His covenant word to Abraham (v. 55; see Gen. 12:1-3; 17:7-8; 22:15-18) and to David (vv. 32-33; see 2 Sam. 7:12-16). Nothing is so sure as God's own word. Luther underscored this once in his own rather crass way. He said, 'If God told me to eat dung, I would do it—knowing it would be good for me.' One would not relish such a prospect, but Luther's point is that if *God told him* to do so he could be sure—because God had said to do it—that it would be good for him. Nothing is so dependable as God's word.

Secondly, we should note where Mary found the material for her praise and prayer. I don't mean she went researching, digging for suitable quotes in some academic way. She doubtless was filled with the Spirit as Elizabeth was (v. 41), but the Holy Spirit does not always do *ex nihilo* work. Geldenhuys admires Mary's psalm and then states: 'It is almost wholly made up of Old Testament quotations.'[3] Hardly anyone discusses Mary's song without pointing out its Old Testament 'twin'—Hannah's song in 1 Samuel 2:1-10.[4] That is the text one should keep alongside Mary's song as a whole. But there are scads of Old Testament allusions and clips and bits and pieces in Mary's piece. You can check them out in this non-exhaustive list:

V. 46   Pss. 34:3; 69:30; 35:9
V. 47   Hab. 3:18
V. 48   1 Sam. 1:11; cf. Gen. 29:32
V. 49   Deut. 10:21; Pss. 24:8; 111:9b
V. 50   Ps. 103:11, 17
V. 53   Pss. 107:9; 146:7
V. 54   Isa. 41:8-10; Ps. 98:3
V. 55   Gen. 12:7; 17:7-8; 22:15-18; Mic. 7:20

Unknown to us, Mary has waylaid us into her school of prayer. If we want to offer praise or engage in prayer, how are we to do so? Use Bible words. No, not in some hammed-up way as if we're saying, 'Note well—I'm quoting!' But rather we should simply recognize that a majority of the praise and prayer we

3. Geldenhuys, p. 84.

4. For a brief exposition, see my *1 Samuel: Looking on the Heart* (Ross-shire: Christian Focus, 2000), pp. 22-26.

will need has already been written in the Old Testament and especially in the Psalms. You so soak yourself in, for example, the Psalms, that their language, their expressions of delight and despair, their turns of phrase, start seeping into the empty nooks and crannies of your gray matter until they begin to shape the way you pray. Mary teaches us that marination in the biblical text is the best preparation for prayer.[5]

5. Cf. Eugene H. Peterson's discussion in *Under the Unpredictable Plant* (Grand Rapids: Eerdmans, 1992), pp. 101-05.

5

Right at the Edge of Christmas
(Luke 1:57-80)

I think it was Theodore Roosevelt's daughter who said that her father wanted to be the bride at every wedding and the corpse at every funeral. In short, to be always and everywhere the center of attention. He loved to dominate the scene, whatever the scene was. And there's a sense in which we should allow God to do the same in Scripture, so that as we study our texts we are always asking: Now what is *God* doing here? Otherwise, we'll get caught up in lesser matters, like: 'Well, they didn't get to call John "Junior," did they?' Or: 'Isn't it precious that Zechariah could speak again so that we have the "Benedictus"?' No, here we are, almost at Luke 2, right at the edge of 'Christmas', but we must keep asking the right question: What is *God* doing here? How is He disclosing Himself? What do we see of Him?

First, we note that **God is so faithful to the little people** (vv. 57-58). We may easily pass these two verses by, but they record the fulfillment of verses 13-14. They are simply saying that God was faithful to do as He had promised. And to whom had He promised? To a childless woman, along in years (v. 7), tucked away in the hill country of Judah (v. 39). Elizabeth was not a mover and shaker; I suppose some might think she didn't really count for much; but God was faithful to her; 'the Lord had magnified his mercy to her' (v. 58). 'And she gave birth to a son' (v. 57b). God's servants rejoice that there

37

are no status requirements for experiencing His faithfulness. One day in the fall of 1874, in a flat in Lower Manhattan, a blind woman answered a knock on her door. On opening the door, she felt some folded paper being pressed into her hand by someone who left without a word. It turned out to be ten dollars. The woman had not had the money fully to pay the rent and so had prayed for the Lord to supply her need. And here it was. So it was later that day Fanny Crosby wrote:

> *All the way my Savior leads me,*
> *what have I to ask beside?*
> *Can I doubt his tender mercy,*
> *who through life has been my guide?*
> *… for I know, whate'er befall me,*
> *Jesus doeth all things well.*[1]

We also have more evidence in this passage that **God tends to do things differently** (vv. 59-66). Neighbors, in general, are wonderful folks, but some of them can be presumptuous and high-handed. And when they came to the priest's home for the infant's circumcision, they kept referring to the baby as 'Zechariah' (or maybe 'Little Zack') in honor of his father. But Elizabeth set them straight. Zechariah had communicated to her what the angel had said (v. 13), probably by scribbling on that overused tablet (cf. v. 63). So Elizabeth put her foot down: 'No, but he will be called John' (v. 60). John, not Junior. Sheer shock. Why, climb where you will, there was no 'John' in their family tree. You can imagine the remark of a neighbor woman to her husband on the way home after the circumcision: 'Well, I never in all my born days heard the like!' Of course, at the time friends and neighbors had appealed to Zechariah. Maybe Zechariah would overrule Elizabeth's nonsense. They had to stoop to charades in communicating to him what they wanted (v. 62), which probably indicates that Zechariah was deaf as well as mute at the time. But on that writing tablet Zechariah was adamant: 'His name is John' (v. 63). Was there an exclamation mark after the word 'John'? That was shock enough, but no sooner had Zechariah written 'John' than he began speaking, 'praising God' (v. 64b). Several guests

---

1. William J. Reynolds, *Songs of Glory* (Grand Rapids: Zondervan, 1990), p. 21.

probably spilled their punch. It was simply unnerving and scary—Luke says fear came over all those there (v. 65a) and that these happenings were all the talk in the hill country of Judea (v. 65b). Folks who pondered it all couldn't help thinking that God must have a special purpose in mind for this child (v. 66).

The child's strange naming, then, and the father's restored voice were both terribly mysterious and different. It surely prompted fear and discussion and thinking (vv. 65-66a). Why did God act so differently, so strangely here? Probably to prompt fear and discussion and thinking. Which would make clear, at least to some, that whatever was coming would be no ordinary, run-of-the-mill affair. Even the birth of Messiah's forerunner is lit up with indicators that something unique is coming.

But, in general, doesn't the text tell us something about God Himself, namely that He is so interesting and fascinating? Of course, you won't see any section in theology books on 'the fascination of God' or run into thirty pages there discussing His unguessable and interesting ways. I don't see material like this in any systematic theology books I know about; but that's still no excuse for not seeing it in the biblical text. God does things with a little spice; He is not caught in the conventional; He is not stuck in a rut. Which is why He is so refreshing.

Now we come to Zechariah's song; he is filled with the Holy Spirit and prophesies (v. 67), and through his song Luke brings before us a third matter: **God stoops down to give a very earthy deliverance** (vv. 67-75). Now that Zechariah can speak, he utters a *prophecy* (v. 67, 'he prophesied,' which means these words are not merely his personal sentiments but God's word), in which he blesses God for the *redemption* He has accomplished (v. 68; the verb is past tense but is anticipatory, pointing to the redemption He will accomplish through the Messiah), and this will be in fulfillment of His *promises*, the one to Abraham (vv. 73-75) in which He promised a people and a place (i.e., land; Gen. 12:1-3, 6-7; and ch. 15) and the one to David (v. 69) in which He promised the person to rule and save His people (2 Sam. 7:12-16; Ps. 132:17-18). But the *salvation* (vv. 71, 74-75) promised here disturbs some. It is 'salvation from our enemies and from the hand of all who hate us' (v. 71), and is part of God's pledge to Abraham 'to grant to us—being rescued from the hand of enemies—to serve him without fear in holiness and righteousness in his presence all our days' (vv. 73b-75). The 'salvation' promised partly but clearly consists of physical security; it is freedom from fear and harm—it is very earthy.

Sadly, but too typically, some commentators try to explain away this emphasis: Luke meant the physical and political-type language in a metaphorical sense to refer to spiritual realities, they claim.[2] This brings to mind the story about Hermann Goering, head of Hitler's air force, when he was playing tennis. His opponent hit the ball where Goering was not, so Goering chided him: 'Can't you see where I'm standing?' Goering's definition of tennis was for his opposite number to hit the ball right to him, so the portly Goering wouldn't have to chase it. That would be 'tennis' as Goering would have it. And one senses some expositors would prefer 'salvation' not so much as Zechariah expressed it—he borders too much on the nationalistic and material.

So ... Zechariah gets only a C+ (on an American grade scale) for his prophecy, as if he speaks of a deficient kind of deliverance—from enemies, as if such earthly security is sub-standard. It's too 'Old-Testament-ish.' But, according to the Old Testament (sorry!), this is what God intends for His people. This provision was one of the covenant blessings, should Israel remain faithful: 'And I shall give peace in the land, and you shall lie down and there will be no one terrifying (you), and I shall remove harmful beasts from the land, and the sword will never pass through your land' (Lev. 26:6). The promise, even to converted gentiles, was that in Yahweh's consummated kingdom, 'they shall sit— each man under his vine and under his fig tree—with no one terrifying (them)' (Micah 4:4). A renewed Israel had a similar promise (Jer. 30:10). Why should we play this down as a part of 'salvation'? Don't you imagine that at this very moment Christians in Myanmar and North Korea and Pakistan and China and Vietnam and Laos and Iran and Syria and Egypt

---

2. See, e.g., W. F. Arndt, *The Gospel According to St. Luke* (St. Louis: Concordia, 1956), pp. 66-67; E. Earle Ellis, *The Gospel of Luke*, 2nd ed., NCB (London: Oliphants, 1974), p. 78; Robert H. Stein, *Luke*, NAC (Nashville: Broadman, 1992), pp. 99-101.

and Nigeria and Somalia long for this very 'salvation'? Is
that unworthy? Shame on us if we're ashamed of this sort of
deliverance! It's almost Advent as I write this—are we *not*
to sing, 'From our *fears* and sins release us'?

This 'redemption' (v. 68) that God has accomplished has
not yet come in its final form. It is yet ahead of us. Whether
one sees it occurring in some 'millennial,' earthly reign of
Christ or in the new heavens and new earth, God's design
is to make His people secure in every way, from all their
enemies, from all their fears. Thankfully, God can be very
earthy.

But, finally, **God also saves by dealing with our real guilt**
(vv. 76-79). Now Zechariah turns to address the infant in the
cradle (v. 76a), to specify his place and mission (vv. 76b-77).
Due to God's tender compassions the 'rising sun' (v. 78,
NIV)—a messianic term however one explains it—will come
and shine on his people in their darkness (cf. Isa. 9:1-2) to
direct their way (v. 79). But John's preparatory function will
be 'to give the knowledge of salvation to his [the Lord's]
people'. One should not miss what is assumed: that it is
God's people who need the knowledge of salvation, and this
salvation consists in 'the forgiveness of their sins' (v. 77).

This boon may stir either cynicism or joy. One current
attitude in our culture is opposed to the very presupposition
behind forgiveness, namely, guilt. Guilt is thought to be
unhealthy, so people deny it or ignore it, or speak of 'guilt
feelings', implying that guilt is only an unpleasant, lingering
sensation that must somehow be dissolved (because it is
unpleasant). I once came up behind a vehicle on the interstate
sporting a bumper sticker that read: 'Screw guilt.' I suppose
you could try, but Psalm 32:5 points to the gospel way. And
there are those of us—and not especially 'emotional' types—
who find forgiveness makes us border on ecstasy. In our
current church, we use the Apostles' Creed every Lord's
Day morning. I know there are perhaps more 'important,'
substantial, and doctrinal parts of the creed, but I can't
help it: my favorite article in the creed is 'I believe … in
the forgiveness of sins.' I know it's way down there, it's
next to the next-to-the-last phrase, but somehow if decorum
permitted and wouldn't throw others off their cadence, I'd

be willing to shout that line. Maybe I'm too obsessed with my own condition, but it is the very gift that Israel—and I—most need (Acts 5:31).

6

What the Bible Packs into Christmas
(Luke 2:1-20)

Things get 'packed' at Christmas—at least in our culture in the west. Secular gurus may disdain the term 'Christmas', but that is the season and merchants salivate over its profits. Stores are packed, schedules are packed—shopping and parties, even church activities, can run one ragged. Parking places may be hard to come by—'no room at the mall.' And Luke's story of the first Christmas is packed as well—but with superb theology rather than seasonal clutter. What then does Luke want us to grasp as we read his story?

He wants us to see, first, **the secret working of God's providence** (vv. 1-5), and to see, for one thing, that this is a 'political' providence. Caesar Augustus (i.e., Octavian, ruling from 27 BC to AD 14) decrees an enrollment (v. 1) and people obey (v. 3).[1] Caesar issues decrees and things happen. He was

---

1. Much ink has been spilt on verse 2, traditionally translated, 'This was the first census that took place while Quirinius was governor of Syria' (NIV, 1984). The rub comes because Josephus places Quirinius' tenure at A.D. 6, whereas Luke (and Matthew) clearly place Jesus' birth near the end of Herod the Great's life, about ten years earlier. So many think Luke must've been in error here. But the term often translated 'first' is capable of other renderings: 'This registration was *before* Quirinius governed Syria'; see David E. Garland, *Luke*, ZECNT (Grand Rapids: Zondervan, 2011), pp. 117-19, for a lucid argument for this option. Or, Nigel Turner still retains 'first,' assuming that it's called first because it was at least the first of two, and then renders: 'This census was *before the census* which Quirinius, governor of Syria, made' (*Grammatical Insights into the New Testament* [Edinburgh: T. & T. Clark, 1965], pp. 23-24; see also Wayne Brindle, 'The Census and Quirinius:

the power of the day. At Augustus' death the Roman empire covered 3,340,000 square miles, more than the mainland of the USA, with a population of between 70-100 million. He was generally well thought of; when Augustus visited Greek Asia in 21 BC, his cult was in full swing; dedications and orations hailed him as 'Savior,' 'Bringer of good tidings,' and 'God, the son of God.' Some argued that in him the long-awaited messiah had come, bringing peace and happiness to mankind.[2]

But there's something subversive going on here. Caesar Augustus is only background for the main act. Luke neutralizes him. The real focus is elsewhere—verse 4—on another, Joseph from Galilee! Yet not so much on the person as on what he represents, for he goes 'to the city of David, which is called Bethlehem, because he was of the house and family of David.' The David-lingo conjures up the promise and covenant granted to David in 2 Samuel 7: 'And your house and your kingship shall be made firm forever before me; your throne will remain established forever' (2 Sam. 7:16). It's almost as if the David-language here functions as code for those in the know. So there is Caesar and his decree and there is Mary's first-born and His feeding-trough. But the real attention is on the latter—and what He represents. Luke knows the meaning of Christmas: Christmas is putting Caesar in his place.

In 1910 US President Taft appointed former president Theodore Roosevelt as the United States' representative at the funeral of Edward VII. After the funeral the German Kaiser told Roosevelt, 'Call upon me at two o'clock; I have just forty-five minutes to give to you.' TR replied, 'I will be there at two, your Majesty, but, unfortunately, I have but twenty

---

Luke 2:2,' *Journal of the Evangelical Theological Society* 27 [1984]: pp. 43-52). The census under Quirinius in A.D. 6 stirred up such a ruckus among the Jews that most remembered it; so Luke might have been saying, 'This census was not *that* one!' Then, just to complicate things a bit, some are now saying that Josephus misdated the census, so one should doubt him on this matter rather than Luke (see, for a start, David E. Graves, 'Fresh Light on the Governors of Judea,' *Bible and Spade* 30 [Summer 2017]: pp. 77-78).

2. For these matters, see Will Durant, *Caesar and Christ*, The Story of Civilization: Part III (New York: Simon and Schuster, 1944), pp. 218, 226, and F. W. Danker, *Jesus and the New Age*, rev. ed. (Philadelphia: Fortress, 1988), p. 53.

minutes to give you.'[3] It was a delightful twist, putting a bit of arrogance in its place. And that is essentially what Luke does here, as if to say: Don't be too impressed with Augustus; keep your eyes on the city of *David* and on the house and family of *David*, because that's where the really important stuff will be happening. And Christians also know this experientially, for if we give Jesus His proper place we are never overly-impressed by Caesar or any other worldly power.

Now there also seems to be a 'prophetic' twist to God's providence here.[4] It's in the geography. There is such a stress on the Davidic connection and Bethlehem that, though Luke does not cite Micah 5:2 ('But you, Bethlehem Ephrathah, small to be among the clans of Judah; from you will come forth for me one to be ruler over Israel'), it lies in state behind the story.[5] But how will Messiah be born in Bethlehem if Joseph and Mary are living in the north, in Nazareth? It's as if God says, 'Let's make Caesar Augustus useful.' Hence, a decree for a census, hence the necessity for Joseph to return to his 'roots,' hence the birth of Jesus in 'Davidsburg'. Emperors can make such fine servants, even if they are utterly clueless about what is taking place.

Now if God's providence is at work in the politics and geography of Christmas, might it not also be operating in your life? God's fingerprints, however, don't make noise, so you'll often find evidence of His presence at some later point as you look back and see the subtle touches and silent traces of His work. It often seems so 'natural'—like a decree for a census. But nothing should surprise you, if He'll even stoop to using an emperor to carry out His plan of redemption.

Next, Luke points to **the clear evidence of Christ's humiliation** (vv. 6-7). Mary's 'time' came while they were in Bethlehem, 'and she gave birth to her firstborn son; and

---

3. Paul F. Boller, Jr., *Presidential Anecdotes* (New York: Penguin Books, 1981), p. 210.

4. I am simply using 'providence' to refer to God's interesting and fascinating way of working out the details in His kingdom and in the concerns of His people.

5. I should think that even Luke's gentile readers would have been taught the 'Bethlehem tradition' from Micah's prophecy. Micah 5:2 is worth detailed study; see, e.g., my exposition in a *Study Commentary on Micah* (Darlington: Evangelical Press, 2010), pp. 101-04.

she wrapped him in swaddling bands and put him to bed in a feeding trough, because there was no room for them in the guest room' (v. 7). Sorry to destroy the 'inn', but it was not there. The word Luke uses here (*kataluma*) occurs also in 22:11, where it specifies the 'guest room' where Jesus will eat Passover with His disciples. Had Luke intended to say 'inn', he could have used *pandocheion* as in 10:34, the inn where the Samaritan brought the beaten victim.

The probable scenario, then, was: Joseph and Mary likely stay in the home of relatives, but, due to other census guests, the guest room is already full. Hence the couple stays in the common room where the family normally slept. At the end of this common room at a slightly lower level was a covered area for domestic animals, where they might be brought in for shelter and safety. In between this common room and the animal area may be some pillars and feeding troughs. So the family likely bedded down at the end of this common room where any number of others may have been. When Mary was not nursing her son, she placed Him in an unused feeding-trough (of wood or stone) right next to her.[6]

But a feeding trough! Let us never be surprised at the humility of God. The Westminster Shorter Catechism asks (Question 27): Wherein did Christ's humiliation consist? Its answer begins: 'Christ's humiliation consisted in his being born, and that in a low condition ....' Its 'scriptural proof text' for that 'low condition' is Luke 2:7. In a feeding trough, needing a mother's breast and a change of diaper. How very incarnate the incarnation is! And yet what encouragement is here. For if Christ stoops so low, to such a 'common' level, does this not sanctify all that seems common and ordinary and unimpressive in the lives of His people? To be quaint and go back a few years—the weaver laboring at his loom, the farmer putting up hay, the mother cleaning her oven; or, the teacher tutoring her 'slower' student in reading, the accountant preparing tax returns, the pastor reading in his

---

6. On this, see Garland, pp. 120-21, for a lucid discussion, drawing in part on Kenneth Bailey; B. Witherington III, in DJG, 1st ed., pp. 69-70; and Gary A. Byers, 'Away in a Manger but NOT in a Barn,' *Bible and Spade* 29.1 (Winter 2016): pp. 5-9. The often hard-hearted 'inn-keeper' has always been a piece of Christian mythology; there is no mention of such a figure in the text.

study, the doctor diagnosing a perplexed patient. Jesus' feeding trough suffuses all the glamorlessness of our callings with a touch of His humble glory.

Thirdly, Luke highlights **the marvelous proclamation of Jesus' person** (vv. 10-12). But it is an angel (v. 9) who does the proclaiming and we should stop and ponder just how essential the angel is here.

Jesus' birth has occurred, and now the angel announces and explains the significance of that birth. We don't always appreciate how necessary explanation is. A few years back we used to hear the claim that God reveals Himself by His mighty acts in history. That's true, as long as you understand it involved both God's act *and* His given interpretation of His act. An act without an explanation may leave us clueless. A child has been born to Mary in Bethlehem. That is the event. But what is the significance of that? What is its meaning? Imagine a dozen people sitting in a circle in a room; each is given a chunk of bubble gum and each chews his/her wad assiduously for several minutes; then one by one they get up, spit their bubble gum into a pan sitting on a chair in the middle of the room, and then leave the room. There are no words, no explanation. What does it mean? Maybe it's a demonstration by the Secure Dentures Club. Or perhaps it was a commemoration of a deceased friend who always chewed bubble gum. But no one knows because no one explains the significance. But God does not leave us in the dark, trying to puzzle it out about Jesus' birth. He sends an angel to interpret it for the shepherds and for us.

Also note that if the angel is essential, he is also polemical— that is, there is a bit of an 'edge' to his words, a kind of 'put down' of prevalent Caesar propaganda. In various proclamations Augustus was called divine, son of a god or god, savior of the whole world, and lord.[7] Verses 10-11 are Luke's way of saying 'nuts' to all of this. The terms the angel uses of Jesus put Caesar in his place. The good news is: 'a Savior, who is Messiah, Lord, was born to you today in the town of David' (v. 11).

---

7. See the various citations in Joel B. Green, *The Gospel of Luke*, NICNT (Grand Rapids: Eerdmans, 1997), pp. 125-26, 133-35.

Hence Jesus is *the one promised:* He is 'Messiah' (or, Christ), the anointed one, the Davidic descendant (2 Sam. 7:12-16) authorized by God to salvage and rule His people; He is *the one able,* for He is 'Lord,' a term already used in Luke's gospel story nearly twenty times of the God of Israel Himself[8]— and yet also used of Jesus (1:43, 76), no one less than deity; and He is *the one needed,* for He is 'Savior', which is good news but also bad news, for it assumes a need. There was a TV commercial a few years back for Scope mouthwash. It showed members of a football team shrinking in anxiety because they were going to give their coach a bottle of Scope. Obviously, the gift presupposed a need. And providing a 'Savior' carries its own offense, for it proclaims a need as well as offering a gift. And this is for 'all the people' (v. 10)— not people in general but the people of Israel, the covenant people.[9] Yes, Israel, the people of God, or by extension and in our lingo, the church folks who attend worship and sing Christmas carols and don't use profanity—they need a Savior. God did not send an economist because our deepest need is not poverty; nor a philosopher because our trouble is not incoherence; He didn't send a psychologist for our problem is not maladjustment; not an entertainer for our problem is not boredom; nor an administrator for we are not disorganized— nor a religious leader because we are not (not many of us anyway) irreligious. 'Savior, Messiah, Lord'—such is the proclamation of Christmas.

Finally, Luke sets before us **the superb responses to God's work** (vv. 15-20). The shepherds' response is very active and eager ('Let's go to Bethlehem ...,' v. 15) and 'they hurried off and tracked down both Mary and Joseph—and the infant lying in the feeding trough' (v. 16). What a top-notch sign that was! How many newborns in Bethlehem would be nestled in a feeding trough? Likely it took a few inquiries at any number of homes but when they saw *that,* there was no

---

8. See the fine discussion in M. Wilcock, *The Message of Luke*, BST (Leicester: Inter-Varsity, 1979), p. 47.

9. Yes, Jesus is Savior for gentiles too in Luke's view. But that is not the scope here. The good news here is not for 'all people' but 'all *the* people', i.e., Israel. See further, Darrell L. Bock, *Luke 1:1-9:50*, BECNT (Grand Rapids: Baker, 1994), pp. 215-16.

doubt. They were openly verbal about what they'd been told (v. 17) and full of praise to God over it (v. 20). Luke takes care to underscore the faithfulness of God: what they'd heard and seen 'were exactly as they had been told' (v. 20b).

If the shepherds' response is primarily active, Mary's is mostly reflective: 'But Mary [emphatic] was treasuring up all these things, turning them over in her heart' (v. 19). Mary keeps 'tossing around' in her mind all that had happened and especially the shepherds' testimony, chewing it over, trying to make it all fit together. Perhaps Mary can be our model of a careful, thinking disciple. Oddly enough, in our day many people don't view Christians as *thinking* people. And Mary here serves as a reminder that not all insight and grasp of truth is instant or immediate, but that it often comes with time and exposure and mulling over what God has shown us.

7

The Waiting Church

(Luke 2:21-40)

Now we meet the account of the double witness (cf. Deut. 19:15) to Jesus from Spirit-directed Simeon and aged Anna. We want to see what Luke wants us to see. However, the first observation may be something Luke implies rather than asserts; he suggests **the high esteem God has for godly, covenant-keeping homes** (vv. 21-24, 27, 39).

As Luke takes up Jesus' post-birth story, he mentions the law *five* times (vv. 22, 23, 24, 27, 39). All that Joseph and Mary carry out is in line with 'the law of the Lord'. Luke falls all over himself trying to make this point. He insists that in every respect Jesus is a very kosher Savior! He refers to Jesus' upcoming circumcision (v. 21; see Gen. 17:9-14), tells how they offer the sacrifices required for His mother's purification from childbirth (vv. 22, 24; Lev. 12:1-8), and how they present their infant as a first-born to the Lord (vv. 22b-23; Exod. 13:2, 11-13)—and likely pay the 'redemption' price (Num. 18:15-16).[1]

All this confirms what Paul says in Galatians 4:4—Christ was 'born under the law'—subject to all the regulations of the Mosaic law. And this was part of what we sometimes refer to as Christ's *humiliation*. If nothing else, all these

---

1. For more detail, cf. Alfred Edersheim, *The Life and Times of Jesus the Messiah*, 2 vols. (1886; reprint ed., Grand Rapids: Eerdmans, 1967), 1:193-96.

procedures underscore that Jesus was born an Israelite, a Jew (cf. Heb 2:17a), part of a people who had been sequentially subservient to Babylon (the exile), Persia (cf. the books of Esther and Daniel), Syria (cf. 1–2 Maccabees), and now Rome. We might say then that Jesus' humiliation certainly consisted in His Jewishness—being part of a despised race, and then also in the relative poverty He shared (v. 24, two turtledoves or two young pigeons were the offering of poorer Israelites [Lev. 12:8]) and in the vicious hostility He would face (v. 34).[2] There are no short cuts in the shaping of our redeemer.

And yet where did God ordain that all this should take place? Within the faith and life of a Bible-devoted, law-prizing family. It's not that God cannot work in a godless family and draw someone to Himself out of such a context. But when He sends His Son among us, He places Him in a family where He will be surrounded by the godly nurture of these pious parents. After all, what is most likely to produce the results of verse 40? Is this kind of home not where He would come to know the Scriptures? Where He would learn to worship? Where He takes His first steps in prayer? No, we know there is no automatic guarantee that someone raised in a believing home will infallibly come to share the faith in which he/she was raised. There are scads of exceptions—and heart-breaking ones—to the 'rule'. But surely it is telling that when God sent His Son to be 'born under the law', He placed Him in a domestic context of quiet faith and humble obedience. Some of our Christian homes may have been more stringent than necessary, and certainly were not ideal in all points, and yet I think I have not yet been able to calculate the boon such a gift has been to me.

Secondly, Luke points up **the marvelous scope and utter simplicity of God's salvation** (vv. 25-33). Here is this Spirit-saturated man, Simeon: three times Luke mentions the Holy Spirit in connection with Simeon (vv. 25, 26, 27). The Holy Spirit had given Simeon a specific revelation that he himself would not die before he had seen the Lord's Messiah (v. 26). Moved by the Spirit, Simeon enters the temple complex and

---

2. On the whole range of Christ's humiliation, cf. the Westminster 'Larger Catechism,' questions 46-50.

recognizes the child when his parents bring Him in. Simeon takes the infant in his arms and blesses God:

> Now you are discharging your slave, O Master,
> in peace in line with your word,
> because my eyes have seen your salvation,
> which you have prepared in the presence of all the peoples
> —a light for revelation to the gentiles
> and glory for your people Israel (vv. 29-32).

Simeon is alluding to Isaiah 49:6. It's one of the 'Servant songs' in which Yahweh is speaking to His Servant:

> It's too trivial—your being my servant
> to raise up the tribes of Jacob
> and to restore the ones preserved in Israel.
> I shall give you as a light to the nations
> to be my salvation to the end of the earth.[3]

The circle of God's salvation will take in but go far beyond Israel, to include the nations. As Yahweh called the Servant himself 'my salvation' (see footnote), so Simeon calls the infant he holds 'your salvation': 'my eyes have seen your salvation' (v. 30). He not only will bring salvation but He Himself can rightly be called 'salvation'; He will not only bring consolation to Israel (v. 25) but He Himself is the consoler. For Simeon, 'salvation' is something he can hold in his arms. And he's doing so.

In one sense we can say that salvation is a plan, God's staggering scheme to have a world-wide Jewish-gentile people as Isaiah 49 says; but salvation is not only a plan but a *person*— Yahweh's Servant-Messiah Himself is Yahweh's 'salvation'. Having Him, we *have* salvation. When my wife and I were in college, we had one Bible professor who sometimes put things in an 'edgy' way in order to make a point. It was a time when a number of groups were taking trips to Israel to see some of the Bible lands sites. Our prof told us what his response was to folks who asked him if he'd 'been to the Holy Land': 'No, I haven't been to the Holy Land, but I know Jesus.' Easy to

---

3. The last line follows Alec Motyer, *Isaiah*, TOTC (Leicester: Inter-Varsity, 1999), p. 311. The servant himself *is* Yahweh's 'salvation'.

forget in one sense the simplicity of it all. Salvation is having Jesus Himself. And Simeon realized that.

In Luke's 'Simeon report' we also hear of **the dark and costly side of God's redemptive plan** (vv. 34-35). There is a hard side to the glorious news, Simeon tells Mary: the Child will divide ('he is set for the falling and rising of many in Israel,' v. 34b), be the object of enmity and hostility ('and for a sign to be spoken against,' v. 34c), and will expose what many belligerent hearts are really thinking ('that thoughts out of many hearts might be revealed,' v. 35b). The hostility and enmity will touch Mary herself ('and a sword will pass through your own soul as well,' v. 35a). The Child will be God's salvation but at great cost and through conflict and opposition (cf. 12:51-53).

It's as if Jesus will simply excite and ignite all sorts of animosity. It just comes. Just recently I was reading a prayer guide published by a Christian relief ministry. It reported what a Muslim in the North Caucasus said to a Christian builder who had come to the area to work and bring the gospel: 'I did not have anything against your faith, yet you have made a mistake. You told your stories when my daughter could hear them. She started to ask me about Jesus. If she becomes a Christian, I will cut off her head. After this, I will find you and will do the same to you.' Where did that come from? Jesus' people share the animosity He receives; He is always a 'sign that is spoken against'.

So there is trouble everywhere Jesus goes, for no one can ever shift into neutral. He makes you either fall or rise; He strips away all the religious candy-coating and exposes your real hostility to Him. There will be some who profess Christ in Christian congregations but, when they see Him more clearly, will be offended and fall away from their profession. Jesus splits, Jesus divides, Jesus angers, Jesus exposes. 'Jesus is God's litmus test for where a person is.'[4]

Besides the section revolving around Simeon, Luke also includes a piece focusing on the prophetess Anna (vv. 36-38). Here it is worth noting **how tenaciously God preserves faithful witnesses to Himself**.

4. D. L. Bock, *Luke*, IVP New Testament Commentary (Downers Grove, IL: InterVarsity, 1994), p. 60.

We read of Anna's roots (v. 36a), her age (vv. 36b-37a; we're not sure if the text tallies her age at eighty-four, or if that number was the time since she was widowed, putting her at approximately one hundred and five), her worship (v. 37b), and her witness (v. 38). She was a widow; she knew what sorrow and doubtless loneliness are like. And, of course, in this passage, she is paired with Simeon. We can't be sure if Simeon was up in years or not, though verses 26 and 29 seem to imply that. Certainly—going back to 1:7, Zechariah and Elizabeth were in their later years. So the remnant church we find in Luke 1–2 has a good sprinkling of 'senior citizen' believers, which suggests that your gray hairs and aching bones and arthritic joints are welcome in Jesus' fellowship. But surely the big point is that such folks are simply here. We walk out of the Old Testament and into the New Testament and begin reading and there they are—the waiting church. They are just there. Zechariah and Elizabeth, Joseph and Mary, and the shepherds, and Simeon and Anna. God always has a true people on earth, worshiping and serving Him through all the vicissitudes and weariness of history. To His praise.

8

Left Behind?

(Luke 2:41-52)

How selective Luke's gospel is! The family returns to Nazareth in Galilee (v. 39). There are no Magi here, there is no night flight to Egypt, no government slaughter of Bethlehem's toddlers, as in Matthew's gospel (Matt. 2). Not that those things didn't happen, but that Luke chooses not to relate them. And then, of course, Luke has none of the tales one finds in the extra-canonical 'gospels', no tales about Jesus bringing twelve clay pigeons to life or stretching a piece of wood that Joseph had cut too short.[1] Instead, Luke has but one episode from Jesus' childhood that climaxes in the very first recorded words of Jesus (v. 49). It might seem like Jesus was inadvertently left behind in Jerusalem, but that, of course, was not the case: 'when they returned, the child Jesus remained in Jerusalem' (v. 43). It was a conscious, deliberate act on His part.

Let us move through the first of the account rather quickly and then focus primarily on the latter part of it. Apparently, Joseph and Mary regularly went up to Jerusalem for Passover (v. 41). Jesus may have accompanied them on previous visits, but Luke focuses on this occasion when Jesus was twelve (v. 42). And now we hear of **a very natural dilemma**

---

1. As in the 'Infancy Gospel of Thomas'; see James R. Edwards, *The Gospel According to Luke*, PNTC (Grand Rapids: Eerdmans, 2015), 90(fn); and NIDB, 5:586-88.

(vv. 42-45). The Nazareth contingent is on its return trip and neither Joseph nor Mary is anxious over spotting Jesus near them — they suppose He's somewhere in the larger group; they would round Him up when they stopped for the night. I don't want to 'contemporize' the account too much, but one can imagine that since Mary and Joseph had other and younger children (see Mark 6:3) and if they also took them along, they may have been preoccupied keeping track of these younger scamps and were likely relieved that, at twelve, Jesus did not require such careful oversight. They weren't neglectful; they didn't need some version of a government social worker hovering over them. He would turn up at nightfall. It was all very natural. They went looking for Him, however, and He was nowhere to be found. A return trip, then, with more than a little foreboding (v. 48).

'After three days' (v. 46a) they find Him. Most expositors take this phrase in an inclusive sense, that is, taking in the day's journey toward Galilee, a day's journey back to Jerusalem, and then finding Jesus on the third day, and **a very surprising discovery** it was: He was in the temple complex, 'sitting in the midst of the teachers, both listening to them and asking them questions' (v. 46b). But there's more here than may meet the eye. Verse 47 indicates that He was actually the center of things: 'All hearing him were amazed at his insight and his answers.' So He wasn't merely listening to the teachers but engaging in back-and-forth with them, and apparently giving rather extended answers in some cases. He was the one with the audience![2] And this leads to **a very understandable reaction**. After their initial astonishment, Mary finds her voice first with a mild rebuke: 'Child, why have you treated us this way? Why, your father and I have been in anguish seeking you' (v. 48). All this sets the stage for the very first recorded words of Jesus and the intended climax of this bit of Luke's narrative.

---

2. W. F. Arndt (*The Gospel According to St. Luke* [St. Louis: Concordia, 1956], p. 101) is probably on target: 'When Joseph and Mary saw Jesus in such a dignified assembly and, at that, not merely as a spectator but as a participant, they were amazed. They themselves, humble Galileans that they were, would never have ventured to intrude into such circles; and their Son, merely twelve years old, was joining in the discussions of the learned Jewish theologians!'

In His response Jesus provides **a very suggestive defense**: 'Why is it that you were seeking me? Did you not know that I must be in my Father's house?' (v. 49).[3] Mary had just alluded to 'your father and I' (v. 48), but Jesus' response about 'my Father's house' clearly does not allude to Joseph. I know of no one who has captured the surprise and import of Jesus' statement more succinctly than David Gooding:

> My Father's house? The learned doctors knew the Old Testament inside out. In all the long biblical record, not even Moses who had built the tabernacle, not David who had longed to build the temple, nor Solomon who had actually built it, no prophet, no king or commoner, not the most exalted of them, had ever referred to the tabernacle or temple as 'my Father's house.' The child was conscious of a relationship with God that none had conceived of, let alone expressed, before. And with that relationship, a compelling devotion: 'I had to be in my Father's house.'[4]

The child Jesus assumed a (unique) relationship with God that no one else had. And—I do not mean any irreverence— He spoke of it in such a matter-of-fact way. Which makes His statement all the more impressive, because, as we know, rather frequently what a person *assumes* packs as much or more punch than what he asserts.

Recently I was reading a biography of Yogi Berra, for years the stellar catcher on the New York Yankees baseball team. Once about 1974, after Yogi's playing days (he was managing the New York Mets at the time), Frank Sinatra was on tour and Yogi's oldest son wanted tickets for one of his shows. He was terribly disappointed because all the near-by shows were sold out. So Yogi told his son, 'Don't worry; I'll see what I can do.' When his son asked what that might be, Yogi said, 'I'll call Frank.' His son was flabbergasted: 'I've been your son all these years and I didn't even know you *knew* Frank Sinatra.'[5]

---

3. For 'my Father's house' as the preferred rendering, see Darrell L. Bock, *Luke 1:1–9:50*, BECNT (Grand Rapids: Baker, 1994), pp. 269-70.

4. David Gooding, *According to Luke* (1987; reprint ed., Coleraine, N. Ireland: Myrtlefield Trust, 2013), p. 59.

5. Allen Barra, *Yogi Berra: Eternal Yankee* (New York: W. W. Norton, 2009), p. 334. Don't mistake a mere illustration as an endorsement of Sinatra.

What is so telling in that anecdote is the simply 'natural' tone in Yogi's 'I'll call Frank.'

And Jesus' words here seem so natural—and yet no one else ever talked like that! Not, 'our Father's house' but 'my Father's house.' Here is a twelve-year-old lad clearly conscious of His unique and intimate (He is 'Father') relation to God and sensible of being under obligation to the Father's will. This last is clear from His use of 'must' (Gr.: dei), which refers to a divine necessity. Already then there is the hint (though not obnoxiously) that He is subject to other and higher authority than His earthly parents. And is there not the hint of a mild reproof in His 'Did you not know…?' Surely what Mary and Joseph already had been told and/or knew (see 1:31-33, 35, 43; 2:10-11, 17-19, 29-32, 34-35, 38) should have factored in and prepared them a bit for something like this? In any case, for now, off to Nazareth and submitting to His parents (v. 51). But don't forget what David Gooding wrote: 'The child was conscious of a relationship with God that none had conceived of, let alone expressed before.'

We mustn't leave this passage without noting that we find **a very appropriate response** here. Well, not so much in verse 50, where we're told they didn't understand what Jesus had said. And yet in one way their non-perception is understandable. W. F. Arndt catches the probable way it was:

> Mary and Joseph did not understand the word of Jesus, that is, they did not realize that He was asserting His divine Sonship. Why not? Did they not know that He had been conceived by the Holy Spirit? Had Mary not heard the simple words of Elizabeth acknowledging her unborn Child as Lord? What of the adoration of the shepherds, of the homage of Simeon and Hannah [=Anna]? Evidently all these things had in the course of time become vague to them. The daily contact with the human Jesus had had the effect of making them almost forget the divine statements about Him. That He, in addition to being a true human being, was the Son of God, they could not perceive in His daily life. It had to be a matter of faith for them, as it must be for us today. At this point the various stories in the apocryphal gospels of miraculous feats performed by the boy Jesus founder. Lk indicates sufficiently that Mary and Joseph witnessed no such things.[6]

---

6. Arndt, p. 102.

But it doesn't end there, for 'his mother was treasuring up all these matters in her heart' (v. 51b). Mary was going over and over these matters, 'chewing' on them, as we say, pondering and trying to think them through. On the whole, it all puzzled Mary—Jesus' remaining in Jerusalem, finding Him in the middle of that 'temple tutorial', those strange words about 'my Father's house'. Yet she's on the right track. What do you do when you find Jesus mysterious and baffling? You begin by mulling it over and over, trying to piece it all together, seeking to make sense out of His mysterious words and ways. There's a sense in which the mystery of Jesus' words and ways has an *inviting* aspect, as if challenging us to make what we can of it all. And eventually the Lord brings light. But Mary has made the right beginning.

I recall the grammatical trouble I had when I was a lad in fifth grade. We had to diagram sentences, were to draw one line under the subject and two lines under the verb. I had no difficulty with subjects but verbs victimized me. For some strange reason, identifying verbs was like a pin-the-tail-on-the-donkey game. I knew—and I think I could quote—the definition of a verb but tended to miss such in a sentence. But then next school year all was different. The difficulty disappeared. I had no problem with verbs, and I could smell them every time. I don't know what happened. Maybe I relaxed over the summer playing sandlot baseball with my friends. In any case, it all cleared up. I am not saying Jesus suddenly makes all things clear; but I'm saying that the mysteries and perplexities Jesus places before us gradually become clearer when we begin 'treasuring up' and pondering and meditating upon the quandaries He sets before us.

9

Where Do We Go After Christmas?

(Luke 3:1-20)

Typically Christians spend a good bit of time during 'Advent' and Christmas in Luke 1–2. But where do we go after Christmas? Luke's gospel suggests that we jump over a bunch of years and find, suddenly, that Zechariah and Elizabeth's infant son (1:57ff.) is now a full-orbed preacher of repentance (v. 3). In fact, we might say that John introduces us to life under the gospel, for verse 18 says that John 'evangelized [*euaggelizomai*] the people'—or, more commonly, 'he preached good news to the people,' even if that included calling them a bunch of snakes and warning about chaff being burnt up with unquenchable fire. What does Luke want to press upon us now that his gospel is breaking out in the open?

First, he wants us to be sure we see **the biggest event** (vv. 1-6). In these verses Luke supplies us with the background (vv. 1-2) and notes the arrival of John and his 'preaching a baptism of repentance with a view to the forgiveness of sins' (v. 3), all of which is in accord with the proper preparation demanded of God's people in Isaiah's prophecy (vv. 4-5; Isa. 40:3-5) as prelude to seeing 'the salvation of God' (v. 6), a term which Simeon had applied to the child Jesus (2:30). There is much in these verses to occupy our attention, but I want to focus particularly on what Luke is doing and saying in verses 1-2 in the background he supplies.

Note the build-up Luke begins as he mentions the prominent and the famous: Tiberius Caesar succeeded Augustus about A.D. 14, so this, his fifteenth year, would be about A.D. 29; Pontius Pilate's tenure in governing Judea ran, it is usually thought, from A.D. 26–36; the Herod who is tetrarch of Galilee is Herod Antipas and his brother Philip was over Iturea and Trachonitis, northeast of Galilee, while Lysanias was located northwest of Damascus; Annas had been booted out of the high priesthood in A.D. 15 but still seemed to share power with his son-in-law Caiaphas.[1] But where is the main grammatical clause in verses 1–2? In 2b: 'the word of God came to John the son of Zechariah in the wilderness.' That is the main event, the big deal. Do you see what Luke has done? He has essentially trivialized the heavy hitters of this age. He itemizes seven of them, then says that the really important event was the word of God coming to John. These world-movers are only the backdrop. Imagine an announcement that said: When FDR was president of the US, Winston Churchill, prime minister of Great Britain, Joe Stalin, head butcher of the USSR, and Charles DeGaulle, the upcoming leader of France, a seven-pound, two-ounce baby girl was born to the George Selloski of Rural Route 3, Puckett, Mississippi. In that imaginary birth announcement, the seemingly insignificant is really the main event that dwarfs the folks who seem to matter the most.

That's what Luke, perhaps tongue-in-cheek (?), is doing here. It's as if he's saying, Here are the movers and shakers of this age, the power-brokers and news-grabbers of the day, and they are mere backdrop for the main feature, namely, that God's word came to John. Do you see the *thinking* that oozes out of the biblical text? It assumes that there is *scarcely anything more vital and important than the public address of God's word to His people.* That is the biggest event. What might this mean, in a derived sense, in our situations? Well, if you are in a congregation where week-by-week the scriptures are clearly explained and carefully applied, must you not say, 'The word of God came—what a treasure!' Or here is a woman, who

---

1. See F. W. Danker, *Jesus and the New Age*, rev. ed. (Philadelphia: Fortress, 1988), p. 82.

spends parts of two days studying a Bible passage, then she goes off to teach it to 8-10 women in a Bible study. What she does there may be of far more importance than all that will clutter the 24-hour news channel that day.

Next, Luke highlights what we might call **the clearest evidence** (vv. 7-14). John was preaching a 'baptism of repentance,' calling Israel, in Isaiah's terms, to 'prepare the way for the Lord' (v. 4)—all of which explains (note the 'therefore' in 7a) how he spoke to his hearers. He addressed them with *urgency*: 'You brood of snakes! Who showed you that you needed to flee from the wrath to come?' (v. 7; see also v. 9). Not the most winsome address (snakes), not the most welcome theme (wrath). But there seems to be a kindness in the severity. If the word about God's wrath is true, it's really kind to know one is facing it. J. C. Ryle captures it all well: 'How plainly John speaks to his hearers about hell and danger.'

Then John presses *necessity* upon them. In view of the coming wrath, 'Produce therefore fruits that are fitting of repentance' (v. 8a). But along with what they must do, he also warns of what they must *not* do: 'Don't begin to say within yourselves, "We have Abraham as (our) father," for I tell you that God is able to raise up children to Abraham out of these stones!' (v. 8b). In other words, John is warning them not to play the 'Abraham card'; don't spout off, he says, about how you are physical descendants of Abraham, that you're in the covenant, that you've been circumcised, and how none of this applies to you. Indeed, John's demand for baptism was a real come-down for Israelite folks. At this time proselyte baptism was probably practiced. That was for gentiles who were attracted to Judaism and wanted to become part of Israel. They were required to undergo an immersion, usually self-administered, and to be circumcised (if male). Then they were said to be 'like a child newly born'.[2] But John was not preaching to gentiles but to Jews, Israelites. They, the covenant people, needed to be baptized and demonstrate genuine conversion.

---

2. NIDB, 1:391. On various washings in Judaism and John's baptism, see Michael Wilkins and David Garland's notes in ZIBBC, 1:24, pp. 209-10.

But if repentance is to be shown by evidence ('fruits,' v. 8), what does that look like? Hence John speaks about the *clarity* of repentance—what 'fruit' will show that repentance is genuine. For the crowds, it is generosity (vv. 10-11): if someone has two tunics, give one to someone who has none; the same with food. Tax collectors should show—surprise!— honesty (no lucrative surcharges, vv. 12-13). Soldiers (perhaps Jewish soldiers serving under Herod Antipas) were to show civility, not intimidating or 'shaking down' folks for extras; rather they should have contentment over their wages (v. 14). So repentance is not some esoteric religious concept but a disposition that could be visible in the flesh and goop of life.

Notice, by the way, what John did *not* say. He didn't tell soldiers to put on a peace demonstration in Rome, protesting 'the military-dictatorial complex'. Nor did he tell tax collectors to quit working for the government and become church custodians. Repentance, then, *is not seen in your doing some extra-ordinary feat but in your living ordinary life in a transformed way.* Repentance is a way of life right where you are. It is not done in Superland. You don't have to go on a retreat or a mission trip or take a seminary class or give an interview on a Christian TV network to show you are walking in repentance.

Don McClure once described a man living near his mission station in Pokwo, Ethiopia. The fellow was a community reject; he was a drunkard, refusing to work, was losing his wife and child because he couldn't keep up the bride payments; he seemed on his way to an imminent death for which few would grieve. Then he became a Christian; he overcame his passion for booze, took measures to get his wife and child back, and was hoeing one of the largest fields in the community. What evidence was there of repentance? Well, for one, hoeing. Not outstanding perhaps but very clear. For John, repentance shows up not in some stellar exhibition but in the brown-paper-package level of life.

Third, we notice how John takes **the lowest place** (vv. 15-18). Folks are speculating about whether John himself could be the Messiah (v. 15), and John puts the clamps on that idea. No, the 'One stronger' is coming and He [emphatic] will bring in the age of the Spirit (v. 16) and carry out a work of separation in Israel (v. 17). John confesses that he is not worthy to untie the straps of Messiah's sandals. That was a task from which even the rabbis exempted their servants—it was thought too menial and degrading. But John claims he is unworthy to perform even this degrading duty. You see then how careful John is not to usurp Jesus' place. One can't help but think of the way the Fourth Gospel puts it when the special Jerusalem Committee asked John who he was: 'And he confessed and did not deny, but confessed, "I am not the Messiah"' (John 1:20; cf. also John 1:8). J. C. Ryle applies John's attitude to Christian ministers: 'A minister who is really doing us good will make us think more of Jesus every year we live.' John's assessment, however, applies to all of Christ's servants as well—we should always have a proper knowledge of our place.

One thinks of Luther's graphic self-assessment. Those who followed Luther's teaching called themselves 'evangelicals', though their enemies called them 'Lutherans', a term Luther loyalists later adopted for themselves, over Luther's protest:

Who is this Luther? My teaching is not my own, and I have not been crucified for anyone. Why should it happen to me, miserable stinking bag of maggots that I am, that the children of Christ should be called by my insignificant name?[3]

We don't have to go to that extreme, do we? Well, if you know yourself, it's a good place to start. Our culture is so bent on how well you can strut, not how quickly you can kneel. And likely you need to keep saying to yourself, like John, 'I am not the Messiah'—five important words, for there are people's foibles and people's lives and your relatives' lives and maybe a few church ministries you'd like to 'fix'. And yourself—or someone—needs to say to you that you are not the Messiah. The lowest place is often the safest place.

Finally, Luke closes this segment by telling us that John paid **the highest price**: 'Now Herod the tetrarch, when he was rebuked by him for Herodias, his brother's wife, and for all the evil things Herod had done—he added this also on top of them all: he locked up John in prison' (vv. 19-20).

---

3. Nick Needham, *2,000 Years of Christ's Power*, 4 vols. (Fearn, Ross-shire: Christian Focus Publications, 2016), 3:121.

In Rome's view Herod Antipas (the 'Herod' of vv. 19-20) was a good ruler, reigning over Galilee and Perea from 4 B.C. to A.D. 39. But Rome is not the only judge. Antipas travelled to Rome about A.D. 29 and at some point in his journey visited a brother, Herod Philip (not the Philip of 3:1) in one of the coastal cities of Palestine. During said visit he fell in love with Herodias, his brother's wife. So Herodias was Antipas' sister-in-law, but she was at the same time Antipas' niece. Herodias agreed to marry Antipas when he came back from Rome, provided he divorced his current wife, a daughter of the Nabatean king Aretus IV. So Herod Antipas married his sister-in-law/niece, two marriages were broken up, for a marriage contrary to biblical law (Lev. 18:16; 20:21).[4] Antipas did not think a little incest was that big a deal. John dared to rebuke Antipas for this union and for other evils (v. 19); hence Antipas threw him in the slammer (v. 20) and later executed him (9:7-9; cf. Mark 6:14-29).

What is Luke showing us? He is telling us that John the Baptist was not invited to conduct Herod Antipas' prayer breakfasts; he is showing us that sometimes there is no 'fulfillment' in ministry; he is showing us that John had to bear the cross before the cross. Luke isn't implying that being Jesus' servant *always* leads to this, but is he not saying that it *can* and *may* lead to this? The Bible never hides the hard stuff in the small print. You could face this, you must be ready for this, in life under the gospel. We must then adopt an attitude that allows for paying this price.

Ulrich Zwingli had the proper attitude in such matters. Zwingli (1484–1531) was the reformer in Zurich when on one occasion the plague swept into and through the community. Zwingli ministered to his people amid the scourge and was eventually laid low himself. It was the plague, not persecution as John faced. But Zwingli's attitude as he faced likely death is the one needed for either. His prayer was, 'Do as you will for I lack nothing; I am your vessel to be restored or destroyed.'[5] Such is the prayer of one willing, if need be, to pay the highest price.

---

4. On Herod Antipas, see H. W. Hoehner in DJG, 1st ed., pp. 322-24.

5. John Woodbridge and Frank A. James III, *Church History Volume 2: From Pre-Reformation to the Present Day* (Grand Rapids: Zondervan, 2013), p. 152.

10

The Standing of Man
(Luke 3:21–4:13)

I want to focus on Jesus' temptations in 4:2b-13 in this section, but one dare not do that without taking account of the context in which Luke places them. Context is so crucial. I still have a couple of notes our middle son left me in his early teens. Early on Saturday mornings I would go off for a prayer meeting with the church's elders, and he left a note on my desk the night before: 'Wake me up before you go to prayer meeting, so I can read the Bible.' Some parents would give anything to have a kid like that. But context makes a difference. Our sons had gotten addicted to watching 'Championship Wrestling' on TV. They spent, in my view, too much time on it. So I proposed a legalistic solution: for every hour they watched Championship Wrestling, they had to spend an hour reading the Bible. (Don't quibble about my parenting.) When you understand that arrangement, that context, you see our son's 'piety' in its true light. And here Luke is supplying the context that will help us appreciate Jesus' temptations in their true light. Hence we take some time on this setting.

First, Luke underscores **the commitment Jesus makes** in His baptism. He tells us that 'when all the people were baptized and when Jesus also was baptized and was praying, heaven was opened and the Holy Spirit came down in bodily form like a dove upon him, and a voice came out of heaven,

"You are my Son, the One I love! I am delighted with you'"
(3:21-22). At His baptism Jesus is praying and is equipped
with the Spirit's power and assured of the Father's pleasure.
But we must not forget what His baptism connotes. According
to 3:3, John's baptism was 'a baptism of repentance with a
view to the forgiveness of sins'. Baptism was for sinners;
baptism was for folks needing to repent. Surely the object of
the Father's pleasure (v. 22) has no sin to repent of and no
need to repent. Why is Jesus, the sinless one, submitting to
something that sinners need? Because, already, at the very
beginning of His public work, Jesus is 'saying' that He has
come to stand in the place of sinners. The shadow of the cross
falls across the waters of the Jordan. In His baptism Jesus
commits Himself to take the sinner's place.

Then Luke points out **the contrast Jesus displays** in His
genealogy (3:23-38). Before we get to that 'contrast', however,
we should take a little space to discuss the genealogy, because
it is a bit of a puzzle no matter how one cuts it.

The scope of the genealogy takes in seventy-seven names
from Jesus back to Adam inclusive. Some think there are
eleven groups of seven names, but Luke doesn't call any
attention to such a structure.[1] As one 'reads' his way back to
Adam, one gets the impression that this is a long, slow story
that has at last reached its goal in the moment of Jesus.

Notice also the pattern or the direction of this family tree: it
is retrojective, it moves backward through history rather than
forward like Matthew's (Matt. 1:1-17). Not only so, but Luke
takes his genealogy clear back to Adam, whereas Matthew
starts his with Abraham. And Luke's placement differs from
Matthew's: Matthew begins his gospel with the table of
ancestors, but Luke places his between Jesus' baptism and
His temptation. More on this later.

Part of the 'problem' with Luke's genealogy is that it is
so different from Matthew's, and not simply in its scope and
'direction'. The names in the two texts between David and
Jesus are almost in total disagreement. Of course, Matthew
traces David's descendants via the 'royal' line of Solomon and
Judah's kings, while Luke follows a line through another son

---

1. Darrell L. Bock, *Luke 1:1–9:50*, BECNT (Grand Rapids: Baker, 1994), p. 350.

of David, Nathan (3:31). So there are bound to be substantial differences. Some think Matthew gives the legal line of descent from David, while Luke 'gives the actual descendants of David in the branch of the family to which Joseph belonged'.[2] There is also the quandary of how to explain the differing precursors of Joseph (Jacob in Matt. 1:16, Eli in Luke 3:23); there are possibilities, but they are largely speculative.[3]

There are these difficulties, then, and there is no clear explanation for them. At this point it's important not to do something stupid. What would that be? It would be stupid to make definite judgments about these (currently) inexplicable perplexities. It would be folly to allege that Luke used a screwed-up genealogy and didn't realize what he was doing here. We are wiser to assume the ignorance is ours and not to pontificate on such a basis.

Now back to 'the contrast Jesus displays'. As noted, Luke takes Jesus' lineage all the way back to Adam (3:38), and right after he mentions Adam, we read: 'Now Jesus, full of the Holy Spirit, returned from the Jordan and was being led by the Spirit in the wilderness, for forty days being tempted by the devil' (4:1-2a). Adam and temptation. This combination is Luke's way of saying, 'Read this temptation story in light of Genesis 3.' If space permitted, I think I could show that Matthew in his 'temptation' account (Matt. 4:1-11) wanted to contrast Israel's unfaithfulness (cf. Num. 14) with Jesus' faithfulness, but Luke by mentioning Adam and then the temptation wants us to contrast Jesus and Adam. We are to put Luke 4 beside Genesis 3. So there the first Adam was tempted, here the second 'Adam' is tempted. In Genesis 3 Adam faces the tempter in the richness of the garden, in Luke 4 Jesus faces him in the desolation of the wilderness; Adam is surrounded with provision, Jesus with destitution. Genesis 3 depicts the fall of man, Luke 4 reports the *standing* of man. Here is a bit of 1 John 3:8 in action. Jesus reverses, or begins to reverse, the ravages of the fall. Here is the second Adam, the representative head of a new humanity.

2. Cf. the discussion in I. Howard Marshall, *The Gospel of Luke*, NIGNT (Grand Rapids: Eerdmans, 1978), p. 158.

3. See discussion in Robert H. Stein, *Luke*, NAC (Nashville: Broadman, 1992), p. 141 (fn 38).

Then we should notice **the conflict Jesus faces** (4:1-2). It is worth noting the intensity of Jesus' temptation. I take 'forty days' in verse 2a with the participle 'being tempted' — 'for forty days being tempted by the devil.' There was a *continuing* barrage of temptation for forty days; then verse 2b introduces the *climactic* temptations that come near the end of that period (vv. 2b-13). Clearly, there weren't merely three specific temptations; there was an ongoing ordeal of temptation. One can't say everything about these selected, climactic temptations; however, one fruitful way to get at them is to consider what they reveal about Jesus' faith.

The first temptation, then, shows that *faith prefers to wait for God than to deify its own need* (vv. 3-4). The focus is on *necessity*. 'If you are the Son of God, tell this stone to become bread' (v. 3b). It's as if the tempter says: You have a genuine need here (acute hunger) and your Father has left you in this need and is apparently making no provision to satisfy your hunger. But in light of the fact that you're the Son of God,[4] you can act on your own and supply your own need. God has called you His Son whom He loves and yet He has left you in need; but you are not 'up the creek' as we say — you have power to meet your own need and act independently of your Father. That seems to be the tempter's 'pitch'.

Jesus' retort is both brief and biblical; He cites Deuteronomy 8:3, 'Man will not live by bread alone' (v. 4). That whole verse helps us to interpret Jesus' short citation of it. That text speaks of Yahweh afflicting Israel, causing them to hunger, and feeding them with manna to show them 'that man does not live by bread alone, but that man lives by all that comes out of the mouth of Yahweh.' So it refers to Yahweh feeding Israel with manna in the wilderness. But what is this 'all that comes out of the mouth of Yahweh'? We might say it refers to His word. Yes, but what sort of word specifically? It seems that in Deuteronomy 8 Moses is saying that it's not strictly the manna/bread that sustains Israel (or 'man') but what stands behind the manna. What is that? It is Yahweh's daily decision to give them manna — that's what 'comes out of the mouth

---

4. The 'if' in the text is not suggestive of doubt; the Greek construction here shows it='If, as is the case,' almost equivalent to 'since'.

of Yahweh,' not the word of God in some general sense but Yahweh's day-by-day decision for Israel to live, and so He supplies them with manna. In short, Israel's sustenance does not depend on the bread itself but on the will of God that decides to give the bread. I think that is where Jesus is resting here—in the will, and time, of God.

Perhaps we can see Satan's intent: he wanted Jesus to fixate on His need, to put His need in the driver's seat. Sometimes we may do that, even with legitimate needs, and when we do, we 'deify' our own needs.

There's a 'Peanuts' cartoon that highlights this problem. Lucy asks Charlie Brown why 'we are put here on earth'. Charlie responds, 'To make others happy.' Lucy becomes reflective. 'I don't think *I'm* making anyone very happy,' she says, but then adds, 'Of course, nobody is making *me* very happy either.' All of which goads her to scream at Charlie Brown, 'Somebody's not doing his job!' My need, whatever it is, must have supreme place.

Misunderstanding is easy, so let me insert a qualifier. I'm not saying that God doesn't care about our needs, nor am I denying that we have genuine needs. And so on. So don't overread me here. But because our present western culture, especially our psychologically-saturated culture, pummels us about our needs and harps on how important and legitimate and proper they are and about how urgent it is to have them met, you may so elevate your needs that they become your idol and God becomes your servant who must take care of and tend your 'idol'. Your culture—and sometimes even your church culture—will seldom say to you, 'Wait in the wilderness and see what God will do for you.'

Luke's second temptation account shows that *faith prefers worshiping the true God to ruling the whole world* (vv. 5-8). The focus in this temptation is on *immediacy*: 'You therefore, if you worship before me—all will be yours' (v. 7). Actually, 'all the kingdoms of the world' (v. 5) had already been promised to the Messiah in Psalm 2:8 ('Ask me, and I will give nations as your inheritance, and the ends of the earth for your possession'). Daniel 7:14 depicted the same: 'and to him [the one like a Son of man] was given dominion and glory and kingdom, that all peoples, nations, and languages should serve him …' (rsv). But this was, at least partly, a temptation to take the short cut rather than the long obedience. 'You can have all the glory now, Jesus.' But Jesus had committed Himself to a certain procedure in His baptism—to stand in the sinner's place, which meant that suffering must precede glory. We might say the first temptation suggested there was no need to wait for divine attention, while the second implied there was no need to follow the divine program. There is that God-ordained order, suffering then glory, for Jesus, and for His people (Rom. 8:17; Acts 14:22).

But the primary point at issue had to do with worship—'if you worship me' (v. 7, niv). Notice with what simplicity Jesus faces this temptation. He does not enter into debate over the devil's claim (v. 6b), does not draw out the implications of the verb 'handed over' (again, v. 6), does not inquire into or haggle over the tempter's view of last things—He never turns aside to discuss side issues but goes straight for the jugular, for the heart of the matter, the 'worship' issue of verses 7-8. And Deuteronomy 6:13 settles it (v. 8b).

This is worth thinking through and considering the implications of Jesus' response. Is not Jesus by this statement/quotation (v. 8) in this setting—is He not saying that it matters more to worship the true God than to possess the whole world? Is that not a very interesting view of worship? Doesn't it suggest that there's a primacy worship has above all other 'activities' or achievements? This same estimate of worship is assumed in the desperate cries in the Psalms:

> What profit is there in my blood,
> when I go down to the pit?
> Will dust give you thanks?
> Will it declare your faithfulness? (Ps. 30:9)

What is David saying? In part he is saying that if he dies, he will no longer be able to praise and worship Yahweh. Dead folks don't get to sing 'Great Is Thy Faithfulness' in public worship. That in turn implies that really his whole purpose for existence is to engage in praise and thanksgiving to the only true God. Such considerations tend to solve deep questions like, 'What is the purpose of my life?'

The final temptation (in Luke's order) shows that *faith prefers to trust God than to test God* (vv. 9-12). We might say the focus is on *certainty* here. Can we be sure of God and His care? In particular, can Jesus be sure of God and His care, and, if so, is He ready to demonstrate that He believes it? The scene, then, is 'the wing of the temple complex', a quite elevated place, and the devil says, 'If you are the Son of God, throw yourself down from here' (v. 9), for, he adds, there's an assurance in Psalm 91 of God's complete protection. The design is not to make a grand display before people but to force God's hand into supplying dramatic protection. All the temptations seek to drive a wedge into the relationship of the Son with the Father.

The pitch, we might say, is to suggest that since Jesus is the Son of God, God will be all the more attentive in caring for Him—but Jesus should prove that. Do you really believe that, Jesus? Do you believe the Bible, Jesus? All that stuff about the shelter of the Most High and the shadow of the Almighty? Look here—here's one of those it-is-written affairs: Psalm 91:11-12. Can You stand on the promises, Jesus? How far will You trust Your Father? How much faith do You have? Are You willing to take the leap of faith?

Here is part of the catch. What is faith? We're not always clear about what something means. We're like that older woman who came bubbling over to Will Moorhead, a congressman from Pennsylvania. In 1960 he'd made what he thought was a good speech on housing for the elderly. Afterward this woman accosted him with, 'Oh, Congressman, your speech was superfluous! Simply superfluous!' Moorhead thanked her, not sure whether she was ignorantly sincere or intentionally mocking him. So he said, 'I'm thinking of having it published posthumously.' She responded with, 'Oh, that's wonderful! The sooner the better!'[5]

'Faith' is like that. Sometimes we get muddled over the meaning of it. Sometimes we may catch ourselves almost thinking that faith is convincing yourself of something you know isn't true. Or—as here—is faith making or taking stupid risks? Is it faith to push on God to give dramatic evidence

---

5. Paul F. Boller, Jr., *Congressional Anecdotes* (New York: Oxford, 1991), pp. 100-01.

of His care? Is it faith to jump off the wing of the temple complex, hollering 'I believe ... in Psalm ... ninety ... one ...' as you go down?

This temptation packs important correction: genuine faith doesn't need sensational proof of God's attention. To press for that is testing God, not believing God. Hence Jesus' retort from Deuteronomy 6:16: 'You are not to put the Lord your God to the test.' To try to push God for proof of His protection or deliverance is a sign of *lack* of faith. Imagine a wife telling her husband, 'You didn't bring any flowers home for me today'; 'you haven't bought me any expensive perfume'; 'you haven't taken me out to dinner for nine days—so how can you say you love me?' 'You didn't call me today on your noon-hour break'; 'today was one of our half-anniversary dates, but you didn't give me a card.' She's putting her husband to the test; she's making him overtly prove himself over and over—and it simply shows a lack of trust in his love.

So what about Jesus? How does Jesus show His faith? By turning around and walking away from the pinnacle of the temple. Which ought to teach us that God can be trusted when He is not sensational. Faith is not demanding the spectacular but remaining content with the ordinary. All of which leads us back to the prayer we must always pray: 'And do not lead us into temptation, but deliver us from the evil one' (Matt. 6:13).

11

A Sizzling Sabbath

(Luke 4:14-30)

We are on our way to Nazareth, Jesus' hometown. But the 'transition text' of verses 14–15 is important. It shows, as James Edwards says, that Jesus does not return from combat with Satan as 'a limping survivor', battered and mauled by the tempter, but returns 'in the power of the Spirit into Galilee' (14) and He 'was teaching in their synagogues' (15). Right up front, then, Luke hits us with **the task of Jesus**, the teaching and preaching of the word of God (see also vv. 43-44). As Edwards notes, moderns are more often impressed by ministries of compassion or 'presence' than by teaching and preaching—but this was the activity at the core of Jesus' ministry.[1] If it holds primacy for Jesus, it ought to be supremely prized among His people.

Once Thomas Hogg's (d. 1692) servant, William Balloch, lay gripped with fever and more: with doubts and fears. He crawled from his bed and up the stairs to Hogg's apartment to ask his counsel. But Hogg was preparing to preach and refused to speak with him then. Yet Hogg's dwelling was also his chapel and since the walls were thin, Balloch heard from his bed the whole of Hogg's sermon. And amazingly all the matters involving his temptations and despair were

---

1. James R. Edwards, *The Gospel According to Luke*, PNTC (Grand Rapids: Eerdmans, 2015), p. 133.

addressed in Hogg's preaching.[2] I know it sounds dated and simplistic, but sometimes you don't need a skilled counselor or a wise mentor—you just need good preaching, the lively, public explanation and application of the word of God. That's what Jesus was up to; He was teaching in their synagogues.

Now Luke does something that's a bit 'shifty'. I don't mean dishonest; but he shifts this Nazareth episode, which apparently happened a bit later in Jesus' ministry (see Matt. 13:54-58; Mark 6:1-6), to the very beginning of his account of Jesus' work. Nothing devious about it; clearly, we can tell from Jesus' allusion in verse 23 that He had already had a ministry in Capernaum. But Luke brings this incident forward and places it front and center, because it furnishes the perspective, the lens, through which he wants you to view Jesus' ministry. There are matters that sometimes affect or 'control' a whole scene. A number of years ago, the University of South Carolina baseball team was playing a game against a 'convict' team at the state penitentiary. A South Carolina batter was about to dispute a called third strike and the prisoners' coach yelled out: 'You'd better not argue with that umpire. He's doing life for murder.' Well, that was a vital piece of information! And I'm sure it governed the demeanor of all those college players throughout the game. That's the way with this Nazareth episode. Luke places it here because he wants it to govern the way you look at all of Jesus' ministry. You need to see it all in light of Isaiah 61.

What does Luke want to stress in this specially selected episode in Nazareth's synagogue? Well, he wants us to hear **the claim of Jesus** (vv. 16-21). Without bothering to offer proof right now, this is likely what initially aggravated His hearers (cf. v. 22b). Jesus is given the privilege to exhort the people on this Sabbath; He stands up to read and the attendant hands Him the scroll of Isaiah. 'When he unrolled the scroll, he found the place where it was written ...' (v. 17b). Note: Jesus *deliberately* sought and selected the passage from Isaiah 61. Scholars generally agree that in the first century A.D. the synagogue readings from the prophets were not pre-selected—

---

2. M. MacDonald, *The Covenanters in Moray and Ross* (Inverness: Melven Bros., 1892), 98-99. I have found the surname spelt both 'Hog' and 'Hogg,' depending on the source.

expositors had the freedom to choose a prophetic passage, and Jesus on purpose zeroed in on Isaiah 61.

Jesus reads from Isaiah 61:1-2a and we could bury ourselves in a mass of details regarding this text.[3] But I think we'll feel Jesus' point better if we primarily look at His text in the context of Isaiah's prophecy.

We start with Isaiah 59, and it's pretty sad. This chapter moves from *accusation* of Israel's sins (vv. 1-8) to *confession* (vv. 9-15a; note the first person plurals, 'we,' 'us') on to *intervention* (vv. 15b-20; things were so hopeless Yahweh Himself plunged in and set them to rights), which section closes on the note that 'A redeemer shall come to/for Zion, even to those in Jacob who turn from rebellion' (v. 20); then the chapter climaxes in an *affirmation* (v. 21) that deserves some attention.

In Isaiah 59:21, then, Yahweh begins, 'As for me, this is my covenant with them.' With whom? With those in verse 20 who turn away from rebellion, i.e., with the repentant remnant of Israel. He continues, 'My Spirit which is upon you ….' Upon whom? The 'you' is masculine singular. Isaiah has already noted that Yahweh will place His Spirit upon the coming messianic king (11:1-2) and upon His (suffering) 'servant' (42:1). The text goes on: 'And my words which I have placed in your mouth ….' Again, this summarizes how Yahweh equipped His Servant to speak His word, as 49:2 and 50:4 show. (Remember that as the 'Servant' revelation moves along from chapter 42 to 49 to 50 to 52 and 53 the stress is

---

3. For example, who are the 'poor ones' (*ptōchoi*), v. 18? Obviously, from what follows they are the captives, the 'blind,' the shattered (v. 18b) and the same as the 'mourners of Zion' (Isa. 61:3). *Ptochoi* here (and in LXX) translates Heb. *'anawim* in Isa. 61:1. English renderings of the word in the OT run a gamut: afflicted, helpless, humble, meek, oppressed. The use of *'anāwîm* in the Psalms is instructive: there they stand in contrast to the 'wicked' (Pss. 10:12; 37:10-11; 147:6), while parallel descriptions are 'his people' (Ps. 149:4) and those who 'seek God' (Pss. 22:26; 69:32). So they are Yahweh's people, His remnant, who are often in dire and dismal circumstances, beaten down in the world. Jesus also stops His quote before it mentions 'the day of vengeance of our God'. Jesus was not negating that idea; it was just not His purpose to stress it here. Clearly the 'day of vengeance' and the 'year of redemption' (see Isa. 63:4) stand together, for there is no deliverance/redemption for God's people unless God represses and judges their enemies. There is also a line from Isaiah 58:6 in Jesus' text ('to set at liberty those who are oppressed,' ESV); I assume that Luke edited it in because it paralleled similar lines in Isaiah 61:1-2. I omit discussion of links with Qumran and the Dead Sea scroll community.

on His suffering, but 42:1-4 clearly implies this 'servant' is also royal). Then there is the affirmation in the last of the verse: 'they [i.e., especially the words of Yahweh] will not depart from your mouth or from the mouth of your seed or from the mouth of the seed of your seed ... from now on and for all time.' Yahweh will just never allow His people to ever be without His revelation given through His Servant. His word will have a continuous and 'always' place among the Servant's people.

That's Isaiah 59:21. So then we come to chapters 60–62; the sustained theme of these chapters is the future and glorious restoration of Israel. And right in the middle of this comes 61:1-3. All of a sudden someone is speaking in the first person ('me'), the same first-person lingo as the Servant used in 49:1-4 and 50:4-9. Must not the 'me' here in 61 be the same person? Moreover, he refers to God as 'Lord Yahweh' (61:1a) just as the Servant did in 50:4, 5, 7, and 9. And—'the Spirit' is upon him, once more as with the royal-servant figure of 11:1-2 and 42:1—and 59:21!—and he is to proclaim Yahweh's word (again, as in 49:2; 50:4; and 59:21). So here in 61:1-3 we come upon the messianic Servant-prophet who announces the arrival of the stellar age of restoration (= chs. 60–62).

Which brings us to the claim of Jesus: 'Today this scripture has been fulfilled in your ears' (Luke 4:21). He did not mean that all of Isaiah 60–62 had been consummated but that this new age had arrived, that the fulfillment had begun, that He (the royal, servant-like, prophetic figure Isaiah had tracked through his prophecy) was the announcer and bringer of it. Quite a claim for a local carpenter to make! There were many who were sleepless in the synagogue that day. And this is vintage Jesus. He may anger you, fluster you, upset, disturb, and infuriate you, but He won't let you yawn. You, He says, have got to deal with who I am.

This brings us to **the offense of Jesus** (vv. 22-27). The Nazareth congregation began to have trouble with Jesus almost immediately. True, 'they were marveling over the gracious words' He spoke, yet they began to say, 'Is not this Joseph's son?' (v. 22b). There was the rub. Oh, it was a 'bonnie' sermon, but that Jesus is the royal-like, servant-like, prophet-like figure of Isaiah who announces the arrival of the new age as taking place on that particular Sabbath in Nazareth's synagogue—well, that was simply too much. It stretches credulity to believe that a local carpenter who made Aunt Tillie's chest of drawers or Azariah and Beulah's kitchen table could possibly be some messianic-type figure. As J. C. Ryle said: 'How apt men are to despise the highest privileges when they are familiar with them.'[4]

Then Jesus takes up what the crowd was already murmuring:[5] do here the sort of things we heard you've done in Capernaum. But, apparently, Jesus won't. He likely senses their response and announces a sort of proverbial saying: No prophet is accepted on his own turf (v. 24). He then illustrates that saying from the days of Elijah (1 Kings 17) and Elisha (2 Kings 5) in the northern kingdom of Israel. Jesus points out a strange phenomenon: there were scads of widows in Israel in Elijah's time, during the great drought; but God didn't send Elijah to any of them; He sent him to Zarephath in Sidon, to Pagansville in Baal country, to a gentile widow there (vv. 25-26). Likewise, Israel had many lepers in Elisha's day, but the only one cleansed under Elisha's ministry was a pagan Syrian army general (v. 27). What crabbed the Nazareth folks was not merely that Jesus spoke of God's benefits going to unwashed gentiles but what those Elijah-Elisha narratives implied—for example, in sending Elijah to be helped and to help that widow in Zarephath *Yahweh was passing by His own people*.[6] And Jesus implies something similar is happening in Nazareth—the works done elsewhere (cf. v. 23) will not be done in Nazareth: God in His judgment is passing them by. That is not the sort of thing the citizens of Nazareth want to hear, especially from one of their own, who, if anything, ought to be pro-Nazareth.

It is at this point that Luke points us to **the destiny of Jesus** (vv. 28-30). Instead of road rage we hear of 'church' rage; fury possesses them, and they haul Jesus off to heave Him

4. J. C. Ryle, *Expository Thoughts on the Gospels: St. Luke*, 2 vols. (New York: Baker & Taylor, 1858), 1:120.

5. So E. Earle Ellis, *The Gospel of Luke*, NCB, rev. ed. (London: Oliphants, 1974), p. 97.

6. See M. B. Van't Veer, *My God Is Yahweh* (St. Catharines, Ontario: Paideia, 1980), p. 88.

off a suitable ridge. But, somehow, Jesus slipped through the crowd and went on His way (v. 30). Luke doesn't tell us how He managed that, but wouldn't the Bible be boring if it stopped to explain every conundrum in detail? What we do see in these verses is a preview of what will happen at the last, when the mob cries 'Away with this man' (23:18) and there is a cross instead of an escape. Speaking a bit loosely, the crucifixion begins at Nazareth.

'Jesus is rejected not in Sodom and Gomorrah, but in Nazareth.'[7] Being familiar with Jesus can prove dreadfully dangerous.

---

7. Edwards, p. 142.

12

A Capernaum Sabbath

(Luke 4:31-44)

We might think of 4:14–5:16 as 'an introduction to Jesus' ministry'. Within this segment the Nazareth episode (4:14-30) strikes a negative note, while the Capernaum report (4:31-44) carries a more positive tone. Not that Jesus won't have a hard word for Capernaum (see 10:15), but here at least it forms a contrast to Nazareth. As Jesus casts out demons and heals the sick here, we see what the Isaiah 61 ministry announced in 4:18-19 was to look like.[1] So Luke says Jesus 'went down' to Capernaum (v. 31) and he wasn't kidding. Nazareth is about 1,300 feet above sea level, Capernaum above 700 feet below sea level, quite a drop.[2] Here we are on the northwestern shore of the Sea of Galilee and 'authority' is the buzz word among the people (vv. 32, 36).

Luke probably intends us to see verses 33-37 as a premier event. It is the first miracle of Jesus that Luke records and is probably meant to be viewed as a *signal* miracle; right at the first of Jesus' ministry He demonstrates His power and victory over Satan and His minions. Luke is telling us that **Jesus' power is assuring,** for if Jesus vanquishes demonic power in this paradigm episode, then surely He is also the

---

1. Mark L. Strauss, 'Luke,' in ZIBBC, 4 vols. (Grand Rapids: Zondervan, 2002), 1:364.

2. Robert H. Stein, *Luke*, NAC (Nashville: Broadman, 1992), p. 162.

cosmic Lord who will banish Satan and all his lackeys at the last. This miracle, rightly seen, provides the people of God with a most settling, 'eschatological' assurance.

But one can't leave these verses without calling attention to a dire warning they contain. There is this man in the synagogue with 'a spirit of an unclean demon' and he screams, 'Let alone; why are you meddling with us, Jesus of Nazareth? Have you come to destroy us? I know who you are, the Holy One of God!' (v. 34; cf. also v. 41).[3] That last statement is where the danger lies. It's actually more than the folks at Nazareth would say. And it is a confession of *truth*, but not a confession of *faith*. So you can know and say true things about Jesus and yet have no saving interest in Him. J. C. Ryle put it pointedly: 'We may go on all our lives saying, "I know that, and I know that," and sink at last into hell, with the words on our lips.'[4]

Next, Luke shows us that **Jesus' power is promiscuous** (vv. 38-41). It is not confined to the synagogue but serves Peter's mother-in-law 'in the grip of a severe fever' (v. 38). Her healing was so complete that she immediately got up and re-joined the kitchen crew (v. 39). Then when the sun went down (v. 40a), that is, when the Sabbath was officially over and folks wouldn't get chewed out for breaking the Sabbath, a whole menagerie of sick and afflicted folks descended on Peter's house and received Jesus' personal attention ('he laid his hands on each one of them,' v. 40b). Jesus held nothing back.

Here, however, I think it's especially instructive to compare verses 33-37 (the synagogue scene) with verses 38-39 (Peter's mother-in-law), for one sees that for all the *cosmic* implications of Jesus' work in casting out a demon, He is yet the *domestic* Savior of verses 38-39. He is the Christ who conquers the evil one and yet the Christ who provides in the home. He works in the public place but also enters into private need. There is always something heartening in seeing this sort of thing. John Hay, a

---

3. 'Why are you meddling,' etc., is lit., 'What to us and to you?' My rendering here leans on Nigel Turner, *Grammatical Insights into the New Testament* (Edinburgh: T. & T. Clark, 1965), pp. 43-47. 'Have you come to destroy us?' could be construed as a statement: 'You have come to destroy us!' A marvelously comforting word though spoken by a demon.

4. J. C. Ryle, *Expository Thoughts on the Gospels: St. Luke*, 2 vols. (New York: Baker & Taylor, 1858), 1:125-26.

young man who was one of President Lincoln's secretaries, once noticed Fanny Seward, the shy, teenaged daughter of Lincoln's Secretary of State, standing rather forlorn and alone at a White House reception. Hay went to her side and told her that he hoped she did not know all the various people there because it was 'so pleasant to tell who people were'. So for the next hour they chatted together as Hay informed her about the celebrities around them.[5] It was a fine touch, seeing an ill-at-ease girl at the social and kindly coming to her rescue with a bit of personal attention. We see something of that pattern in Jesus here. He's in the synagogue but also in the sick room. He carries on a public ministry but is not allergic to private troubles. He both quells the raging of demons and takes care of mothers-in-law.

Finally, Luke shows us that **Jesus' priority is preaching** (vv. 42-44). After what must have been an exhausting and exhilarating day of ministry, Jesus seeks a remote place. Luke does not explicitly say (as Mark does, Mark 1:35) that Jesus prayed, but does he need to do so? In any case, He is besieged by the people of greater Capernaum and pressured to stay among them (v. 42b). This He had to refuse because He was under a divine 'must'—He must 'preach the good news of the kingdom of God' (v. 43) in the other towns as well. That, to preach the kingdom, is why He was 'sent.' He means sent by God. God sent Him to preach.

The content of Jesus' preaching is 'the kingdom of God.' This (in v. 43) is the first exact occurrence of the phrase in Luke's gospel. In all it appears 32 times (along with seven references to God or Jesus' kingdom without 'of God'). Alan Thompson offers a fine summary:

> In Luke's Gospel the kingdom is: both present (10:9, 11; 11:20; 17:21) and future (13:28-29; 19:11; 21:31); both God's (4:43, passim) and Jesus' (22:30; 23:42); and granted by both the Father (12:32) and the Son (22:29) to Jesus' disciples (8:10) who are "the poor" (6:20) or "humble" who "receive" Jesus (18:16-17) and therefore "enter" the kingdom, God's saving rule (18:24-26).[6]

---

5. David Herbert Donald, *"We Are Lincoln Men"* (New York: Simon & Schuster, 2003), p. 183.

6. Alan J. Thompson, *Luke*, EGGNT (Nashville: Broadman & Holman, 2016), pp. 81.

Jesus had already preached this way at Nazareth when He proclaimed the fulfillment of Isaiah 61 and Himself as the proclaimer and bringer of the fulfillment. And that we may possess (6:20), see (9:27), seek (12:31), receive (18:17), enter (18:25), and wait for (23:51) the kingdom implies that we must make a proper response to Jesus' proclamation.

Again, I think there is a warning note for God's people in this little segment. Did you note verse 42b? 'They came to him and tried to hold him back from going (away) from them.' Can't blame them in a way; it was wholly natural. But doesn't this point to a repeatable trouble? We like to 'manage' Jesus; we want to conform Him to our own wishes, to 'shape' Him to fit our own purposes.

Arnold Dallimore in his biography of George Whitefield has an interesting account of Anglican Whitefield's visit to Scotland in 1741. He preached for Ralph and Ebenezer Erskine (the 'Seceders'). They had a fine rapport on the whole but the latter were eager for Whitefield to confine himself to their group, so they could set him right on church government; they would not insist just yet on his subscribing to 'the solemn league and covenant' but wanted him to preach solely for them until he had further light.[7] And we—not just Capernaumites—can make the same mistake with Jesus: we try to finagle Him to meet our expectations, to fall in with our program, to meet our designs of what Jesus ought to do or be like. Again and again He may have to remind us that *we* do not write His script.

---

7. Arnold A. Dallimore, *George Whitefield*, 2 vols. (Westchester, IL: Crossway Books, 1979), 2:88-89.

13

A True Fish Story

(Luke 5:1-11)

My teen-age years passed near Aliquippa, Pennsylvania, where J & L Steel was big. Aliquippa and steel were semi-synonymous at the time. And the Lake of Gennesaret, as Luke calls it, or, more commonly, the Sea of Galilee, was alive with fishing. William Barclay claims that in the NT period there were 'nine townships clustered around its shores, none of them with fewer than 15,000 people'.[1] Fishing was 'in.' There are apparently between eighteen and twenty-five species of fish in the Sea of Galilee (the number depends on whom one consults). But we're already veering off-track, for we know Luke does not tell us this fish story for us to admire fish but to see Jesus.

Already in the preface to the story (vv. 1-4), we can see **the courtesy Jesus displays**. Here, especially in verses 1 and 3, the focus is on the word and teaching (in line with 4:43-44). Simon's boat, however, becomes the object of Jesus' creativity, for it allows Jesus a little space from the press of the crowd in order to teach them. In the loan of his boat Simon was really

---

1. William Barclay, *The Gospel of Luke*, Daily Study Bible (Philadelphia: Westminster, 1956), p. 52. Scholars discuss the relation of our passage with Mark 1:16-20. The main options in my view are: they are the same incident but Luke includes much more detail that Mark's account passes by, or, Luke's story tells of a separate incident. Those wanting to delve into this can begin with Darrell L. Bock, *Luke 1:1-9:50*, BECNT (Grand Rapids: Baker, 1994), pp. 448-51.

assisting in the ministry of the word—in his own indirect way, he was a servant of the word. Hence, in verse 4, Jesus wants to give him a 'user's fee' for occupying his boat—a tip for his service, and Jesus always tips well. It's a bit of Jesus' courtesy, and it somewhat reflects what Jesus had said in Matthew 10:42:

> And whoever gives just a cup of cold water to one of these little ones because he is a disciple—I assure you: He will never lose his reward (HCSB).

There is no service, be it ever so small or apparently insignificant, that Jesus forgets. Not even the loan of a boat.

This should prove a bit heartening to us. Let's say you are a Christian father and you may not feel especially eager to drag yourself upstairs at 8:30 in the evening to have a brief talk with your eleven-year-old daughter over a difficulty she had faced at school that day. But up you went. You listened and spoke with her and prayed with her. Not a big deal. Twenty minutes at the max. But Jesus doesn't forget the small stuff, like boat loans and daughter talks. It's part of the sheer courtesy Jesus displays.

The center of this account records **the foolishness Jesus commands** (vv. 4-7). 'Put out into the deep water,' Jesus said, 'and let down your nets for a catch!' (v. 4). The text doesn't convey tone of voice or precise attitudes, but one senses Peter is exercising patience in verse 5: 'Master, all night long we've toiled and taken nothing; but *at your word* [emphatic] I will let down the nets.' Perhaps Peter recalled that he had already seen the effects Jesus' word produces (4:39, and probably he also witnessed 4:35-36). One still wonders, however, if he's not skeptical about a carpenter directing a professional fisherman in the latter's area of expertise. But then—a 'huge number of fish,' breaking nets (v. 6), emergency help, sinking boats (v. 7)! But it all seemed so foolish, simply so wrong-headed.

For one thing, Jesus' command was *insensitive*—He had already tied up Peter's boat for His teaching time and Peter & Co. were likely exhausted from their all-night foray (v. 5); and it was *irrational*—fishing out in the deep in the daytime was a sort of 'bonkers' suggestion. The Sea of Galilee seemed to yield more profitable hauls close to shore; and the nets used in deep water could be seen by the fish in daytime and so avoided.[2]

Here we must enter a caution. It's one thing to see in the text that Jesus commanded something apparently foolish and ludicrous. It's another thing what you do with that. Don't turn the point on its head and start thinking Jesus *only* works in strange and bizarre and unexpected ways and never in the ordinary and run-of-the-mill and seeming rational. That's when we see some fellow get up and say he believes the Lord is calling him to quit his job, uproot his family, solicit donors (naturally), and move to Paraguay and start a faith mission there. Probably not. That's more likely his own ego speaking than the Shepherd's voice. So don't let this point go to seed, so that you say that if it seems weird, then Jesus must be in it. Rather, if it seems weird, it may just be weird.

All that said, Jesus *does* at times seem to operate in 'foolish,' irrational ways that don't make much sense. It reminds me of the company commander sometime during the Battle of the Bulge who told one of his platoon leaders to 'take' a house in a German-occupied village. The lieutenant was a 'replacement' fresh from the US; he apparently didn't know to throw a grenade in, kick in the door, and enter guns blazing. Hence the commander was horrified as he watched his lieutenant walk up and knock on the door and talk to the German sergeant who answered it, resplendent in undershirt and suspenders. The sergeant barked orders—German guards behind a fence and barn came out with hands up; a hidden machine gun crew surrendered. How did it happen? Oh, the platoon leader simply *asked* the Germans to turn over the house and surrender.[3]

And verse 4 is strange like that—let down your nets in deep water in daytime. But sometimes Jesus' foolishness is simply a cover for His goodness that can sink your boats! Jesus does

2. See Joel B. Green, *The Gospel of Luke*, NICNT (Grand Rapids: Eerdmans, 1997), p. 232, citing a study by David Bivin; also Carl J. Laney, 'Fishing the Sea of Galilee,' in *Lexham Geographic Commentary on the Gospels,* ed. Barry J. Beitzel (Bellingham, WA: Lexham, 2017), pp. 165-73.

3. Stephen E. Ambrose, *Citizen Soldiers* (New York: Touchstone, 1998), p. 284.

sometimes work in outlandish ways that baffle us to no end. We simply note the pattern here. So … sometimes you'll ask: Why is He leading me in this way? Or, Whatever could He possibly have in mind with this strange re-arrangement of my circumstances? What on earth is He up to now? Sometimes Jesus orders a bit of foolishness.

Third, we see **the insight Jesus brings** (v. 8): 'When Simon Peter saw (it), he fell at Jesus' knees, saying, "Go away from me, because I am a sinful man, O Lord".' Peter saw himself differently; he got a new view of himself. What brought this on? Verse 9 may give a partial explanation—'For amazement had come over him and all those with him over the catch of fish they had taken.' Peter & Co. knew what was likely and what was near impossible in fishing Gennesaret; they knew this should not have happened; they smelled something supernatural. Hence their amazement.

Of course, we might look at Peter's response here and compare it to the vision Isaiah had of the majestic holiness of God (see Isa. 6:5), and yet what overwhelmed Peter was not a devastating view of God's holiness but an experience of the overwhelming goodness and kindness of Jesus.[4] And notice that Peter's is a *spiritual* response: He does not say, 'I am a lousy fisherman,' but 'I am a sinful man.' Jesus has no reason to have any truck with him at all.

Don't think Peter's attitude is merely an impulsive impression. There is a change of language in the way he addresses Jesus, which may be revealing. In verse 5 he calls Him 'Master' (*epistatēs*), whereas in verse 8 he addresses Him as 'Lord' (*kurios*). Depending on context, *kurios* can mean 'Sir' as well as 'Lord,' but James Edwards argues that 'Lord' has been used thirty times in the Third Gospel at this point, all with reference to the Lord God. So he infers that Luke surely intends his readers to hear 'Lord' as a divine title here.[5] Is it

---

4. If you're worried about 'techie' matters, don't be; i.e., how could Peter fall at Jesus' knees without de-stabilizing the boat and so on. A few years ago, a boat was discovered in the Sea of Galilee, dating from the first century A.D. It was twenty-six and a half feet long and seven and a half feet wide. No flimsy canoe. See Robert H. Stein, *Luke*, NAC (Nashville: Broadman, 1992), p. 169.

5. James R. Edwards, *The Gospel According to Luke*, PNTC (Grand Rapids: Eerdmans, 2015), p. 155.

that Peter sees who Jesus is (Lord) and that helps him to see who he is (a sinful man)? Calvin has famously written that 'no one ever attains clear knowledge of self unless he has first gazed upon the face of the Lord.'[6] I suppose (and I may be wrong) that part of Peter's self-repulsion came from shame over his arrogance and perhaps subtle disdain in verse 5, which may stand behind his grudging consent ('but at your word'). Peter seemed for all his acquiescence to have assumed a certain superiority to Jesus. Now all that is in tatters.

I think it may be helpful for us to note when this insight came home to Peter, if we may 'typify' it in terms familiar to us. You note from Peter's use of 'Master' in verse 5 that he already had had some association with Jesus, indeed, some degree of allegiance to Jesus, so that we would probably not call this Luke 5 episode a 'conversion' experience but a post-conversion experience (as I believe Isaiah's was in Isaiah 6). This means that you may come to this frightful awareness of your own sinfulness and utter ungodliness *after* you've been a follower of Jesus for some time. This realization does not necessarily hit you when you first come to Christ, but He may bring this home to you after you've been His for a time.[7] If it is shattering, it is also liberating—you sense that you've finally got *truth*. And there's something settling about that.

We mustn't leave this passage without noting **the constancy Jesus shows** (v. 10). This may be a greater miracle than the fish of verse 6 or the confession of verse 8. 'Don't be afraid,' Jesus says, 'from now on it's men you will be catching' (v. 10b). Here Jesus shows He is not only competent to catch fish but gracious to accept sinners. Let's put it this way: there are some believers who can get verse 8 into their mouths but can't get verse 10 into their ears. Isn't it heartening to consider what Jesus' response was *not?* What if Jesus came back with: 'Yes, well, I'm totally shocked. This puts a whole different light on our association. It looks like I will have to pull up stakes and start with somebody else.' But that was not it.

---

6. John Calvin, *Institutes*, trans. from French ed. of 1541 by Robert White (Edinburgh: Banner of Truth, 2014), p. 2.

7. See John 'Rabbi' Duncan's reflections on having not done a sinless action in his seventy years; A. Moody Stuart, *The Life of John Duncan* (1872; reprint ed., Edinburgh: Banner of Truth, 1991), p. 150.

Jesus' comeback was: From now on I have work for you. He doesn't throw His sin-riddled servants under the bus. Here is the constancy Jesus shows.

Bobby Richardson played second base for the New York Yankees in the 1950s-60s, part of the time under legendary manager Casey Stengel. But Stengel liked to shuffle line-ups, platoon players, and Richardson found it unsettling. But Stengel, like most Yankee managers, was eventually fired, and Ralph Houk became manager. He didn't try to keep things unsettled. In fact, he told Bobby Richardson at the first of the 1961 season that he didn't care if he was in a batting slump or whatever, he was going to be his second baseman; he'd be playing every day. It was just the sort of assurance Richardson needed to make him thrive. One sees a similar tenacity on Jesus' part in the text here. Jesus doesn't let go of His servant. Peter says, 'I am a sinful man, O Lord,' and Jesus so much as says, 'I think I can use you—I have work for you to do.'

Looking back over this fascinating passage we would do well to let a couple of questions hang over us: (1) Do I allow place for the 'foolishness' of Jesus?, and (2) Have I grasped that the first step for Christian usefulness is in verse 8?

14

'Lepers Are Being Cleansed!'

(Luke 5:12-16)

The rubric for this section comes from Luke 7:22, part of Jesus' answer to John the Baptist, in which He piles up evidence that He is indeed the 'coming one.'[1] And here we meet 'a man full of leprosy' (v. 12). But is his 'leprosy' really leprosy? The reason for that question is that the traditional translation 'leprosy' does not seem to specify what we (since the nineteenth century) know as 'leprosy,' i.e., Hansen's disease. It seems, especially in Leviticus 13-14, to cover, at least in humans, a range of ritually defiling skin maladies, perhaps like psoriasis, eczema, favus, and leukoderma. Perhaps such 'leprosy' could include 'Hansen's disease,' but it was not limited to that.[2] But in our passage it doesn't matter: the fellow on the ground in front of Jesus did not have some minor dermatological disorder—he was, Luke says, 'full of leprosy.' Whatever form it was, his was a severe case. Which meant he lived something like a living death. As Leviticus 13:45-46 required, he wore torn clothes, let his hair hang loose and untended, and, should anyone get near,

---

1. One could consider vv. 1-11, vv. 12-16, and vv. 17-26 together since they all begin in a similar fashion (*egeneto de* in v. 1, and *kai egeneto* in vv. 12 and 17), but vv. 17-26 also fit with the 'conflict' stories that follow, so I treat that passage with those sections and have chosen to deal with vv. 12-16 by themselves.

2. NIDNTTE, 3:105-7; see also G. J. Wenham, *The Book of Leviticus*, NICOT (Grand Rapids: Eerdmans, 1979), pp. 194-201; and Jay Sklar, *Leviticus*, TOTC (Downers Grove, IL: InterVarsity, 2014), pp. 183-84.

he was to cover his upper lip and holler out, 'Unclean, unclean!' He could not live at home. He must live by himself (or maybe with other lepers, cf. 17:12), no coming to the synagogue, no joining in public worship, no morning coffee at the local café, no hugs from his kids or his wife. Relatives might leave food for him at a designated place; but he was cut off from human contact. If he were fortunate, he might find a reasonably comfortable cave.

Clearly, we see this man's **faith in Jesus' power** (v. 12). And we see his faith by noting his sheer gall. This fellow was not supposed to be there! The surprise appears in Luke's 'Behold' (see AV), which most recent versions don't translate as such, perhaps because it sounds too stilted now. But one could translate, 'And— why, of all things!—a man full of leprosy.' He 'fell on his face' before Jesus. What is he doing there? Why didn't he observe quarantine? What is he doing 'in one of the towns' where his ritual uncleanness might defile others? How did he get through? Apparently he had heard of Jesus' work, perhaps he had seen some of His healings at a distance. He was absolutely convinced that his case would be a 'piece of cake' for Jesus. If only Jesus were willing. Desperation joined with conviction and produced a recklessness that drove him, in spite of all hindrances and barriers, to Jesus. In his 'Lord, if you will ...' one hears an echo of Charles Wesley's hymn: 'Other refuge have I none, *hangs my helpless soul on thee.*'[3] Here is not some unclean human specimen for our condescending pity but a schoolmaster to bring us to Christ and to show us where all true faith in Jesus must begin.

Then verse 13 sets before us **the marvel of Jesus' work**. Observers must have been aghast—'he reached out his hand and touched him.' Imagine what that in itself meant to this leper. He hadn't felt a human touch probably in years. It was a touch of compassion and fearlessness and power. The crowd would know that the moment He touched the leper, Jesus would contract 'uncleanness.' But, of course, that wasn't the case: Jesus did not contract uncleanness but communicated cleansing. His mere word brings immediate cleansing. When the prophet Elisha had directed Naaman's cleansing (2 Kings 5), it was via a process (washing in the Jordan).

---

3. From 'Jesus, Lover of My Soul,' stanza 2.

But there was no process here; at Jesus' word healing was immediate.[4] So the touch points to Jesus' compassion and the immediacy of the healing points to His power. It is always the combination Jesus' disciples need, not some sort of helpless sympathy nor sheer brute force but the perfect harmony of both. Joseph Hart caught it nicely in his hymn, 'Come, Ye Sinners, Poor and Wretched,' right at the beginning:

> Come, ye sinners, poor and wretched,
>> weak and wounded, sick and sore;
> Jesus ready stands to save you,
>> *full of pity joined with power.*

That is the fully-equipped Savior Luke shows us here.

Though there's nothing mundane about Jesus' cleansing of this leper, we must not miss **the routine in Jesus' command** (v. 14) in what follows. Jesus commands him to silence and then tells him to 'go off and show yourself to the priest, and offer for your cleansing just what Moses specified, for a testimony to them.'[5] It's marvelous to be cleansed from leprosy, but there's also some 'paperwork' involved; there's a procedure to be followed in which the priest must validate the cleansing and offer the appropriate sacrifices. It's all spelled out in Leviticus 14. As Bock notes, it was a week-long process, spelled out in some detail.[6] It had been set up under Moses and Jesus was not about to circumvent those requirements. The man cannot burst into his house with a 'Hi, honey, I'm home!', but must jump through all the hoops that Leviticus 14 lays out for him. The miracle does not negate the duty to follow the requirements of the word of God that were still in effect. Jesus did not think it a negligible routine.

I wonder if there's not a sense in which this sort of affair is still often a principle in Jesus' work. For example, let's say a university coed is in weekly worship or on an overnight student retreat and suddenly the gospel 'comes home' to her,

---

4. David E. Garland, *Luke*, ZECNT (Grand Rapids: Zondervan, 2011), p. 239.

5. The 'testimony' could be simply authentication for the priest that the man had been healed. Or it may be something more—a witness of the power of Jesus now let loose in Israel.

6. Darrell L. Bock, *Luke 1:1-9:50*, BECNT (Grand Rapids: Baker, 1994), p. 476.

the Holy Spirit enlightens her, and all things become new. It is so staggering and astounding. Now what is the next thing Jesus would have her do? If one might presume, something like this: 'Be sure to attend your classes on Monday and go to your work-study job in the library afterwards.' Sometimes Jesus follows up His out-of-this-world work with a very down-to-earth demand. No testimonies please—just go show yourself to the priest and do everything he says to do.

Finally, I think Luke gives us a glimpse of **the peril in Jesus' success** (vv. 15-16). But word got out (v. 15a; cf. v. 14a) and huge crowds of folks kept coming to hear His teaching and be healed of their illnesses. In face of all this scurry and stir and popularity, Luke appends a note that Jesus kept 'withdrawing to isolated places and praying' (v. 16). I think there's more here than at first meets the eye. Could we say Jesus felt compelled to withdraw and pray because the situation proved a danger to His own soul? Did the plaudits of the crowds perhaps conjure up a familiar voice that repeated, 'All will be yours' (4:7)? Oh, it's a bit different from Satan's original pitch but the innuendo is similar: there's a way of acclaim and popular approval open to you; you don't need to hold to the commitment of your baptism. Doesn't it feel wonderful to be liked and wanted? Jesus, knowing the danger of such moments, went off by Himself and gave Himself to private prayer. This implies that Jesus' temptation was not simply an event that occurred in Luke 4, but an intermittent and ongoing assault which required frequent recourse to the Father's presence.

Ryle calls on Christian disciples to follow Christ's example:

> There are few professing Christians, it may be feared, who strive to imitate Christ in this matter of private devotion. There is an abundance of hearing, and reading, and talking, and profession, and visiting, and almsgiving, and subscribing to societies, and teaching at schools [and—might we add?—attending conferences and writing blogs and posting on Facebook and tweeting and texting]. But is there, together with all this, a due proportion of private prayer? Are believing men and women sufficiently careful to be frequently alone with God?[7]

---

7. J. C. Ryle, *Expository Thoughts on the Gospels: St. Luke*, 2 vols. (New York: Baker & Taylor, 1858), 1:139.

Jesus' example is all the more necessary when we realize, as Jesus did, that success can destroy. It's a troubling paradox that what may seem the best moments in our Christian experience may actually be the most dangerous.

15

The Trouble with Jesus
(Luke 5:17–6:11)

Luke now has a whole block of material that we could dub 'Jesus and His critics,' very similar to 2:1–3:6 in Mark's Gospel. Here is a series of 'conflict' stories, and because of this common thread in them I think it well to take them all together. One then can't treat each in as much depth, but I think sometimes there's more value in seeing the connectedness in a whole swath of text. Here, then, are these episodes that make you look at Jesus through the eyes of His opponents. This is likely good for us, for sometimes we can become so 'accustomed' to Jesus that we fail to see *what's wrong with Him*. That is, in the view of others. We need to listen to these critics—they'll tell us what the trouble with Jesus is.

First, they are upset over **the authority Jesus assumes** (5:17-26). Right off Luke mentions the major attention Jesus was attracting ('Pharisees and law-teachers were sitting there—they had come from every village of Galilee and Judea, even Jerusalem,' v. 17a) and the major provision He had at that time ('the power of the Lord was present for him to heal,' v. 17b). Then we meet two surprises. One is the ingenuity of faith (vv. 18-19). Men come toting a paralyzed friend on a stretcher but can't get him to Jesus because of the crunch of the crowd, so 'they went up on the roof and let him down through the tiles, with the stretcher, into the middle [of people] right in front of Jesus' (v. 19b).[1] And Jesus 'saw their faith' (v. 20a), not their mess. Then comes the second surprise: the irrelevance of Jesus. Jesus says to the paralytic: 'Man, your sins are forgiven you' (v. 20b). That must have buffaloed the paralytic and his friends; they brought him for healing not forgiveness. But Jesus always sees deeper, sees the real need behind the obvious need.

That sets off the rumbling. 'The scribes and the Pharisees began thinking, "Who is this who speaks blasphemies? Who is able to forgive sins but God alone?"' (v. 21). Their first question is off the mark but their second one is spot on. So Jesus asks them why they are thinking the thoughts they're thinking. Then Jesus so much as says: Look, we're not playing religious games here. It's easy to say things like 'Your sins are forgiven' or 'Get up and walk.' It's easy to *say* either; the problem comes with the second pronouncement—if nothing happens, it leaves one looking like a dolt. Then the lesson begins; He is going to teach His critics that 'the Son of Man has authority on earth to forgive sins' (v. 24). Note: He did not say He announced or declared forgiveness in God's name or that He was merely assuring the paralytic of forgiveness. No, He Himself forgives sins. He gives a clear sign: He orders the paralytic to get up, pick up his stretcher, and go home (v. 24b). It happened immediately (v. 25). Once more, it's as if Jesus said: You can't *see* sins being forgiven, but you can see that when I say something is to happen, it happens. So when I speak forgiveness, it really occurs—just as when I told this paralytic to get up and tote his stretcher home, he really did it.

'Who is able to forgive sins but God alone?' (v. 21b). Jesus is acting like deity in forgiving sins, and this poses a huge dilemma for His critics. For when Jesus claims to forgive sins and acts like deity, He either is, or, if He is not, then He is indeed uttering blasphemies (v. 21) and can in no way be a good person or upright teacher. Of course, He might just be lulu, walking around forgiving sins until the fellows in the white coats come and take Him away. But no one ever took

---

1. Some have raised flack, claiming a Palestinian house would not have roof 'tiles.' But it's not a problem; see the discussion in Darrell L. Bock, *Luke 1:1-9:50*, BECNT (Grand Rapids: Baker, 1994), pp. 480-81.

Jesus that way; no one ever seemed to think He was simply a nut-case. They thought He was as serious as judgment day. Right here in Luke 5, Jesus means to face you with an either-or. All this reminds me of a scene in the movie 'Hoosiers.' Norman Dale has become basketball coach in a small-town Indiana school. Some of the players' parents quite vocally oppose him. Hence there's this scene in the gymnasium; one of the players' fathers is reaming out the coach and part of his speech goes like this: 'Mister, the way I see it, there's two kinds of dumb. There's the guy who gets naked and runs out in the snow and barks at the moon—and the guy who does the same thing in your living room. The first you can mostly ignore; the second, you're sorta forced to deal with.'

That's it; Luke implies that Jesus is like the guy who gets naked and barks at the moon in your living room. You're sort of forced to deal with Him. He is either deity or deceiver; He is either right to act as God or He is scum lower than Lucifer. You may have trouble with the authority Jesus assumes, with His forgiveness.

But Jesus' critics also get annoyed over **the company Jesus keeps** (vv. 27-32). Jesus enters into the most offensive associations. He causes a mini-problem in the call of Levi (aka Matthew). Verses 27-28 sound very matter-of-fact as one reads them, but Jesus' call to Levi must've aggravated the locals. Levi would have been one of those hired from the native population for his job, working in the revenue operations of Herod Antipas, probably collecting taxes and tolls on caravan goods. He had to be able to communicate in several languages and to possess an adequate level of 'office' skills. But such men were hated by kosher Jews— they were collaborators with the Romans or their lackeys and tended to be shysters and cheats. Someone like Levi would be disqualified from being a judge or witness in court and would be excommunicated from the synagogue.[2] Therefore when Jesus calls such a low-life to follow Him it constitutes a small scandal.

But Levi goes on to cause a maxi-problem—he 'made a huge reception for him [Jesus] at his house, and there

---

2. See the very helpful article in M. Silva, ed., NIDNTTE, 4:480-84.

was a huge number of tax collectors and others who were reclining at table with them' (v. 29). Levi invites in a bunch of his work-mates; he wants the other fellows at the tax office to meet Jesus. This was no mere chip-and-dip affair: they were 'reclining' at tables; this was first-class, top-drawer entertainment. And it sets off the Pharisees and their scribes who gripe about it to Jesus' disciples (v. 30). Some of the guests may have been rich and many raunchy, and Jesus and His men were dining with them. With the 'wrong' set. Likely these critics would say that such folks, even if Jews, were outside the covenant. A scurvy lot indeed. Their concern was that godly folks shouldn't expose themselves to such circles, i.e., to such contamination. But Jesus might say, Yes, but they need to be exposed to *Me*. In any case, here was an offensive association; they were upset with Jesus' fellowship, with the company He keeps.

Jesus, though, counters them with a very logical defense: 'The healthy do not have need of a doctor but those who are sick' (v. 31). We might elaborate the logic. Do you blame a doctor for being around sick folks? A plumber for cleaning out a sewer? A mechanic because he works with broken-down vehicles? A mortician because he messes with corpses? If Jesus is a physician, where should He be but among the terminally ill? That is actually such good news, good news that ironically will ooze out of the Pharisees' complaining in 15:2.

Yet Jesus pushes for more; He doesn't simply defend His conduct but sets an edgy appeal before the Pharisees & Co. in verse 32: 'I have not come to call righteous folks but sinners to repentance.' I know there's some debate here, but I think Jesus is being ironic. When He says 'righteous folks,' it is a subtle dig almost in the sense of 'those who wrongly imagine they are righteous.' I think Jesus is trying to drive His critics to see themselves in another category, as sinners; He's seeking to rouse them to a sense of their need.

Category shifts, however, are difficult to make. This matter always brings to mind an incident I've noted before. I was a lad of eight-ten years old and went on a 300-mile trip with my parents to attend a Bible conference for several days. We stayed in a motel, obviously before the days of card keys. One had a real metal key to the room, attached to an oblong piece of green plastic that had the motel name and address on it. One morning as we were getting ourselves cleaned up and ready, my father confessed he could not find the room key. He had looked in all pants and jacket pockets, everywhere possible in the room; no key. My mother made the wild suggestion that maybe he had left it in the outside lock when we had come in the night before. He knew that was absurd. I can still recall his pacing across the room toward the door, with his lower lip stuck defiantly out, and muttering, 'Oh, I wouldn't do that—that'd be *dumb!*' With that he opened the door and pulled the key out of the outside lock. He simply couldn't conceive of himself in the category of 'dumb.' And first-century Pharisees and their contemporary descendants often find it unthinkable to see themselves in the 'sinners' category. Which may mean that you have no need of Jesus because you can't see how desperate your condition is—you are sure you are among the 'healthy.'

The interchange between Jesus and His critics continues (v. 33a) and morphs into another problem they have with Jesus, **the atmosphere Jesus encourages** (vv. 33-39). Their complaint asked why Jesus was bucking the standard religious pattern, for 'the disciples of John fast frequently and offer prayers—likewise also the disciples of the Pharisees, but yours are eating and drinking' (v. 33). Well, just look, they might have said, at the remains of Levi's dining room. So where are the fasting periods and the set prayers? There was one required fast for Israel in OT times, the day of atonement (Lev. 16:29-34; 23:26-32), but by the NT period the Pharisees were usually fasting every Monday and Thursday (cf. 18:12).

Jesus' answer argues first from *propriety* (vv. 34-35). He essentially says it is wedding time in redemptive history. The 'bridegroom' of Israel has come.[3] You don't tell folks at a wedding to drop their punch and cake and begin fasting. It's not appropriate, it doesn't fit. (Jesus does say there will come a time for His disciples to fast—when He is 'taken' from them [v. 35]; hence already the cross is before Him). So we don't send a sympathy card to newly-weds, do we? Unless

---

3. On the bridegroom imagery, see James R. Edwards, *The Gospel According to Mark*, PNTC (Grand Rapids: Eerdmans, 2002), p. 90, and NIDNTTE, 3:436.

it's done as a gag. Or, what about a different analogy? You're having a birthday party for your child and have invited three or four other six-to-eight-year-olds over for the party. When it's time to eat, do you bring in a tray filled with little cut-up sprigs of broccoli and cauliflower, complete with a center bowl filled with a sugar-free, salt-free, taste-free dip? Perish the thought, healthy as you may deem it. No, they are to have birthday cake and ice cream, so that they can return to their parents on a three-hour sugar high. Is there something wrong with the vegetarian alternative? 'Wrong' is the wrong word—it's *inappropriate*. You simply don't go serving broccoli and cauliflower at a kids' birthday party. Nor is fasting proper when Israel's bridegroom has shown up.

But then Jesus also argues from *principle* in verses 36-38. He says there are some things that must not be mixed: new patches and old clothes and new wine and dried-up wineskins. If you tear a patch-piece from a new garment and use it to patch up an old one, you are guilty of double stupidity: you've just ruined a new garment and the new piece won't match the faded color of the old garment anyway (v. 36). And new wine percolating with its fermentation will blow open old wineskins, so both wine and the skins are lost (vv. 37-38). In short, it's no good trying to squeeze Jesus into your old molds, thinking that Jesus has just brought some additional religious ideas you can tack on to your pre-formed traditions. No, Jesus has brought the new age, and it's disastrous to mix the tedious traditions of Judaism with the new age of the kingdom.

Where, then, do we hit upon the keynote in all of this? Surely in verse 34, and William Lane is surely on target to highlight it:

> The central comparison between the wedding festivities and Jesus' disciples lies in *the joy which they possess in their master*. Jesus emphasizes this with his answer to the critical question. The reason for the fundamentally different position of his disciples is that 'the bridegroom is with them,' and in his presence they experience joy.[4]

---

4. W. L. Lane, *The Gospel According to Mark*, NICNT (Grand Rapids: Eerdmans, 1974), pp. 110.

That's it: the joy they possess in their master. Nor is this only true of the original disciples, for Peter describes how even later believers regarded Jesus: 'whom not having seen you love, in whom though not seeing him now but believing, you rejoice with joy inexpressible and packed with glory' (1 Pet. 1:8). The gospel, the bridegroom, brings joy to His people.

We must never sell short the attraction of this. J. B. Phillips, the New Testament translator, had had little happiness in his younger years, thanks partly to a nasty beast of a stepmother. But there were several incidents God used in his early university days to draw him to faith. One was at the Keswick Convention in 1925. Phillips was nineteen and impressed that 5,000 people could be packed into the Big Tent for moving singing, heartfelt prayer, and powerful preaching. He spoke of the people as 'earnest, but by no means joyless Christians.' Some would call the people he was with 'fundies,' but Phillips said they were plainly devoted to Jesus Christ and he was convinced he must throw in his lot with 'these lovable devoted people.'⁵ What was the attraction but the joy they possessed in their Master? It's not that Christians flout some sort of phony, worked-up optimism; but when people know that 'the bridegroom is with them' (v. 34), they are always ready to celebrate.⁶

Still the 'trouble with Jesus' continues—the Pharisees et al. are livid over **the tradition Jesus defies** (6:1-5, 6-11). The disciples are 'caught' snacking on heads of grain as they were walking through the fields. Some of the Pharisees are around and accuse them: 'What you are doing is not lawful on the Sabbath!' (6:2).⁷ It was certainly lawful, for Deuteronomy 23:25 permitted such snacks-in-transit. Ah, but this was the Sabbath and such picking and rubbing of a few grain heads was 'work,' it was 'reaping' and 'threshing,' it was unlawful. Not according to biblical law but according to biblical law sifted through the sieve of their tradition. So in

5. J. B. Phillips, *The Price of Success* (Wheaton, IL: Harold Shaw, 1984), p. 56.

6. Not everyone welcomes this 'newness' Jesus brings. That is Jesus' point in verse 39: by and large Israel will prefer the 'old wine' as 'good enough' (NASB).

7. It's enough to drive one to distraction; Jesus and His men can't even walk through a grain field without a couple of Pharisees popping up to bother them.

the *Mishnah* one finds thirty-nine kinds of 'work' forbidden on the Sabbath: sowing, reaping, etc., but also making two loops, weaving two threads, separating two threads, tying a knot, loosening a knot, sewing two stitches (*Shab.* 7. 2). Rabbi Meir, however, said that one was not guilty if he could untie the knot with one hand (*Shab.* 15.1). In face of this clutter Jesus goes to Scripture and cites the account in 1 Samuel 21, when David and his men ate the bread of the presence—technically, only the priests were to eat it. It was an occasion where necessity trumped restriction. The point is all the more pointed if, as rabbinic tradition suggests, David did this on the Sabbath.[8] In any case, Jesus as 'Lord' of the Sabbath has authority to declare what is right or wrong on the Sabbath.

Then there's this case of a man with a 'withered' right hand (6:6).[9] Healing would naturally be regarded as 'work' on the Sabbath, and only in the case of mortal illness was medical help permitted on the Sabbath.[10] This case was not an emergency—the fellow could've been healed the next day or the day after. Here the consideration of mercy seems to determine Jesus' action. His critics were eager beavers for what was lawful on the Sabbath and so Jesus asked them: 'Is it lawful on the Sabbath to do good or to do evil, to save life or to destroy?' (v. 9). In view of what they were contemplating for Jesus (v. 11), His words may have been loaded. 'And when he had stared them all down, he said to him, "Stretch out your hand." And he did so—and his hand was completely restored!' (v. 10). And His critics went berserk (v. 11).

Contemporary application of this section can be difficult because overtly strict Sabbath observance is hardly a problem among God's people today. But it helps if we can get to the heart of the matter and J. C. Ryle nailed that when he observed: *What excessive importance hypocrites attach to trifles.*[11] When we look at it like that we realize we have our own way of being in bondage to trivia that we've given almost

8. Bock, p. 524.

9. Luke, as opposed to Matthew (12:10) and Mark (3:1), specifies that it was his 'right' hand that was affected. Doctor's observation?

10. Cf. *Mishnah* (*Yoma* 8.6).

11. *Expository Thoughts on the Gospels: St. Luke*, 2 vols. (New York: Baker & Taylor, 1858), 1:159.

biblical status. In some circles in my country, any faithful Christian parents will (it is implied) certainly place their child in overtly Christian schools or else carry on home schooling. Certainly not in state-supported 'public' schools. Or there may be others who decry dating for Christian young people—'courting' is the only way. There are some clergy types who tout their 'freedom' and love their alcohol and cigars but insist that there can be no celebration of Christmas or Easter in the churches they serve. Or you yourself may simply slip into a pattern of hyper-kinetic Christian activity that you feel you 'have to do'—a veritable treadmill of Bible studies and 'circle' meetings and volunteering to help para-church ministries and service projects, so nights and even days can be taken up in 'good' Christian activities and yet it is little more than an exercise in exhausting tyranny. And where is the freedom that Christ has given? Must I myself defy the bondage of a self-imposed 'tradition' in order to walk in Jesus' freedom once more?

Luke takes a good hunk of text to show you 'what's wrong with Jesus.' You had better, then, look Him over very carefully before signing up for discipleship.

16

An All-Nighter

(Luke 6:12-16)

Many of us can likely look back to college and university days when periodic 'emergencies' arose, emergencies that were often a fruit of poor planning, sloppy scheduling or even a dash of indolence. But there is a term paper due or an exam to be taken on Thursday, and Thursday is tomorrow, and so on Thursday you might bump into a spent-looking soul, bleary-eyed from popping caffeine pills, who tells you that because of an exam or paper deadline he had to 'pull an all-nighter.' Luke tells us that Jesus had His own all-nighter: 'and he was going through the night in prayer to God' (v. 12). He apparently felt the necessity for it—though, unlike collegians, not for any previous deficiency on His part. These five verses are a brief transition text before an extended section of Jesus' teaching (vv. 17-49), but they merit separate attention.

Let us take up Luke's theme of prayer. He seems to highlight, first of all, **prayer as the necessary discipline of the Son of God** (vv. 12-13a). Luke is the only one of the 'synoptic' gospels that mentions Jesus engaging in prayer at this point (cf. Matt. 10:2-4; Mark 3:13-19). Why such necessity and intensity on Jesus' part that He takes up all night in prayer to God?

The preceding context suggests a partial answer. All of 5:17–6:11 consisted of 'conflict stories,' a whole series of occasions in which Jesus patiently yet pointedly answers the gripes and complaints of the Jewish religious leaders. The last episode and the final note of it are especially ominous. The scribes and Pharisees were eye-balling Jesus on that Sabbath in the synagogue. After He 'had stared them all down' (6:10), He healed the man with the withered hand, and then Luke concludes: 'But they, they were filled with rage and began discussing with one another what they might do to Jesus' (6:11). One needs little imagination to grasp the sort of options they were considering. The whole 'conflict' section comes to its crescendo on that note. And at a time like that Jesus spends a night in prayer (6:12), doubtless seeking grace to endure, to press on in the path of suffering that was all too sure to come. One dare never face a cross prayerlessly.

Then there is a prospective need as well. Next day He would choose the Twelve (v. 13) out of a far larger number of His disciples. Choosing 'apostles' shows that Jesus has a long-term project in view, called the church. These twelve are to be the initial leaders and guides of His people and so there is every reason why Jesus should seek the Father's direction as He was about to choose these men. What He has faced and what is ahead of Him brings Him to all-night prayer; a double need requires a single night in prayer.

That Jesus 'goes through the night' in prayer suggests a certain arduousness or 'driven-ness' about this undertaking. If the Son of God cannot short circuit this discipline of seeking the Father's face, dare any of His disciples try to do so?

Secondly, Jesus' choice of His men suggests **prayer as the mysterious companion of the providence of God** (vv. 13b-16). We needn't run down all the identities of the Twelve.[1] Prominence does not seem to have been a criterion behind Jesus' selection. But what especially grabs a reader is the final entry: 'and Judas Iscariot, who became a traitor' (v. 16b). He was not one yet, but He 'became' (*egeneto*) such.[2]

---

1. For this, cf. Alfred Plummer, *The Gospel According to St. Luke*, ICC (New York: Scribners, 1902), pp. 172-75. Likely, Bartholomew = Nathanael (Jn. 1:45), Matthew = Levi elsewhere, and 'Judas of James' = Thaddaeus.

2. Judas Iscariot's place among the Twelve is important for at least two reasons: (1) it supports the case for the reliability of the NT story. One could imagine that the early church may have wished to expunge the shameful record of Judas, but there

But how could that be, why would it be, when Jesus' selection process had apparently been bathed in prayer? And yet Jesus' earnest prayer did not magically prevent the disaster of Judas. We may be tempted, pragmatists that we are, to say, 'But isn't that why we pray? To be able to avoid such screw-ups and messes and debacles?' Is it? In any case, Jesus prayed; and Jesus chose Judas.

Doesn't this text highlight what many believers know by experience? That along with our prayers the mysterious providence of God is at work. And it is useful to see this, for it may keep us from a sort of 'presto' view of prayer, thinking that if we are praying, well then, 'of course' God is going to make all turn out fine. But not always. Prayer may not always resolve mysteries but may intensify them. And it doesn't hurt the Lord's people to ponder that.

---

it stood; the early church didn't 'air brush' the portrait of Jesus' apostles; and (2) Judas becomes a standing warning that closeness to Jesus and faithlessness to Jesus can easily co-exist. See James R. Edwards, *the Gospel According to Luke*, PNTC (Grand Rapids: Eerdmans, 2015), pp. 189-90.

17

Kingdom Regimen

(Luke 6:17-49)

Now Luke provides us with an introduction to Jesus' teaching. Luke's record is sometimes called 'the sermon on the plain,' an allusion to the level area on the hillside where Jesus taught (v. 17). Gobs of ink have been spilled over the relation of Luke's material to the 'Sermon on the Mount' in Matthew 5–7. Briefly, I think both versions reflect the same occasion: the settings are similar (Matt. 4:23-25; Luke 6:17-19), they have some sort of 'beatitudes' at the beginning, and similar conclusions as well (Matt. 7:24-27; Luke 6:46-49). Luke's material here is only a third as long as the collection in Matthew. Luke apparently made his selection of what to include here. Anyone wanting to delve into the relation of the two can find ample discussion elsewhere.[1] Luke's preface to Jesus' teaching highlights the wide attraction of Jesus (vv. 17-18a) and the promiscuous benefits of Jesus (vv. 18b-19)—then follows the demanding teaching of Jesus in verses 20 and following. It is one thing to receive Jesus' gifts, but to be His disciple you not only receive His benefits but order your life under His word.

However, we must not pooh-pooh the folks in verses 18-19. In a day without 'advanced' medical expertise and when much superstitious quackery prevailed, to have One who

---

1. E.g., Darrell L. Bock, *Luke 1:1-9:50*, BECNT (Grand Rapids: Baker, 1994), pp. 548-60.

willingly heals diseases and neutralizes demons is a boon no one would want to miss. So verses 17-19 tell us of the terrific generosity of Jesus — which exemplifies verses 35b-36.

In this exposition I prefer to emphasize the broad highlights of Jesus' teaching rather than trying to explain every text in detail. This procedure can be both helpful and frustrating, but hopefully more of the former.

First of all, Jesus stresses the theme of **division** (vv. 20-26). Note that He speaks 'to the disciples' here (v. 20a), not to the world, not to everyone. Far more than His disciples were there (vv. 17-19), but Jesus' primary audience consists of disciples. Jesus calls them 'poor' (v. 20b), a term referring to God's beleaguered people.[2] They also hunger and weep (v. 21) and in the fourth 'beatitude' Jesus tells us why:

> How blessed you are
> when men hate you,
> and when they ostracize you
> and insult you
> and throw out your name as evil
> because of the Son of Man (v. 22).

Seems like Jesus is saying their destitution and sorrow will be because men will hate and despise them because of their allegiance to Jesus ('because of the Son of Man'). But, pray tell, who are these folks who will hate them like this? After Jesus tells them to rejoice and assures them of stellar reward, He adds: 'for their fathers kept doing the very same things to the prophets' (v. 23b). It's not something unusual; this is the way it has always been. But who are 'their fathers'? They are the ones who hated, opposed, and tried to silence Yahweh's prophets in what we call OT times.[3] The men, then, who will hate Jesus' disciples (v. 22) are the descendants of 'their fathers' (v. 23), that is, they will be the then-contemporary generation of unbelieving, Son-of-Man-rejecting Israelites. The persecutors of Jesus' disciples here are not unwashed pagans or the world

---

2. See exposition of 4:14-30, footnote 3.

3. Cf., for example, Ahab's treatment of Micaiah in 1 Kings 22, Amaziah's opposition to Amos in Amos 7:10-17, or, if you have a high threshold for pain, follow the repeated attacks on Jeremiah (Jer. 11–45).

at large but *fellow Israelites* who will despise and seek to rub out Jesus' people—and stand under Jesus' 'woe' (vv. 24-26). Nothing could be clearer: Jesus says there are two 'Israels' and one of them belongs to the seed of the serpent (cf. Gen. 3:15).

Jesus calls His disciples to rejoice and leap for joy (v. 23a) when they suffer 'on account of the Son of Man' (v. 22) for two reasons: (1) their reward is great in heaven, and (2) they have the honor of belonging to *a suffering tradition* of the people of God. That's what the last of verse 23 implies—Yahweh's true people have always been a suffering people and that will not change in the life of Jesus' kingdom.

My wife and I graduated from a small midwestern college. Every year the college choir would go on tour, stopping at various churches and venues to present their concert repertoire. They ended every such concert with the same selection. It was a tradition. And part of the tradition was to announce at that point that if there were any previous members of the college choir in the present audience, they were asked to make their way to the front, stand with the choir, and join them in singing this final selection. It was a nice touch, a way of honoring choir members from years past. And perhaps Jesus offers something like that in verse 23: God's people have built up a long tradition of suffering over the years, and now, you, my disciples, have the honor and privilege of being part of that tradition. So Jesus speaks of division; He speaks of two Israels; He speaks of the cost of discipleship right from the start.

Secondly, Jesus teaches about **distinction** (vv. 27-35). He begins with:

> But I say to you who hear:
>> love your enemies,
>> do good to those who hate you,
>> bless those who curse you,
>> pray for those who abuse you (vv. 27-28).

Jesus strikes the 'love your enemies' note at the beginning (v. 27) and end (v. 35) of this section. This love is to be the distinctive mark of a disciple.

Just an aside. Be careful not to cast Jesus' words into high contrast to the Old Testament. Some folks thrive on that. But

Exodus 23:4-5 commands an Israelite who sees his enemy's ox or donkey wandering off to bring it back to him; or if he sees the donkey of someone who hates him collapsed beneath its load, he is not to walk by 'on the other side' but assist the hater with freeing his donkey and re-positioning its load.[4] Seems like that's loving one's enemy—in the Old Testament.

Back to verses 27-28. Immediately after these two verses Jesus provides *four examples* of how His disciples ought to act toward their enemies. That is, in verses 27-28 He tells them to love their enemies, to do good to those hating them, etc.; but *how* does one go at that? Verses 29-30 provide specific instances:

> To the one whacking you on the cheek, offer (him) the other as well; and from the one taking away your coat, don't hold back your tunic; give to everyone who demands of you, and from the one who takes your stuff—don't demand it back.[5]

What readers must see is that these instances are *persecution* scenarios. These are all hostile actions from those who will hate (vv. 22, 27) Jesus' disciples. That's why in the third instance (traditionally = 'give to everyone who asks of you') I have, quite legitimately, translated *aiteō* 'demand' (see Luke 23:23). The picture is not of a panhandler on the street asking you for a hand-out—it is a hostile demand by one who is opposing or attacking Jesus' disciple. Calvin saw this clearly:

> [I]t may readily be inferred from the context, that Luke does not here speak of a request to obtain assistance, but of actions at law, which bad men raise for the purpose of carrying off the property of others.[6]

The instances in verses 29-30 depict what happens when disciples suffer 'on account of the Son of Man' (v. 22). In those

---

4. Anyone interested in the technical details involved in the translation of Exodus 23:5 may check Joe M. Sprinkle, *'The Book of the Covenant': A Literary Approach* (Sheffield: JSOT Press, 1994), pp. 180-82.

5. The first instance is not likely a punch to the jaw but an insult, likely a back-handed whack, perhaps in connection with dismissal from the synagogue. Cf. Bock, p. 592.

6. *Calvin's Commentaries*, 22 vols. (Grand Rapids: Baker reprint ed., 1981), 16:300.

situations they are to function with an active non-resistance. Someone makes away with your jacket—then ask him if he wants your T-shirt as well (cf. v. 29b). But the scope of the text has to do with persecution, and it seems some expositors forget this when they arrive at verses 29-30. These are not general injunctions for conduct in life's generic circumstances.[7] They are commands for disciples under duress from those who hate Jesus and them. That is the context that should control interpretation and applications here.

However, when we take account of the particular context, Jesus' commands are still daunting. One might imagine a disciple hearing verses 27-30 and perhaps asking, 'Do you mean to say we are to let folks who hate you and us to walk all over us?' And in verses 32-34 Jesus essentially says, I am not calling you to a conventional ethic but to an *exceptional* ethic. What's so great about treating someone well who has treated you well? Every pagan Tom, Dick, Harry, and Harriet does that. It's the 'good ole boy' system—and there's nothing *different*, nothing *distinctive* about that. But blessing those who curse you, praying for those who abuse you—that's not more of the same old thing. That's surprising and uncommon.

A few years ago we were buying another auto. I knew the car dealer, and I'm sure he conspired to give us an excellent deal. But even I could tell that it was too good. The amount he was allowing us on the car we were trading in was far too generous and beyond its worth. Of course, I was not conferring with the dealer himself at the point of the sale but with one of his sales people. So I told the salesman I was not paying enough difference on the vehicle I was purchasing. I told him he needed

---

7. Jesus is not teaching a general, across-the-board non-resistance, as if he forbids self-defense. Say you are walking to work at your office via a back street. You've just stopped at a coffee shop to get a hot pick-up. Suddenly a fellow pops in front of you, with one hand in his pocket as if he has a gun. He demands you hand over your cash. But just as suddenly you flip the hot coffee in his face, punch him in the solar plexus, and when he doubles over, you bring your knee up and smash him in the chin. If you could do it (risky as it is), Jesus' words do not forbid it. It's beyond the scope of this text. Or when my three oldest brothers were in elementary school, my father ordered them that if some bully on the playground started picking on one of them, the other two were to rush to their brother's aid. Any kid who attacked one Davis kid needed to know he would be fighting all three! Was my father's order contrary to Jesus' teaching? Certainly not. We are not being told to be wimps for Jesus.

to jack up the price two-to-three thousand dollars more. One could visibly observe the look of consternation that crept over the salesman's countenance. He had never had a customer tell him he was charging too little, that he wanted to pay 2K or 3K more than was asked. It simply baffled him. He couldn't figure it out. That's what Jesus is saying in verses 32-34. His disciples' deportment under the pressure of persecution should be so different that it astounds the world; they are to act in a way that no one else acts. They are to be marked with a love that makes the pagans go round scratching their heads.

And they did—some pagans even griped about it. Like emperor Julian 'the Apostate' (d. A.D. 363), who vigorously tried to restore paganism to pride of place and yet admitted:

Atheism [i.e., Christian faith] has been specially advanced through the loving service rendered to strangers, and through their care for the burial of the dead. It is a scandal that there is not a single Jew who is a beggar, and that the godless Galileans [= Christians] care not only for their own poor but for ours as well; while those who belong to us look in vain for the help that we should render to them.[8]

That is the sort of thing Jesus meant. The love that marks His disciples must go beyond the boring reciprocity of this age.

In verses 36-45 Jesus emphasizes **discernment**. His primary concern is for self-critical (rather than other-critical) discernment. The connections are a bit difficult to make out here. Some expositors would connect verse 36 or verses 36-38 with what precedes, with the 'distinctive' love theme. Such love would be an indication of the Father's compassion (v. 36) and displayed in an attitude that is free of carping and condemning and grudging (vv. 37-38). But at least by verse 39 the theme of discernment is front and center.

Well, maybe. Jesus' 'parable' in verse 39 is a bit elusive: 'A blind man is not able to lead a blind man, is he? Won't both of them fall into a pit?' I take this as a warning to Jesus' disciple not lightly to take on the task of leading or teaching others; he must not presume to be qualified, or he could do

---

8. Bruce L. Shelley, *Church History in Plain Language*, 4th ed. (Nashville: Thomas Nelson, 2013), p. 38.

much harm. The objective is to stay 'pit-less,' and a 'fully equipped' (v. 40) disciple could insure that; but an arrogant or impulsive one who is unaware of his own defects and inadequacies will produce nothing but disaster.[9] Jesus presses home the same need for self-criticism and assessment in verses 41-42. 'Why do you look at the splinter that's in your brother's eye, but don't notice the beam that's in your own eye?' (v. 41). He is not saying that we must never assess or critique a fellow disciple but that we must not fixate on the minute errors of others when we've major faults we ourselves have not faced. No splinter-detection without beam-elimination. It's a call for careful self-assessment.

In verses 43-45 Jesus pushes this matter a step further— or deeper. The little causal particle 'For' in verse 43a[10] tells you that verses 43-45 are going to expand upon or explain verses 41-42. The chain of thought is something like this: The hypocrite (6:42) produces bad fruit.[11] When it comes to trees, the quality of the external fruit reveals the internal condition of the tree (v. 43). In botany, there is always a corresponding consistency in these matters: you don't find thorn-plants producing figs, nor thorn-bushes yielding grapes (v. 44). What is visibly produced is tied to what the plant actually is. Jesus then moves from trees and plants to persons (v. 45)— whether they produce good or evil is tied to what they are, particularly their internal condition. For example, 'the good man out of the good treasure of his heart produces what is good.' Jesus is not merely flashing analogies. As Bock says, the 'primary intent is self-examination, not examination of others.'[12] Jesus is calling you to discern yourself. He's not telling you to engage in some morbid, groveling introspection but to assess your own 'fruit' (cf. v. 42) and to ask what that says about the condition of your own heart. Even if you

9. James R. Edwards, *The Gospel According to Luke*, PNTC (Grand Rapids: Eerdmans, 2015), pp. 203-4; and W. F. Arndt, *The Gospel According to St. Luke* (St. Louis: Concordia, 1956), p. 197.

10. The NIV often fails to translate such connecting particles—an aggravating habit of that translation.

11. Alan J. Thompson, *Luke*, EGGNT (Nashville: Broadman & Holman, 2016), p. 110.

12. Bock, p. 616.

consider yourself Jesus' disciple or even a card-carrying
Israelite, you may find you need to plead that God will give
you a new heart and a new spirit (cf. Ezek. 36:26).
Finally, Jesus leaves us facing the matter of **decision**
(vv. 46-49). Here in Luke Jesus begins His 'conclusion' with a
rebuke: 'Why do you keep calling me "Lord, Lord," and are
not doing the things I say?' (v. 46). He is after more than empty
profession. Only doing what He says shows proper esteem for
His person. So in verses 47-49 Jesus sets two alternatives before
His hearers; it's a sort of Psalm 1 of the New Testament.

He speaks of two builders, and the first one exemplifies
the response Jesus seeks. Jesus outlines a proper response in
the verbs of verse 47; He speaks of 'everyone who comes to
me and hears my words and does them ….' Comes, hears,
does. Nothing theatrical. The right response to Jesus puts His
teaching into practice. This sort of response is like a house-
builder who 'digs and goes deeper and sets a foundation
upon rock.' A flood comes, waters slam into the house but
can't shake it—it's too well-built. Hence stability. On the other
hand, there's the one who is fascinated with Jesus' teaching
but doesn't care a lick about submitting to it (v. 49a). He's like
one in a hurry to get something up and is satisfied to build on
top of what is (at the moment) hard ground—but the torrent
smashes it all to bits. Hence tragedy. Jesus doesn't smooth out
His conclusion or try to leave folks with a positive twist. The
last thing we hear is the crash of that flimsy house.[13]

So, there are the two ways. There is the decision one
must make. Jesus intends to head off the emptiness of a
mere enthusiastic profession (v. 46). That sort of thing even
aggravated Hitler. When he visited Italy in 1938 to court
Mussolini, he spent at least four hours in Florence. But the
cheers rending the air were fictitious—they were crowd
effects from an Italian movie and were being relayed from
open windows by scads of amplifiers.[14] Sort of like the
phoniness that calls Jesus Lord but doesn't do what He says.

---

13. Cf. Darrell L. Bock, *Luke*, IVP New Testament Commentary (Downers
Grove, IL: InterVarsity, 1994), p. 130.

14. Richard Collier, *Duce!* (New York: Viking, 1971), p. 142.

18

Jesus and His Friends
(Luke 7:1-50)

A few pages back we dealt with 5:17–6:11 under the rubric 'The trouble with Jesus.' We could have also called it 'Jesus and His critics' (see outline in Introduction). In something of a parallel yet contrasting fashion I propose we come at Luke 7 under the heading 'Jesus and His friends.' Here we meet a centurion, a widow, John the Baptist, and a sinful woman, all of whom Jesus helps or encourages. We may have to go lightly on some details, but I think seeing the whole chapter together will be useful.

First off, we meet a centurion, who points us to **the adequacy of Jesus' word** (vv. 1-10). Theoretically a centurion had charge of a hundred soldiers, but in practice more likely sixty-eighty troops.[1] Much we don't know about this centurion: likely he was a provincial and not a Roman, though clearly a gentile; he may have been seconded to serve under Herod Antipas in Galilee or perhaps he was retired and living in Capernaum. But the text is clear that he is compassionate (he held his slave in high esteem, doing all he could to preserve his life, vv. 2-3),[2] generous (he evidently was friendly to local Jews and had underwritten the cost of synagogue construction,

---

1. Craig Keener, *The IVP Bible Background Commentary: New Testament* (Downers Grove, IL: InterVarsity, 1993), pp. 206.

2. Doesn't the centurion's appeal here suggest that you show the highest love for someone when you go to Jesus on his/her behalf?

vv. 4-5), humble (vv. 6-7a),[3] and believing ('But say the word, and let my servant be healed,' v. 7b). He explains his faith: he himself is placed under Rome's authority and so when he gives any command, what he commands happens. And since Jesus speaks with God's authority, whatever He declares will take place (v. 8). We readers are amazed to read that; indeed, Jesus Himself is amazed at him (v. 9a).

The recovery of the slave appears almost as an after-thought in verse 10; Jesus' words in verse 9b supply the keynote: 'I tell you, not even in Israel have I found such faith.' One would hope Jesus would find faith like that in Israel, among God's covenant people. But He didn't. He saw it in an outsider, a pagan, a gentile.[4] One of the delightful surprises of God's grace is that we happen on to faith where we least expect to find it. Eric Liddell was at an inn in China during the Japanese occupation. Orders were given that the military was going to examine everyone's luggage. Liddell opened up his suitcase to expose a New Testament in full view. The Japanese soldier spotted it, said in broken English, 'Bible; you Christian?', extended his hand and shook Liddell's, turned on his heel and walked away. Who in his right mind would expect to run into a Christian believer in the Japanese imperial army? Yet there he was. Faith in unexpected places. Like a gentile centurion in Capernaum, who was absolutely convinced that Jesus' word was enough. And yet that's sad— for what it says about Israel.

In verses 11-17 we move on to Nain. Capernaum (v. 1) was on the northwest shore of the Sea of Galilee, but 'soon afterward' (v. 11) Jesus is in Nain, six miles southeast of Nazareth. This episode also underscores the adequacy and authority of Jesus' mere word (vv. 14-15) but more as well, for here we meet a widow whose experience depicts **the reach of Jesus' power.**

A funeral was in progress when Jesus and His entourage arrived in Nain; the procession was coming out the town gate.

---

3. Some suggest that he held off Jesus' personal presence because Jesus would contract 'uncleanness' if He entered a gentile's house; but vv. 6-7a imply that his own personal unworthiness was his chief concern.

4. Our centurion here is a kind of harbinger of the faith of gentiles in Luke's second volume, e.g., the faith of another centurion and his household in Acts 10.

Funerals are sad but this one doubly so. Luke tells us the dead man was the 'only son' of his mother and then that she was a widow (v. 12). No husband, but now the 'only son,' who was surely her support, had died. It was more than loneliness; it meant almost certain poverty. There were then no Social Security payments, no retirement accounts, no life insurance, no pensions. In one sense, we might say that her life had ended though her existence continued. A bleak day for a woman in Nain. And Jesus walks right into her sadness (v. 13). Jesus and those with Him could have stood to the side in quiet respect and have allowed the procession to go on. But unasked He intervenes and does something for this widow, without any indication of faith on her part or on the part of others.[5] A marked contrast to what happened in verses 1-10, where the centurion solicited Jesus' help (v. 3). Isn't this often the case with us? Doesn't our Lord frequently bring His help into our need unasked? If every benefit we received depended on our faith or prayers, would we not be poor indeed?

'Don't cry anymore' (v. 13) are among the cruelest of words unless Jesus can do something about the reason for her sorrow. This He proceeds to do. Likely, even touching the dead man's stretcher would convey ritual uncleanness (cf. Num. 19:11ff.), but it doesn't matter since now the contagion will flow the other way! Note that, once more, the transforming work occurs simply at Jesus' word: 'Young man, I say to you [emphatic], Rise!' Jesus was not raising many; He spoke only to this one man. Then we read Luke's delightfully illogical statement—'And the dead man sat up!' (v. 15a). The centurion back in verse 7 had been right: 'But say the word.' Again, Jesus' mere word restored. However, you must not miss the contrast between Nain and Capernaum. There Jesus restored a man on the point of death (v. 2), here one who had already died.[6] It's one thing to prevent someone from dying, but what if the grim reaper has already come through? Hence we must take verses 1-10 and verses 11-17 together, so that we

5. J. C. Ryle, *Expository Thoughts on the Gospels: St. Luke*, 2 vols. (New York: Baker & Taylor, 1858), 1:209.

6. This, of course, was not a resurrection but a restoration to life. The day would come when this man would die again. But the crucial point is that Jesus has power even over the realm of death.

see that Jesus not only keeps one from death but has power to restore even when death has done its worst. This is very instructive: it tells you that *Jesus always seems to be far more than you ever imagined Him to be.* If you've walked with Him for some time, have you not found it to be so?

Don't let the significance of this cancelled funeral be lost on you. This 'little' miracle is telling you that even death is in Jesus' power. Being in the realm of death does not put you beyond Jesus' reach or the sound of His voice. Such a miracle is a sort of acted parable of what Christ will do at His second coming (1 Thess. 4:13-18). Some may raise the objection: Why doesn't the Lord raise bunches of people now? For the same reason He didn't do it *then*, when He was on earth—it's not time yet (see reference above). Jesus restored some people from death to life in the days of His flesh, but He didn't go around emptying cemeteries and putting morticians out of business. These episodes, as at Nain, were clues, pointers, previews of what is yet to come. Even the very description of dead believers in 1 Thessalonians 4:16 pulsates with hope: they are 'the dead in Christ.' They may be dead, but they are still united to Christ! What happened that day in Nain won't take away the misery and sadness of death for us, but, rightly understood, it should take away its despair and horror.

Jesus' deed made a suitable impression. 'Fear took hold of (them) all' (v. 16a),[7] and they said, 'A great prophet has been raised up among us,' and, 'God has looked after his people' (v. 16b). A great prophet indeed—and far more than that. This episode brings to mind those occasions in 1 Kings 17:17-24 and 2 Kings 4:8-37 in which, through the prayers of Elijah and Elisha, young lads were restored to life. I would think that in Nain the Elisha incident in 2 Kings 4 might especially have come to mind. That occurred in Shunem, a site on the south side of the Hill of Moreh (at the east end of the Plain of Esdraelon). The interesting thing is that Nain sits on the *north* side of the Hill of Moreh, about two miles from Shunem.[8] Surely some folks at Nain that day must've recalled what

7. A proper reaction to divine activity (1:12, 65; 2:9; 5:26; 8:37; 21:26).

8. You can keep these straight because Shunem begins with 's' as does 'south,' and Nain with 'n' as does 'north.' Cf. further, my *2 Kings: The Power and the Fury* (Ross-shire: Christian Focus, 2005), pp. 65-69.

had occurred just 'over the hill' some 800 years earlier. But there was something unique about the Nain affair. In both the Elijah (1 Kings 17) and Elisha (2 Kings 4) incidents, a lad's life was restored in answer to the earnest prayers of the prophet. Nothing wrong with that. But at Nain there's more. Jesus does not pray—He *commands* the dead to live. It's like Genesis 1:3: God said, 'Let there be light'—and there *was* light. Who then is this? Here at Nain they have seen a prophet but far more than a prophet, indeed, one who speaks life into being. Luke had the right response in verse 13, when he called Jesus 'Lord.'

John the Baptist is the third friend of Jesus we meet (vv. 18-23), and the teaching point centers around **the evidence of Jesus' identity**. John's disciples had reported to him about 'all these matters' (v. 18), that is, what Jesus had done in verses 1-10 and 11-17. Then John sent two of his disciples to Jesus to ask Him, 'Are you the Coming One or should we expect another?' (vv. 19-20). Where was John that he sent agents? Herod Antipas had thrown him in prison (3:19-20), which was, according to Jewish historian Josephus, in the fortress at Machaerus, five miles east of the Dead Sea.

But why would John have such a question? Hadn't John proclaimed 3:16-17? Yes, but that may have been part of John's problem here, for Jesus didn't seem to be 'burning up the chaff' or fulfilling Malachi 3:2 ('But who can endure the day of his coming? And who will be able to stand when he appears? For he will be like a refiner's fire ...'). It probably didn't help that John was in a dungeon in Machaerus. We don't need to psychologize John, but rotting away in a dungeon hardly stimulates optimism. Apparently John thought there was 'something missing' from Jesus' ministry if He was the Coming One. He didn't seem to be all that John thought He should be. No one less than John the Baptist is doubtful about Jesus.

John's disciples popped their question at a time when Jesus was healing people of various diseases and freeing them of evil spirits (v. 21). So Jesus, alluding both to these works and to such texts as Isaiah 35:5-6, gave them His answer:

> Go, report to John what you've seen and heard:
> The blind see again,
> the lame walk,

> lepers are cleansed,
> and the deaf hear;
> the dead are raised,
> the poor have the gospel preached,
> and how blessed is the one who does not get
> tripped up over me (vv. 22-23).

As noted, in Isaiah 35 such works describe the time when God comes to deliver His people, and these works are signs of the age of Zion's restoration. They constitute evidence that Jesus really is the Coming One, though He has not yet brought the judgment aspect of His work in a pervasive way. It's as if Jesus says: These evidences from Isaiah 35 are already occurring, John, though the Romans are ruling the land, the scribes and Pharisees sniffing around everything I do and say, and you are rotting away in Herod's prison; but—don't you see?—the age of restoration has already begun!

The text carries a spillover for us: Don't be surprised if you have perplexities about Jesus. Often they will be the same in principle as John's: Why isn't He working in the way I had imagined He would? Why doesn't He meet my expectations of what a Messiah should be? Why does He take so long to deliver from this specific distress? Why doesn't He exercise more severity when there are matters that need to be put right?

We cannot yet move on to Jesus' final 'friend,' for Jesus takes more time not to speak to John, but about John to the crowds. The primary teaching point in this section (vv. 24-35) will involve **the exposure of Jesus' generation**. However, first we must look at what Jesus says about John, which has to do with the matter of *privilege*.

Jesus asked the crowds what they had expected when they went out to see John. 'A reed shaken by the wind?' (v. 24c). A sort of wishy-washy wimp? Does the man of 3:7 and 3:19 strike one that way? Did they expect to see some effete elitist, someone sporting nice threads and living the soft life (v. 25)? No, they went out to see a prophet, but John was not merely another prophet; rather he was the prophet designated to announce the coming of the Lord (v. 27). Jesus picks up on Malachi 3:1 in its context. There Malachi was quoting the griping and accusations of the unbelievers in Israel, who in their defiance demanded, 'Where is the God of justice?' (Mal. 2:17). Yahweh immediately responds to this in Malachi 3:1. As if He says: So, you want the God of justice? Well, you shall have Him! Or, as the text itself says, 'Look, I am sending my messenger, and he shall prepare the way before me, and—suddenly—the Lord whom you are seeking will come to his temple, even the messenger of the covenant you are delighted about.' Jesus says, Now those words 'my messenger' refer to John. He is not merely one more prophet (v. 26b). He is the prophet right before the coming of the Lord. He is *the* forerunner of the One who will purify (Mal. 3:2-4) and separate (Luke 3:16-17) Israel. He is the 'hinge' of redemptive history right between the old age and the new.

That means that John enjoys an unparalleled privilege: 'I say to you, among those born from women there is no one greater than John' (v. 28a). What a staggering statement! Alexander the Great, Julius Caesar, Socrates, Napoleon—no matter, none of them come up to the level of this locust-eating prophet. Then Jesus adds another verbal jolt: 'But the least one in the kingdom of God is greater than he is' (v. 28b). It all amounts to Jesus saying that no one is greater than John except those who are greater than John! It's a formal contradiction—to make a point. John as the hinge of redemptive history outstrips all comers in greatness, but the most obscure believer in the age of fulfillment is 'greater' than John (cf. Luke 10:23-24). How are we to understand this?

An analogy may help. Susan B. Anthony worked avidly for women's suffrage in the United States. She died, however, in 1906, fourteen years before the 19th Amendment was adopted. She campaigned for women's right to vote and yet never enjoyed that right herself.[9] She was, I suppose we could say, very 'great' in the suffrage movement. And yet a post-1920 northwestern Iowa farm wife was 'greater' than Susan B. Anthony because she enjoyed the privilege of voting.

And you are not John the Baptist but perhaps only a relatively unknown believer in Jesus, and yet you enjoy a package of privileges: know a suffering Savior and therefore

---

9. She tried to vote in 1872 but was arrested for the attempt. Citing Anthony as a socio-political example does not include approval of her religious views.

having the comfort of a 'Man of Sorrows' in your suffering; standing in the victory of Jesus' resurrection, so living with no final terror; having received the gift of the Spirit and so enjoying the sense of His presence; understanding that Jesus presently reigns at the right hand of God and that therefore you are, in that place, the object of His attention and intercession. And your privileges ought to multiply your gratitude.

Privilege is the positive keynote in Jesus' John-the-Baptist-footnotes. The other is negative: *perversity* (vv. 31-35).

There was a split reaction to Jesus' exposition of John's place in redemptive history (see vv. 29-30). And so Jesus allowed John to go on instructing the people as He spoke of 'this generation' (v. 31). This is the first use of this phrase in Luke's gospel, and it consistently refers to those who are opposed to Jesus.[10] The phrase is not really a time-indicator but a hostility-indicator. Jesus likens 'this generation' to the fickleness of children at play (v. 32). The kids providing the music are frustrated. They tell their playmates, 'We played wedding music for you, but you haven't danced; you just turn crabby and say, "We don't wanna play wedding." So we cranked up a funeral dirge and you say, "Ah, we don't wanna play funeral either."' Jesus is saying that's the way unbelief in Israel is—nothing satisfies it. No matter what 'approach' is taken, it will always find something unsuited to its tastes. Jesus then shows how the playground perversity works out in Israel:

> For John the Baptist came neither eating bread nor drinking wine, and you say, 'He has a demon!' The Son of Man came eating and drinking, and you say, 'Why, a man who's a glutton and a wino, a friend of tax collectors and sinners' (vv. 33-34).

John is too weird, Jesus is too wild. No matter how God speaks to this people, unbelief is not satisfied. Contrary to what we often assume, unbelief is not thoughtful and rational but twisted and perverse.

This scenario reminds me of a fellow who used to come see my father. This man and his wife were former parishioners in

---

10. Alan J. Thompson, *Luke*, EGGNT (Nashville: Broadman & Holman, 2016), p. 121.

one of my father's previous congregations and, occasionally, they would show up for worship at my father's current congregation. Per usual, my mother would invite them for Sunday dinner. I recall scenes as the men sat on our front porch, waiting for the call to the mid-day meal. This fellow seemed to get a new car fairly regularly, and my father, who loved to 'talk cars,' might say, 'Paul, how do you like your new car?' He might respond, 'Well, I'll tell you, Daryl, it seems to use some oil—not real bad, but I have to add a quart about every 800 miles. You'd think a new vehicle would do better.' Another year, another visit, and 'How about your new car?' 'Well, I'll tell you, Daryl, they can't seem to get the front-end alignment right. I've had it in the shop three times, but it's still not right and it's worn out a set of front tires.' Another time, another car, same question: 'Well, I'll tell you, Daryl ....' For Paul no vehicle ever seemed right. That is the trouble with Israel. Whether God brings His word through John or through Jesus, unbelief will always find something wrong with it. That is what an evil heart of unbelief (cf. Heb. 3:12) does, and there's no cure for it, unless the Father gives a totally different disposition (John 6:65).

Finally, we meet the last of Jesus' friends in this chapter, a sinful woman (vv. 36-50), which teaches us **the power of Jesus' forgiveness**. One meets with similar stories in the other gospels (Matt. 26:6-13; Mark 14:3-9; John 12:1-8), but in my view this story is not the same as those and so is unique to Luke.[11]

We run into a surprise at the very beginning: Jesus accepts an invitation to lunch from a Pharisee (v. 36). If Jesus has come to seek and to save the lost (19:10) and if the Pharisees by and large are lost (v. 30), then why shouldn't Jesus spend time at Simon's dinner table? If Jesus didn't ever associate with moral-living, religiously-arrogant Pharisees, why, a good number of us would not be in the kingdom of God!

Luke describes the setting (vv. 37-39). Simon's is a serious dinner-party, for the guests are 'reclining' (v. 37), resting on couches with their left elbows on the table and feet extended

11. See James R. Edwards, *The Gospel According to Luke*, PNTC (Grand Rapids: Eerdmans, 2015, pp. 225-26 fn.

out. This was no light or quick lunch. Such occasions were not tightly closed off—interested and uninvited observers were allowed to stand on the sides and listen in on conversations.[12] In spite of such normal freedom, teeth must've clenched and nerves have gone taut when 'the woman' came up to Jesus' feet. Luke is so gracious: Yes, she's a 'sinner' in the city, but he withholds her name and doesn't elaborate on the sort of sin in which her expertise lay. Pharisees (and some preachers) may imagine what they like but we don't need to know. Luke builds his description. He uses four participles to set the scene: 'having known' where Jesus was, 'brought' (a phial of fragrance), 'stood' (at His feet), 'weeping'—this last implying an ongoing action. Then he switches to 'main' verbs: she 'began to wet' His feet with her tears, and 'wiped (them) dry' with the hairs of her head, and 'kept on kissing' His feet and 'anointing' (them) with the fragrance. It was considered shameful for a woman to unbind her hair in the presence of men, but apparently she was so overcome that normal social restraints were forgotten. The air was both uneasy and electric, but Simon kept his thoughts (or so he thought) to himself: 'If this fellow were a prophet, he would know ...' and He would repulse such attentions (v. 39).

Then Jesus wants to tell Simon something—a story (vv. 41-42). Not much of a story; simply about two fellows in debt to a money lender, one for 500 denarii, the other for 50. That's approximately the equivalent of two years' wages and two months' wages respectively. Then the wild punch-line: 'Not having anything with which to pay him back, he forgave them both' (v. 42). No one does that, of course; if you think otherwise, go in and ask your banker to forgive your mortgage. And watch the look on his/her face. But Jesus doesn't stop there: he has a question for Simon (v. 42b), who with his mathematical mind will surely answer correctly (v. 43). But we should stop here momentarily. Notice: we may not have the whole gospel in verse 42a, but we have a large chunk of it. The gospel brings together hopeless condition and 'impossible' gift.

---

12. ZIBBC, 1:388. Why not be there instead of reading about it in the paper the next day?

Simon had said that he assumed the one forgiven more would love more. Jesus agrees and goes on to apply His story and to offend Simon. Jesus turns toward the woman and asks, 'Do you see this woman?' (v. 44).[13] Then Jesus proceeds to contrast the deficient hospitality of Simon with the fervent devotion of the 'sinner.' It was *your* house I entered, Jesus says, but there was no water for My feet, no kiss of greeting, no oil for My head—none of the proper (or at least possible) courtesies were offered. Three times Jesus emphatically refers to the woman's conduct with 'But *she* ...' (vv. 44, 45, 46). She washed Jesus' feet with her tears and, possibly having no towel, daringly dried them with her hair; she hasn't ceased kissing Jesus' feet in contrast to a non-existent welcome on the cheek; she anointed His feet with fragrance while Simon didn't even supply cheap oil for His head.

Scholars are divided on whether Simon should be faulted on his hospitality. Some hold that these tokens of hospitality were not really required (e.g., Howard Marshall). But Jesus goes to some pains to point out Simon's deficiencies and so I come down with those who see Simon's practice as a studied indifference—his lack of normal courtesies may have been a calculated attempt to demean Jesus.[14] By commending the woman's attentions He critiques Simon's negligence—and that was a social no-no. One was never, ever to show any disapproval for a host's conduct or provisions. One simply didn't do that. But Jesus does, and in detail. Jesus is willing to be an offensive social klutz if it will awaken Simon to his own need. 'The one forgiven little loves little' (v. 47b). His utter lack of even courtesy toward Jesus may well indicate he's a total stranger to the forgiveness of sins. Maybe Simon will think.

---

13. I have to confess—with no irreverence intended—that Jesus' question amuses me. Of course Simon sees the woman. He hasn't been watching much else for the last however many minutes! But I often think how Simon would've answered had he been from the southern US with our practiced evasiveness: 'No, really, is there actually a woman there? Well [stretching his neck], of all things, there *is* a woman there. I hadn't actually noticed!'

14. See especially Kenneth E. Bailey, *Poet and Peasant* and *Through Peasant Eyes*, combined ed. (Grand Rapids: Eerdmans, 1980), pp. 4-5, 14-15, and the superb comments of David E. Garland, *Luke*, ZECNT (Grand Rapids: Zondervan, 2011), pp. 328-29.

A couple of matters must be straightened up. One is the theology of the text, especially verse 47a, when Jesus says to Simon, 'For this reason, I tell you, her sins which are many, have been forgiven, for she loved much.' A superficial take on the text might assume it teaches that her great love led to her forgiveness. But that is all wrong. Jesus' little parable (vv. 41-42) makes the order clear: forgiveness comes first and produces the response of love. So in 47a Jesus is saying that her love is the *evidence* of forgiveness already received. The other 'matter' is the woman. Jesus was dealing with Simon most of the time. But here is this woman on her knees at the end of the couch, in a hostile setting, many eyes probably staring daggers at her. Jesus gives her clearly needed words of assurance (vv. 48, 50), especially, 'Your sins have been forgiven.' The verb form carries the sense 'have been and remain forgiven.' What could be more welcome?

I frequently recall a Sunday School picnic in which men and boys from our church were playing softball with those of another church group. I was twelve or thirteen, was playing first base for our team, and a fellow from the other team got a base hit and was there at first base. He was probably twenty and fairly well built. He said something about knocking me down if he had to do so—I don't know why his ego told him to pick on a puny Presbyterian kid. I was naturally a bit unsettled and jittery from his threats. When our team went in to bat my next older brother, Jim, was there. He was twenty-one. He must have observed Mr. Macho intimidating his kid brother and told me, 'If that guy gives you any trouble, tell him to come see me.' Well, words have power! Jim had just liberated me. Simply a statement, just an assurance—but desperately needed and totally effective. And that's what this woman needed in a hostile environment and with a memory full of her past; simply a dogmatic assurance from Jesus: 'Your sins are forgiven.'

Luke will not let loose of you until he tells you the thoughts of the diners: 'Who is this who even forgives sins?' (v. 49). Jesus didn't declare forgiveness in God's name; He Himself forgives. Luke has already faced us with this in 5:21. He doesn't want you to think you can dismiss the 'deity question.'

19

Mega-Parable: Keep Your Eyes on Your Ears

(Luke 8:1-21)

Jesus is the one who said it: keep your eyes on your ears (v. 18a).[1] It's really impossible to do, unless one looks in the mirror! But we know His intent: *You must be very careful about how you hear the word of God*, especially the word that God's kingship has at last arrived and has done so in the person of Jesus (v. 1), and so your relation with the word of God begins with how you respond to Jesus Himself. In this connection Jesus tells the parable about the sower, seed, and soils. Of all Jesus' parables this is the mega-parable, the leading parable. It has pride of place in each of the synoptic gospels (see Matt. 13 and Mark 4). Note that aside from 5:36-37 and 6:39, it is the first one that Luke relates. It stresses that listening is not a passive matter and that how you hear the word of God determines everything. What then does Luke set in front of us here?

Look first at the material before and after the parable. Here Luke shows us that **Jesus gathers a congregation around His word** (vv. 1-3, 19-21). These two brief segments form a kind of wrap around the parable and its explanation. Verse 15 (in the explanation of the parable) shows that there will

---

1. English versions tend to 'unliteralize' it to 'consider carefully' (NIV) or 'take care' (ESV), but the verb is *blepō*, to look, see.

surely be a true congregation, and in these two segments we get a glimpse of it. Verses 1-3 show that these folks in the congregation of Jesus are people with a *past*. As Jesus was moving about and preaching we are told:

> And the twelve were with him and some women who had been healed from evil spirits and diseases: Mary, called Magdalene, from whom seven demons had gone out, and Joanna, wife of Chuza, Herod's financial manager, and Susanna and many others, who were serving them out of their resources.

Some would probably be troubled about the women. There seemed to be a general opposition in Judaism to teaching torah to women. It's not difficult to cough up nasty comments by various rabbis.[2] The problem with these women was not so much their gender as their past. They had had their day under the devil's regimen: 'healed from evil spirits and diseases.' Mary Magdalene's was a severe 'case.'[3] And now a bond of gratitude held them to Jesus. And kept holding them, for these women were there at the cross and burial and empty tomb (23:49, 55; 24:10) as well.

It's often this way among Christ's people. During Martyn Lloyd-Jones' first pastorate in South Wales, there was quite an 'alcohol' problem in the community. Dock workers might receive liquor as part of their wages. But some of these men got washed, sanctified and justified. So a man would stop at the manse, hand a bottle to Mrs Lloyd-Jones, and explain: 'I asked the Doctor to keep this for me ... it's good stuff, the Captain gave it to me when I finished the job.'[4] He had been converted but couldn't trust himself to keep the liquor in his own home. As a result, Lloyd-Jones ended up with a whole cupboard full of fine booze! They were fellows with a past— they were a bunch of sops, but they had come to Jesus.

---

2. See TDNT, 1:781-82; however not all such comments should be taken in an unfiltered way; see NIDNTTE, 1:615-16.

3. There is no reason to identify the 'sinful woman' of 7:36-50 with Mary Magdalene or to assume that she had been a prostitute. Seven demons is bondage enough without laying more on her.

4. Iain H. Murray, *David Martyn Lloyd-Jones: The First Forty Years 1899-1939* (Edinburgh: Banner of Truth, 1982), 221fn.

Then in verses 19-21, we hear that Jesus' people are blessed with *privilege*. Jesus' mother and brothers arrive and can't get access to Him because of the crunch of the crowd. Three times in three verses 'mother and brothers' are mentioned. But Jesus puts a new twist on the relational language: those who stand in family bonds to Jesus are those 'who hear the word of God and do it' (v. 21). Prizing the word of God like that is what determines nearness to Jesus. What higher privilege could one have than to be among the family of Jesus and to be mother, brother, and sister to Him? Hence verses 1-3 and 19-21 depict a two-fold miracle: Jesus kidnaps people from Satan's landfill and makes them part of His family. All of which should be instructive for us: don't ever forget what you *were* (vv. 1-3, plus perhaps 1 Cor. 6:9-11), but in view of verses 19-21 don't forget what you *are*.

Secondly, Luke says **Jesus brings judgment through the word** (vv. 4-10, 16-18). Here we need to touch on Jesus' teaching by means of parables (vv. 4, 9-10). Let me paraphrase a common approach one sometimes reads or hears. It goes like this: 'Jesus uses the common, well-known, simplest and familiar items of country and village life to make divine truth plain and clear; He has no truck with labored, technical, doctrinal points; there's no complicated jargon or five-syllable theological words; He tells you about a farmer! What could be clearer and closer to home than that?' But that is pretty much rubbish.

You may disagree. You may say, as you look back over verses 4-8, 'But it is all so basic and obvious.' If you think that, it's because you've cheated and you are subversively pulling in verses 11-15 into the smoke-filled room of your mind. You subconsciously have Jesus' explanation floating around in the back of your head. But drop that out of your memory. Just look at verses 4-8 by themselves. In the last of verse 8 Jesus implies you need to get the point ('The one who has ears to hear, let him hear'). But that's the point. What *is* the point? And, if you think you know the point, how do you know it's the point?

Take a kitchen situation. Suppose I walk into our kitchen and there on the counter are several racks of freshly baked cookies. They are there in all their potential sustenance. Now what am I to make of it? There is no note or any indication of what these specimens are for. Am I to hear my wife's voice saying, 'You'll like these—have three or four'? Or am I to understand an admonition? 'Don't mess with these; they're for the dessert party over at the Jablonski's house tonight.' It's not clear, not as obvious at all as we like to think. That's the way with the parable. Like the disciples (v. 9), the original audience would be scratching their heads. What's He talking about? What is the seed? Who is the sower? How is it 'simple' and 'clear'?

What does Jesus say He is doing? 'To *you* [emphatic; the disciples] it has been given to know the mysteries of the kingdom of God, but to the rest it comes in parables, in order that "seeing, they may not see, and hearing, they may not understand"' (v. 10). Jesus seems to say: I use parables to conceal and hide and obscure the word of God. Then He quotes from Isaiah 6:9. There (in eighth century B.C. Judah) the word of God had been given but persistently rejected and so Yahweh withdraws His word. The idea seems to be that as Isaiah brings the word (Isa. 6:9-10) it will have a 'densifying' effect on the hearers. So they won't be able to 'get' it. I suggest Jesus is saying that there is an 'Isaiah situation' in Israel at this point. Even recently in the text we've heard and seen Israel's unbelieving flip-floppiness (7:31-35) and hard-hearted arrogance (Simon in 7:39-46). Parables then are (at least in part) an expression of judgment upon an unbelieving Jewish nation.[5] They were designed to conceal.

When our boys were small, I read them a multi-volume work called *Journey Through the Night*. The setting was Germany's occupation of Holland during World War II. At one point one

---

5. 'The parable is a sign of judgment' (E. Earle Ellis, *The Gospel of Luke*, NCB, rev. ed. [London: Oliphants, 1974], pp. 125). I also agree with Ellis' overall assessment: 'Why did the preaching of Jesus and of the early Church get so little response from the people of Israel? Indeed, why did the kingdom message find a true and lasting response only in a minority of Gentile hearers? The parable answers this question with the doctrine of the remnant (cf. Rom. 9:27). For most people the Devil, temptation, cares, and riches are effective deterrents to the gospel message. The parable tells a story of rejection. In turn, this rejection becomes a ground for teaching in parables. The parable is a sign that the rejectors are themselves rejected by God (10). Jesus, like the New Testament generally, sees in the negative response of the Jews the hidden purpose of God (cf. Rom. 9-11). The conclusion (16-18) applies the parable as a warning to everyone to "take heed how you hear". The unbelieving Jewish nation which "has not" the truth of God shall lose even what it "thinks" that it has' (p. 124).

Dutch farmer, Vander May, phones up another farmer, DeBoer, and tells him he has some *puppies* to deliver. By that he meant he had some Jews to bring to DeBoer's place for the latter to hide. But since Nazi ears may have been listening in on the phone lines, he said 'puppies.' It was designed to conceal the truth from Nazi snoops. That is Jesus' point about the parables. Verses 16-18 carry a similar warning note, although in these verses Jesus isn't speaking of 'the rest' (v. 10) but to the disciples. Expositors differ on the thrust of verses 16-18. Some think they are urging the disciples to be 'light' and spread the word of the kingdom. But that is not Jesus' concern here. 'Watch out therefore how you hear' (v. 18a)—it's about how His disciples receive His word. So, briefly, verse 16 shows the intention of the revelation Jesus brings. Perhaps there's a bit of 'Oh-no!' humor in the picture. One doesn't light a small clay lamp only to put a container over it and snuff it out. Nor does one put it under a couch, which would also obscure what light there was (or, maybe, set the couch on fire and make more light than wanted). Verse 17 may suggest that the revelation Jesus brings will become progressively clearer. But what really matters is 'how you hear' (v. 18). God is at work among those who hear Jesus' word. Those who receive and welcome His word will find that God gives them even more light and insight, while those who stiff-arm His word will find that God 'takes away' even what they thought they had.

Verse 18 brings to mind a story once carried in *Leadership* magazine. There was a city-bred fellow who bought a farm and several milk cows. When he was in the feed store one day he lamented that his best cow had gone dry. The proprietor asked if he was feeding her right. The man said that he fed her what the store owner had sold him. Next question: 'Are you milking her every day?' Answer: 'Just about. If I need six or eight ounces of milk for breakfast, I go out and get it. If I don't need any, I don't get it—I just let her save it up.' The city fellow had to be told it didn't work that way. That's the way it is with Jesus' truth. You don't dare play around or piddle with it or manipulate it at your convenience; rather you need to lay hold of all you can—if you want more.

Back to parables. These are not quaint, nostalgic, home-spun, aw-shucks stories for folks to understand, but they are part of the judgment of God for failure to hear the word of God before. And if you do understand, it is only by divine gift ('to you it has been given,' v. 10). It is the 'sweet and gentle' Jesus who says that you will only understand the secrets of God's rule and Jesus' person if God gives you the ability to understand. So, like the disciples, you need to ask![6] But get the point: if you have no use for the word of God, no real care for it, no hunger for it, it will be taken from you; if you continue to despise the gospel, Jesus will hide it from you. Jesus brings judgment through His word.

Finally, **Jesus pictures our danger in relation to His word**—we see this in Jesus' interpretation of the parable (vv. 11-15). We seem to be left looking at a good bit of failure of the word (vv. 12-14). It won't do, of course, to get picky over parabolic details, e.g., asking why the sower threw seed in such poor places. It's a disputed matter, but some claim that at this time sowing usually, though not invariably, preceded plowing.[7] If so, the farmer was only on the first step and wanted to sow promiscuously. In any case, Jesus shows us our danger. We can only deal with a couple of examples.

For one, the rocky layer (v. 13). Jesus doesn't refer to soil with a lot of rocks mixed in with it but to areas where there is a limestone layer of rock with a very thin bit of topsoil above it. It can warm up in no time, seeds may sprout quickly, but whatever moisture there is can dry out, and 'wither' is the name of the game. In terms of hearers, 'they receive the word with joy' and 'believe for a while.' Like the 'starter' fire in a fireplace, the newspaper and kindling burst into flame but soon peter out if some hefty dry logs have not been added.[8] In a time of testing they fall away; perhaps they become disappointed with God because He is not the safety valve they imagined.

---

6. Cf. David Gooding, *According to Luke* (1987; reprint ed., Coleraine, N. Ireland: Myrtlefield Trust, 2013), pp. 142-43.

7. See Craig S. Keener, *A Commentary on the Gospel of Matthew* (Grand Rapids: Eerdmans, 1999), pp. 376-77; cf. also James R. Edwards, *The Gospel According to Mark*, PNTC (Grand Rapids: Eerdmans, 2002), p. 128. The scenario in Isaiah 28:24-26 has plowing precede sowing.

8. For a graphic 'rocky ground' illustration, see C. H. Spurgeon's 1860 sermon in *The New Park Street Pulpit*, vol. 6 (reprint ed., London: Banner of Truth, 1964), pp. 177-78.

Here contemporary readers must beware of a wrong reaction. For someone is liable to say, 'Well, but though it would not be advisable to be rocky-layer hearers, nevertheless such folks are "saved," aren't they?' Where would you ever get that idea? 'They believe for a while.' That is not saving faith. See Mark 13:13. People can receive the word with joy, be impressed and overwhelmed with the gospel, perhaps be enthusiastic witnesses for Jesus—and fall away as lost souls.

Then there's the seed among the thorn-plants (v. 14). The problem here is not pressure (as in v. 13, 'a time of testing') but preoccupation: 'as they go along they are choked by the worries and riches and pleasures of life.' Other 'stuff' takes over. Maybe it was only meant to be temporary. But Christ just gets squeezed out. The scary item here is a Greek participle, *poreuomenoi*, 'as they go along.' The worries, riches, and pleasures don't make a sudden assault; rather over a period of time they simply ooze their way in—the 'choking' is only the last, fatal step. Gradual danger is hard to notice.

This phenomenon is like kudzu. It's a twining vine that was introduced into the US from Japan in the late nineteenth century. Originally it was marketed as an ornamental plant for shading porches. But things gradually got out of hand. Now one can drive down highways in the southeastern United States and see large patches of kudzu covering and smothering trees and undergrowth. One source says it now covers over seven million acres in the southeastern US. Power companies spend $1.5 million/year to repair kudzu damage to power lines. But it's been gradual. Still is. During growing season kudzu grows about one foot per day. One usually doesn't hear or see that.

It may be that one of these culprits (worries, riches, pleasures) may put more 'squeeze' on the word in your life than another, but, whether all or one in particular, the subtlety is frightening: 'as (you) go along'—it's a gradual, slow, turtle-like, kudzu-creeping development that you may not see.

There is a 'conflict,' then, that the word of God appears to have with three of these soils (vv. 12-14), and it seems that frequently the word of God loses the battle. Is that the case with you? Are you reading your biography in these soil samples of Jesus?

20

Above All Earthly—and Sinister—Powers
(Luke 8:22-39)

Luke's style seems almost lackadaisical as he takes us into another section: 'Now it came about on one of the days ...' (v. 22a). So begins a segment that parallels Mark 4:35–5:43, consisting of four episodes exhibiting Jesus' power. This whole section (= 8:22-56) could be dubbed 'Jesus and His triumphs,' for it depicts Jesus' control over danger (vv. 22-25), demons (vv. 26-39), disease (vv. 43-48), and death (vv. 40-42, 49-56). However, we are not simply looking at samples of Jesus' power. These four samples consist of *worst-case scenarios*, instances in which folks are in the most desperate or hopeless of circumstances. And yet Jesus shows He is fully adequate for each one. I'm convinced that at the end of this section Luke (no less than Mark) wants his readers to throw up their hands and shout, 'Hallelujah! What a Savior!'

Because the whole text is so long, I will divide it up and treat only verses 22-39 in this chapter. And the first incident (vv. 22-25) focuses our attention on **the Creator's voice.** Jesus and disciples are on the Sea of Galilee heading for the southeastern side. It was Jesus' idea (v. 22b). Jesus falls asleep and all chaos breaks loose with one of those capricious windstorms that can blast its way down on the lake.[1] It kicks up

---

1. For background, see Gordon Franz, 'What Type of Storms Did Jesus Calm: Wind or Rain?,' in *Lexham Geographic Commentary on the Gospels*, ed. Barry J. Beitzel (Bellingham, WA: Lexham, 2017), pp. 175-82.

the waves and the boat is being swamped (v. 23). They shake Jesus awake with their alarmed 'We are perishing!' (v. 24a). It's a significant panic, for some of these men are veterans of any number of storms on this lake. They are 'old salts,' have been caught in many squalls before, and for *them* to be alarmed tells us their trouble is doubly dire. Fully awake, Jesus 'rebuked' the wind and waves, they ceased, and 'it became calm' (v. 24b).

A couple of observations. One has to do with Luke's style. I know this can be subjective, but it seems to me that Luke is very 'these-are-the-facts' in his description in verses 22-24. His prose seems 'severe,' not including any extra details, refusing to 'fluff up' the account with more fascinating items of interest. I suggest that may be because he's more interested in the aftermath (v. 25) than in souping up the drama itself.

Note too the verb used of Jesus in verse 24b: 'he rebuked (*epitimaō*) the wind and the waves.' This verb is used in LXX in Psalm 105:9 (=106:9 in our Bibles) where it says that Yahweh 'rebuked the Red Sea, and it became dry.' It may also be used in Psalm 106:29 (LXX; =107:29 in our Bibles), also of Yahweh, 'He rebuked the storm and it calmed into a breeze'; however, the better reading in this text seems to be 'he commanded' (*epitassō*), which, please note, is the verb used when the disciples speak in verse 25 ('he commands even the winds and the water'). We shouldn't pass by what may well be an allusion to these OT texts, telling us, then, that what Yahweh does, Jesus does, and when Jesus 'rebukes' and 'commands,' wind and storm cease. What then does Jesus intend for us to think of Him?

The 'teaching moment' comes in verse 25, where we meet two questions. Jesus asked the first: 'Where is your faith?' He is not implying they have no faith in Him at all; rather he's asking where their faith was in this circumstance.[2] Why didn't it show up? Jesus is not suggesting that they should

---

2. Cf. Bock's excellent comments in *Luke 1:1-9:50*, BECNT (Grand Rapids: Baker, 1994), p. 763. Cf. Richard D. Phillips' comment: 'It was faith that Jesus was interested in. He did not comment on the terror of the storm, for it was no surprise to him. He did not boast regarding his wondrous work. What drew his notice was what the storm revealed about their faith' (*Mighty to Save* [Phillipsburg, NJ: Presbyterian & Reformed, 2001], p. 95). Phillips' volume is a fine exposition of the miracle accounts in the third gospel.

have expected to see something like what Jesus did, but that they might at least have considered that since Jesus was *there*, nothing could really harm them. If Jesus was in the boat with them, that should count for something. We may hear Jesus repeating the same question to us again and again.

The disciples ask the second question: 'Who then is this that he commands even the winds as well as the water—and they obey him?' (v. 25b). Note what moved this question. Luke says, 'They were afraid.' Now likely they were afraid in the storm when they cried, 'We are perishing' (v. 24a). But Jesus had taken care of that. It was calm now. Their fear is noted *after* the storm and it is tied to what Jesus did. If at this moment we could have been 'skyping' with the disciples, we might ask, 'Why are you trembling? The storm's over, the danger's past.' They would tell us that we don't understand— they are not shaking because of the storm but because of Jesus. Think what they had to think about: they are sitting in a boat with a man at a certain latitude and longitude on the Sea of Galilee and He tells the winds to stop blasting away—and they do just that. Who can command winds and water but the Creator, the God Psalms 106 and 107, for example, speak of? And yet He's sitting with them in a boat! And a short time before He fell asleep (v. 23a). He has all the normal needs of humanity and yet speaks with the voice of deity and that's enough to cause brain tremors.

Secondly, verses 26-39 show us **the Conqueror's prize**. Luke takes us over to the 'region of the Gerasenes' to the southeast of the Sea of Galilee, Gentile territory, where we are not surprised to run into pig farming (v. 32).[3] And here we run into a tragic case. No sooner is Jesus on land than a certain man, demon-possessed, meets Him. Luke takes some trouble describing him: his humiliation ('for a long time he had worn no clothes,' 27b), his isolation ('he was not staying in a house but among the tombs,' 27c; 'he was being driven by

---

3. Matthew locates the incident in the region of the 'Gadarenes' (Matt. 8:28), while Mark and Luke read 'Gerasenes' (Mark 5:1, Luke 8:26). Please note 'the region of.' No gospel claims the incident happened *at* Gadara or Gerasa. On the whole matter, see Todd Bolen, 'Where Did the Possessed-Pigs Drown,' in *Lexham Geographic Commentary on the Gospels*, ed. Barry J. Beitzel (Bellingham, WA: Lexham, 2017), pp. 196-218.

the demon into desert places,' 29c), his subjection ('For many times it [the unclean spirit] had dragged him away,' 29b), and his fragmentation ('he said, "Legion," because many demons had entered into him,' 30). What a specimen of degraded, mangled humanity! Yet in the middle of this heart-breaking description Luke includes what we might call a comforting terror, for 'when he saw Jesus, he cried out and fell in front of him, and with a loud voice said, "Would you leave me alone,[4] Jesus, Son of the most high God? I beg you, do not torment me"' (v. 28). The terror is the demon's, the comfort is ours. It's as if as soon as Jesus comes, there is an invisible compulsion that propels these denizens of darkness to show submission to the Sovereign they so intensely despise and to confess the truth of His supremacy. This leaves us in no doubt about how the so-called cosmic conflict will play out. The terror of the demons is the hope of the church.

Luke tells us that Jesus had commanded the unclean spirit to come out of the man (v. 29a). Then he also gives us some 'invisible information' in verses 31-32. There is no way we could come up with this background data by our own insight or observation. It has to do with the demons' request of Jesus not to commit them to the 'Abyss'; they apparently wanted to 'inhabit' something and so begged permission to enter the herd of nearby swine. Jesus allowed this—one might say He heard the demons' prayer. You can say what you want about this, but you would have no clue about it unless Luke had 'revealed' it to you. Then he follows up this invisible information with very observable evidence: the pigs rushed down the slope into the lake and were drowned (v. 33). How do you know the demons left the man? Well, look at that mad panic that possessed those pigs. Naturally, the text stirs all sort of questions, as Darrell Bock notes: How can animals be possessed? Why would Jesus allow such a use of animals? What happened to the demons? Why did the spirits feel compelled to dwell somewhere rather than roaming the earth? The text gives no answer.[5] The local chapter of People

---

4. Cf. W. F. Arndt, *The Gospel According to St. Luke* (St. Louis: Concordia, 1956), p. 240.

5. Bock, p. 776.

for the Ethical Treatment of Animals might be upset, but the Bible is silent about these sudden swine suicides. Luke provides still more observable evidence of Jesus' work in verses 34-35. The pig herdsmen fled the scene and told town and countryside what had occurred; folks came to see, came to Jesus and 'found the man from whom the demons had gone out sitting—clothed and sane—at the feet of Jesus' (v. 35b). They looked at that wholeness, that quietness, that submission, that sanity—'and they were afraid' (v. 35c). There is a fear that may draw you to Jesus (see v. 25), and there is a fear that may drive you from Jesus. It's the latter in this case. They heard (v. 36), they saw (v. 35), and the whole crowd of the Geraseneans asked Jesus to 'go away from them' (v. 37a)—for they were seized with a great fear (v. 37b). Luke includes no explanation. Did they fear Jesus would wreck the pig industry and the whole local economy? No answer. Maybe Luke simply wants the sadness of folks asking Jesus to leave them alone to sink into our souls. And Jesus complies (v. 37c)—which should grip us with greater fear.

At the end of his account (vv. 38-39) Luke supplies a heavy layer of irony (which is also apparent in Mark 5:17-20). J. C. Ryle summed it up well: The Gerasenes begged Jesus to leave them and their request was granted; and yet the man from whom the demons had departed asked that he might be with Jesus—and his request was denied.[6] Jesus continues to baffle us, but also to instruct. Clearly, there is more than one way in which to serve Christ, and sometimes our place is bearing witness precisely where we are.

However, in one sense—and this is the deeper irony—Jesus did *not* grant the Gerasenes' request. Oh, to be sure, He Himself left them and yet in a sense He didn't. He sent His home-grown evangelist back into their midst to bear testimony to them. One might almost speak of the guile (guiltless guile, to be sure) of Jesus. It reminds me of a story Australian missionary Dick McClellan told of Christians in Ethiopia.[7]

6. J. C. Ryle, *Expository Thoughts on the Gospels: St. Luke*, 2 vols. (New York: Baker & Taylor, 1858). 1:274-75.

7. I have referred to this in my *The Way of the Righteous in the Muck of Life* (Ross-shire: Christian Focus, 2010), p. 32; originally, it's from McClellan's account in *Warriors of Ethiopia*.

He tells of a number of evangelists from the Wolaitta tribe in southwestern Ethiopia who wanted to take the gospel to other tribes in the Gofa region. The men moved their families to Gofa, rented land, built houses, planted crops, had new neighbors in, and spoke the gospel to them. Some received the Savior; prayer houses were built; worship began. But too many changes took place—converts no longer frequented witch-doctors, no longer paid the priest-tax to Orthodox priests, no longer slipped bribes to government officials for favors. So a police lieutenant arrested the evangelist Atero, chained his wrists together, clamped his ankles together in heavy iron rings so he could only hop, not walk. He paraded Atero in front of the market-day crowd to make it clear that this is what would happen to any who followed the 'new religion.' He ordered Atero, 'Go back to Wolaitta … and take your Jesus thing with you! We don't want your Jesus here!' Then Atero hopped forward and said, 'O Sir, listen. Please listen. I can go but the Gospel will stay. By the power of God I planted Jesus in Gofa. He is planted in the hearts and souls of the Gofa people. I can go but Jesus will stay.' That is the gracious defiance of the gospel to the crabby rulers of this age. And that's Jesus' procedure in this text. It's the supreme irony: Jesus can go, but Jesus will stay, because there is loose in the territory of the Gerasenes a demon-deprived evangelist who can't stop talking about what Jesus had done for him.

21

A Tale of Two Daughters
(Luke 8:40-56)

When Ann Landers had her 'advice column' in newspapers, a woman sent Landers her story. Her story was simple: my mother died; I was crushed; I was sitting in her funeral service still overwhelmed. In mid-service the church door opened, a flustered-looking young man entered and sat down beside her. Perplexed, he whisperingly asked her why the minister kept calling Aunt Mary Margaret. Answer: because that was her name—no one called her Mary. Another subdued exchange confirmed that this was *not* the Lutheran church; the latter was across the street; he was at the wrong funeral, and the deep grief both felt threatened to erupt in inappropriate laughter. The follow-up pow-wow in the church parking lot afterwards proved to be the prelude to twenty-three years (to date) of a very happy marriage.

Now one does not expect that. One doesn't imagine two separate funerals getting tangled together to produce a marriage. But sometimes that sort of thing happens. What should be two separate dramas gets intertwined, interlocked, in a way none of us could have foreseen. That's the way with this passage. Among the crowd welcoming Jesus back from the Decapolis is Jairus, whose only daughter is dying. Will Jesus come? What ought to be simple isn't. On the way to Jairus' house his story gets mixed with someone else's story. There's an interruption and, since Jesus never seems in a hurry, He accepts the intrusion. Jairus' daughter must be placed 'on hold.' Even in terminology Luke seems to mesh the two stories: the term 'daughter' is used by Jesus toward the woman (v. 48) and for Jairus' girl (v. 49). Then there is an interesting chronological overlap: Jairus' daughter is about twelve (v. 42) and the woman's affliction had been endured for twelve years (v. 43). One had had twelve years of life, the other twelve years of misery. So the two episodes are tied together; the one intrudes upon the other; and as a result we can see that *Jesus is a Savior you can trust in your desperation, or even in your death.*

Let's pick up the woman's story first and think about **the touch of faith** (vv. 43-48). She'd suffered from 'a flow of blood' for twelve years, some abnormal, chronic vaginal bleeding. An Israelite woman was technically or ritually unclean during her monthly period (Lev. 15:19-24), but this sort of aggravated, ongoing condition kept her in a perpetual state of uncleanness (Lev. 15:25-30). Anyone who sits on her bed or on a chair she has occupied contracts 'uncleanness.' So life simply shrivels out of life. She couldn't go to anyone's place for dinner. Few, if any, would come in to visit her. Synagogue services were off limits. Physical debility and then social isolation to the max. Not that she hadn't tried—she'd 'spent all her resources on physicians' (v. 43),[1] help likely mixed with quackery.[2] On this day, with Jesus near, desperation took over. She had heard of Him and had apparently convinced herself (see Mark 5:28) that if she just touched His clothes she would be healed. She had no promise to that effect. Could one call it a holy hunch? At least it was a convinced conviction.

We must admit that we don't have all the fill-in details. Surely she would normally be recognized if she had tried to circulate publicly. Did she wear different clothes or cover herself in such a way as to avoid recognition? Was she

---

1. There's some debate about the original text here, whether the spending-on-physicians note is original or not. Dr. Luke may've preferred to exclude it. Likely, however, it's original.

2. Cf. some of the later 'cures' proposed in the Babylonian Talmud; see David E. Garland, 'Mark,' in ZIBBC, 1:237. Who would ever want to start a cure by getting a barley grain from the dung of a white mule?

counting on getting 'lost' and unnoticed in the crush of the crowd? No doubt this was her hope. Desperation and drama and deliverance all collided in a moment as she 'came near from behind and touched the edge of his cloak—and immediately her flow of blood stopped' (v. 44). (That 'immediately' will also appear in vv. 47 and 55). She tried to slink a few feet further behind. But Jesus had stopped. He asked, 'Who touched me?' (v. 45). Joy over a healed body froze with panic over public exposure. Perhaps Peter's air-tight logic will protect her. His point was that practically everyone was touching Jesus, given the jostling of the crowd (v. 45b). But Jesus knew otherwise. As someone has said, Many pressed around Him, but one touched Him in faith.

She can only face the 'severity' of Jesus (vv. 46-47). She had craved anonymity and now she may well fear His anger and certainty of being publicly exposed before everyone. Scared, embarrassed, a spectacle 'before all the people,' she gave what proved to be both a confession and a testimony. She simply told the why and the how (v. 47b). And one word dissolved her fears—'Daughter' (v. 48). This is the only time in the Gospels that Jesus addresses someone with this affectionate term.[3] Her fear runs into Jesus' tenderness—and also His clarity. He says to her, 'Your faith [emphatic] has made you well; go in peace.' This is likely a necessary corrective lest she or others surmise that superstition works. At any rate, Jesus sees behind what may have been her superstitious surmises to the faith that drove her. The benefit did not come via some magic in His clothes but through the faith in her touch. And Jesus wanted her to know that. Yet whatever weaknesses or misconceptions she may have had, she was totally convinced of the sufficiency of Jesus.

Secondly, Luke depicts **the trial of faith** (vv. 40-42, 49-56). Here we come back to Jairus. He already had a trial when he came to Jesus: his 'only daughter' was dying (v. 42). Let's pause a moment to note what a common trial this has been for servants of Christ. It's easy to think of Christian names and not realize the sorrows they faced. Of John Owen's eleven children, only one reached adulthood. Charles and Sally

---

3. Mark L. Strauss, 'Luke,' ZIBBC, 1:399.

Wesley had eight children but watched five of them die in infancy or early childhood. B. M. Palmer lost a small boy and four adult daughters to death. With medical advances such losses may be comparatively fewer today, but still they occur. In any circles of Christian friends or in any local church, you find parents who have faced the loss of a child, or even more sadly, of children. Jairus, in our text, understandably, would prefer not to be one of them.

Jairus' trial was partly a matter of *time*. He wanted Jesus to reach his house before his daughter succumbed. Now I admit I am inferring from the circumstances in the text something that the text does not state. But my hunch is that Jairus may've been more than a bit itchy. Here is a crowd impeding Jesus' progress. And then there is this woman with her chronic bleeding. And Jesus takes time, makes time, for her. One is only too glad that she's healed of such bodily affliction, but time is of the essence.

But time ran out. The trial that was a matter of time now becomes a matter of *fact*. 'Someone came from the synagogue ruler's place, saying, "Your daughter has died; don't trouble the teacher anymore"' (v. 49). Jairus now becomes even more hopeless than the bleeding woman had been. His messenger's suggestion made sense—no need to bother the teacher. No one can do anything now. Matters are beyond hope. It borders on irreverence but could you imagine Jesus saying, 'Jairus, I do appreciate your seeking me out and if I can ever be of some help to you in the future … sorry about this time, can't always beat the clock …'? No, instead, Jesus had another word: 'Don't be afraid; only believe and she shall be made well' (v. 50).

And this means that Jairus' trial becomes a matter of *revelation* (vv. 50-55). Jesus is careful to take His eye-witnesses with Him—Peter, John, and James, in addition to the parents. But there's no doubt. Everybody knows she's really dead (v. 53). Yet when Jesus' hand grips hers He reaches across the chasm of death and conquers it. 'And I have the keys of Death and of Hades' (Rev. 1:18). True, this was a restoration not a resurrection. Understand that the day would come when she would die again (though she likely would bury her parents instead of their burying her). But don't you see the significance? This was meant to show Mr. and Mrs. Jairus and all Jesus' people that Jesus has power even over the realm of death. The D-word is not the last word. No, the time for resurrection hasn't come yet, but Jesus is showing us who *He* is. One could say that that trip to Jairus' house shows us that 'Don't trouble the teacher anymore' is never a right response in our troubles.

There is a bit more. We should back off and look at both episodes in a general way in order to see **the teaching of faith** Luke's account leaves with us.

He shows us that *Jesus may seem most severe when He is doing us much good.* Take the bleeding woman. He involved her in public embarrassment. One can only imagine how she shuddered when she heard Jesus' 'Who touched me?' But His intent was not vicious but gracious—He wanted to clarify her faith and personally assure her. Then, by His delaying, Jesus set Jairus up for shattering disappointment and all He could cling to was an 'Only believe.' But these instances teach us that Jesus' 'severity' may be only the wrapping or prelude to His goodness. They should remind us of that delightful twist in Cowper's hymn: 'behind a frowning providence he hides a smiling face.'

Then too *Jesus tends to lead us to see more of Himself.* Think of Jairus' case. Verses 41-42 clearly show Jairus' faith as well as his humility. But in verses 49-50, after he receives news of his daughter's death, Jesus calls him to a deeper, higher step of faith. It's as if Jesus was saying something like: You trusted Me in what was urgent, now trust Me in what is hopeless; you trusted Me in what was alarming, now trust Me in what seems irreversible; you thought I was adequate for that original situation—but what about this? Can you trust Me, can you believe that I am adequate for this very different, much more difficult one? So we run into a point we've made before: whether for Jairus or for us ... Jesus is always *more* than you can imagine.

Sometimes married people find this principle in operation in their spouses. I recall one Valentine's Day when I was diligently teaching my Old Testament class at Reformed Seminary. On exiting the classroom, I was met by four ladies in red gowns called, I believe, the 'Sweet Adelines.' They began singing, as they looked semi-adoringly at me, 'Let Me Call You Sweetheart' and a couple of other romantic ditties. It was very well done, but it never seemed to stop, though it may have been only five or six minutes. It was hugely embarrassing, not least because students and other professors were all around in the foyer observing the spectacle. Yes, my wife had paid them to do this and to waylay me on my work-site. I never suspected her. One lives with someone for years and assumes one knows her, but there are obviously depths of deviousness latent in her that I have never discerned. It's the fortune of many married couples, I think—one discovers there is far more lurking within that familiar person than one has ever imagined. This, I think, is what Luke is saying, only in a positive sense, about Jesus. In our walk with Him we go on discovering that He is far more than we have ever perceived.

Here then is a tale of two daughters that shows Jesus is a Savior you can trust both in desperation and in death. His severity brings comfort, His delays lead to joy.

22

An Introduction to Jesus' Discipleship
(Luke 9:1-50)

When I was a lad we took an annual summer trip to Kansas to see my grandmother. We'd leave soon after 4:00 a.m. from our home in western Pennsylvania and soon would be in Ohio. But Ohio was a problem for me. Unlike Indiana, which was much 'skinnier,' Ohio (though only 220 miles east-west) seemed to go on and on forever. There was just so much of it. Luke 9:1-50 is a bit like that. It's a big chunk of text. And if I deal with every section in detail, it will take a long time to get through it. But this huge text has a common concern: the instruction of disciples. Disciples pop up everywhere (e.g., vv. 1, 10, 12, 14, 16, 18, 28, 32, 40, 43, 49—these are only the explicit mentions). So Luke 9:1-50 has to do with 'The Training of the Twelve.'[1] Our exposition, then, cannot deal with the whole raft of details but will stick with the main concern—What were the disciples to learn?

They were meant to learn **the sufficiency of Jesus** (vv. 1-17). The text begins with the gifts of Jesus:

> Now when he had called the twelve together, he gave them power and authority over all the demons and to heal diseases; and he sent them to preach the kingdom of God and to heal the sick (vv. 1-2).

---

1. To cite the title of the classic work by A. B. Bruce (New York: Harper & Brothers, orig. pub. 1871).

The twelve had a mission of preaching, healing, and casting out demons. 'Preaching the kingdom of God' (v. 2) likely involved proclaiming the nearness of the kingdom (cf. 10:9-11), especially in the word and works of Jesus, and calling to repentance in light of it. These verses also show that the kingdom involves trampling on Satan's power and restoring people to whole-ness—a preview of the way 'things ought to be.' They were to travel light (vv. 3-4). Hence they went through the villages 'evangelizing and healing everywhere' (v. 6). Reports of their mission in Jesus' name even pricked Herod Antipas' curiosity and conscience (vv. 7-9).[2] But the power and authority for this mission was the gift of Jesus. The sufficiency of Jesus explains it.

When the apostles report on their mission, Jesus tries to withdraw with them to Bethsaida on the north shore of the Sea of Galilee (v. 10).[3] But the crowds track them down, so Jesus welcomes, preaches and heals (v. 11). The twelve become anxious over 'crowd control.' Did they think Jesus may have been oblivious to the potential problem? They argue then for an early dismissal so folks could find lodging and food (v. 12). Yet Jesus was perfectly serious when He replied, 'You [emphatic] give them something to eat' (v. 13a). That was ludicrous. Their only resources were paltry (5 loaves, 2 fish)—unless they were to *buy* food for 'all this people' (v. 13b). This latter suggestion may have been made to underscore the hopelessness of such a venture. Conceivably there could have been an ideal response. Couldn't they have thought or said: as in the Galilee mission (vv. 1-2) Jesus gave us the authority and power we didn't have in ourselves, so now in face of this we must look to Him to supply what we need. But they didn't think that way. And we can partly understand that. David Gooding makes an excellent observation here:

---

2. Rightly seen, there is something tremendously comforting in Herod Antipas' words, 'John I have decapitated.' In this context, Herod's words, vicious and horrid as they are, are actually a confession of *failure*! It's the perennial problem the rulers of this age have. They snuff out the servants of God, but the kingdom of God just keeps on coming. It must gall and alarm them—if they ever think about it.

3. The exact location of Bethsaida is a matter of debate. Josephus indicated it was east of where the Jordan entered the Sea of Galilee and on the shore. For detailed discussion, see the articles by Gordon Franz and Benjamin Foreman in Barry J. Beitzel, ed., *Lexham Geographic Commentary on the Gospels* (Bellingham, WA: Lexham, 2017), pp. 142-43, 271-75.

Now the apostles had never seen a miracle on this scale before. They had witnessed the healing of individuals .... But to feed this tremendous mass of people, numbering some five thousand males let alone women and children, was altogether a different proposition.[4]

It was, then, a sort of novel situation for them.

Jesus takes over. Breaking up the people in groups of roughly fifty would make it easy to have estimated the numbers. Jesus blessed the provisions and broke them up and then 'kept on giving' (imperfect tense, continuing action in past time, v. 16a) them to the twelve to pass out. The twelve baskets of extras clearly testified that they hadn't merely squeaked by.

We can't castigate the twelve for being 'slow' about seeing the adequacy of Jesus. We contemporary disciples can spend most of our lives having to learn the same. For we run into new and unknown circumstances as well: a new period in life, a new wrinkle in family relations, new conditions in the workplace, a new trial of a type we've never had to face before. And we don't necessarily think back to how competent and providing Jesus has always been before. We have to learn all over again a very basic truth: the sufficiency of Jesus.

The next section, verses 18-45, is a rather long one, but it hammers home one major matter: the disciples must learn **the mission of Jesus**. One can divide this segment by considering the confession (vv. 18-27), the mountain (vv. 28-36), and the miracle (vv. 37-45).

Luke places the disciples' (or Peter's) confession right after the feeding of the five thousand.[5] Jesus asks them about what the crowds say about Him. After the report from the polls, He presses them with 'Who do *you* say I am?' Peter answers, 'The Messiah of God' (v. 20b). We must not minimize this confession. The twelve knew the guesses and opinions of the

---

4. David Gooding, *According to Luke* (1987; reprint ed., Coleraine, N. Ireland: Myrtlefield Trust, 2013), p. 166.

5. Some scholars speak of the 'great omission' in Luke in going right to Peter's confession after the feeding of the five thousand. By doing so Luke leaves out all the material Mark has after the 5,000 (=Mark 6:45-8:26). But that's no problem. Luke is not Mark's slave.

proverbial 'men in the streets,' but they went beyond these with a definite conviction in the face of popular speculation. They are to be commended.

However, Jesus 'rebuked' them! That's what the verb (*epitimaō*, v. 21a) usually means. In this verse most English versions have 'strictly warned' or 'strictly charged' or the like. But the verb occurs twelve times in Luke's gospel, everywhere else meaning 'rebuke,' and so it should here.[6] Peter & Co. give the right answer—and get rebuked! Jesus put the clamps on their telling this to anyone (v. 21b). Why? Because most Jews at the time, including the disciples, packed the wrong freight into the term 'Messiah.' Not that the Messiah was not the conquering and reigning king promised in the Davidic covenant but all that was not yet. The term now needed to be front-loaded with what many in Israel had ignored: the shame and suffering and spurning of 'the Son of Man,' as Jesus referred to Himself (v. 22). This was all God-ordained—it 'must' (Gr.: *dei*, v. 22a) take place. So no talk about 'Messiah' until you understand what Messiah should connote.

Verses 23-27 logically follow from verse 22. If their Master is headed for suffering and rejection, then His disciple will face this as well. Here Jesus speaks to 'all,' (v. 23a), which I take to mean all His professed disciples. Since He will be a suffering Son of Man, whoever wants to come after Him must 'deny himself and take up his cross daily and go on following me' (v. 23). What does denying oneself mean? Earle Ellis puts it memorably: it means 'a person must become apostate from his egocentric self.'[7] And they'd lived in Roman-occupied Israel long enough to know what taking up a cross meant. It was the cross-piece a doomed person carried to the place where he was to be crucified. To take up one's cross was to be ready to die for Jesus' sake. Of course it may not always come to that. That's the hint of the word 'daily.' Coming after Jesus involves making a daily deathly decision—to be ready, if need be, to go to the death for Him.

---

6. See David E. Garland, *Luke*, ZECNT (Grand Rapids: Zondervan, 2011), p. 390.

7. E. Earle Ellis, *The Gospel of Luke*, NCB, rev. ed. (London: Oliphants, 1974), p. 140.

All that probably fell like a ton of bricks on Jesus' hearers, but notice how Jesus appends arguments or considerations to this demand in order to stimulate a willing response. Don't miss that little causal particle 'For' at the beginning of verses 24, 25, and 26. Jesus is giving reasons or incentives for taking the denial-and-death option. These arguments center on paradox (24), profit (25), and pressure (26).[8] This is vintage Jesus: His severe demands are often supported by solid encouragements. Nor should we miss His allusion to 'coming in his glory' (v. 26b). He is now placing His suffering and rejection front and center, but that does not for a moment dissolve His coming glory in its proper time.

Now we come to the mountain scene, Jesus' transfiguration (vv. 28-36).[9] Here we meet with the transformation in Jesus' appearance (29), the visitors He receives (30), and the conversation they are having (31). What is the purpose of this occasion? In a text that seems so disciple-oriented, we are apt to neglect Jesus. So we should ask first what the transfiguration must have meant to Him.[10] In a word, encouragement. His splendor here must have been a reassurance of the divine glory that was essentially His even in His present 'humbled' condition. The fact that Moses and Elijah spoke of His 'exodus' (v. 31) must have heartened Jesus tremendously. The word 'exodus' can mean 'departure' in death (see 2 Pet. 1:15); it certainly focuses on that here but may also include His resurrection and ascension. But here were men who would *talk with Him* about His suffering and

---

8. Don't pass by the quiet implication of verse 24, 'Whoever loses his life *on my account.*' Who could demand or expect or express such a notion except someone who is deity? For someone who is merely human to expect such would be conceit in excelsis. Note also that the 'pressure' in verse 26 probably comes from a persecution situation in which one is tempted to deny allegiance to Jesus.

9. Debate swirls around verse 27 and Jesus' assurance that there were some standing there who would 'never taste death until they see the kingdom of God.' Since the transfiguration immediately follows verse 27, some think the saying is fulfilled in the glory Peter, John, and James saw on the mountain. Others, sensing 'never taste death' seems to imply something more removed, suppose it refers to the resurrection-ascension of Jesus as He takes up His reign and pours out its power in the Pentecost and post-Pentecost period of the church. For more, see Bock, pp. 858-60.

10. Here I am drawing upon Donald Macleod's exposition in *From Glory to Golgotha* (Ross-shire: Christian Focus, 2002), pp. 69-76, which I have found immensely helpful. See also A. B. Bruce, *The Training of the Twelve*, pp. 192-95.

death, when His disciples seemed to stiff-arm the whole matter (cf. vv. 44-45; Matt. 16:22-23). How relieving it must have been to recognize the 'elephant in the room.' And then the Father's voice, underscoring His election and approval of Jesus must have gladdened Him (v. 35), perhaps bringing to mind shades of His baptism (3:21-22).

What were the three disciples to receive from this startling occasion? Probably *assurance*. 'They saw his glory' (v. 32), so when the days of Jesus' suffering arrived, hopefully at some point these men would, in the face of all that, recall that they had seen Jesus in His splendor and ponder that that divine splendor must still be real in spite of His sufferings. They were going to see at Jerusalem Jesus despised and humiliated and executed, and they needed an assurance on record that the suffering did not negate the splendor, that His rejection did not falsify His reign, that His misery did not cancel His majesty. So the transfiguration is for them a sneak preview of Jesus' glory. No matter what it looks like when Jesus undergoes His 'exodus,' the glory is nevertheless real.[11] Admittedly, this assurance was likely eclipsed in the short term.

As it turned out, the transfiguration was meant as *correction* for the disciples. They were having trouble with sleep but 'became fully awake' (v. 32) and saw both Jesus' glory and His conversationalists. When it looked like the consultation was breaking up, Peter makes his suggestion about three shelters, apparently wanting to prolong the experience. After all, when Moses and Elijah show up, it's obviously major stuff. While Peter is talking, however, 'a cloud came and began to cover them' —which scared them (v. 34). I don't know that the disciples thought of it, but in the book of Numbers, whenever Israel or folks within Israel opposed or were ready to assault Moses, the glory-cloud of Yahweh's presence appeared (see Num. 12:5; 14:10; 16:19 and 42; and 20:6 in their contexts). Now God's cloud comes in defense of Jesus, we might say.

---

11. Consider an analogy. Here is a man who usually wears jeans and T-shirts, lives in a modest home, mows his own yard, and drives an auto eight-ten years old. You, however, are his personal accountant; you know he is fabulously rich because you keep his books, do his taxes, and have seen his resources. The transfiguration was to give the three disciples such an inside look—which didn't 'take' until a later time.

Out of this cloud comes a voice. The Father specifies Jesus' competence via nine Greek words in verse 35. Drawing on OT background, the voice declares that Jesus is the 'Son,' who will reign over the nations (Ps. 2:7), the 'Chosen One' who is the suffering servant who gives His life for the sins of His people (Isa. 42:1, plus 49:1-7; 50:4-9, and 52:13-53:12), and the prophet like Moses who instructs God's people in the word (Deut. 18:15). And what are the disciples to do? 'Listen to him!' 'To him' is emphatic. They are to accept Jesus' word. And what was that word? It was the word about the cross (vv. 21-22) and about the cost (vv. 23-26). The disciples, however, didn't 'get' this (v. 45; also 18:31-34). They probably could not put together, like most of their Jewish contemporaries, the idea of a suffering Messiah. 'Suffering Messiah' seemed a contradiction in terms; it was like saying 'delicious vomit' or 'clean dirt.' Hence they urgently needed to 'hear him,' when Jesus clearly instructed them otherwise.

We might draw a couple of inferences from this account. One is that we can have a genuine Christian confession (v. 20) and yet have much progress to make in knowing *what kind of Christ* we believe in. We must always let Jesus define Himself. You must quit casting Jesus into your own image of what you want Him to be.

We should also learn from Peter's suggesting that the 'glory' experience be prolonged (v. 33). It was meant to be a secret, passing glimpse of Jesus' glory. Meant as an encouragement but not intended as an ongoing experience, meant to be temporary. Are contemporary disciples sometimes guilty of the 'Peter glitch'? Do we make the same error in principle? Some of us may long to recover the special joy or freshness or excitement of our early Christian experience. Perhaps you had a dramatic conversion and all things seemed new and delightful, yet, somehow, now that 'pizazz' is not there anymore. Nothing wrong with that desire. But does it occur to us that perhaps God provided that excitement in order to carry us through the hurdles and temptations our nascent faith faced, that perhaps that was meant to be a temporary provision? Or there was a particular period of spiritual growth and maturing—the Scriptures seemed so alive with instruction and comfort, prayer seemed wrapped in such a closeness to God. Perhaps this happened when you were a part of a certain church fellowship and you long to find that sort of church or to recover that atmosphere again. Granted, we do not enjoy the 'dry times,' the days of Christian 'plodding.' But could it be that sometimes we take what God intends as momentary, along-the-way encouragement and try to make it a permanent arrangement? 'Let us make three shelters.' Do we make an idol of our experience or feeling or excitement (that we've idealized), so that we prefer our experience to Jesus Himself?

Now we come to the 'miracle' (vv. 37-45), the last section on the mission of Jesus. One could say that Jesus comes down from the majesty on the mountain into the misery in the valley—and yet He shows His glory in both. Here then is a sad case of demonic affliction. It is all packed into the boy's father's description in verse 39: the spirit seizes him and suddenly screams, brings on convulsions and foaming at the mouth, smashing and bruising him up. Satan salivates to destroy. Luke's account of this episode is much briefer than Mark's (Mark 9:14-29).[12] Luke clearly depicts Jesus' mighty work but does so with a severe economy.[13] And yet Luke is the only one of the synoptic gospels (see Matt. 17:14-21; Mark 9:14-29) to record the impression this miracle made upon the crowd.[14] Indeed he clearly links the crowd's amazement to Jesus' next assertion of His coming arrest and suffering (vv. 43-44). It was *'while* all were marveling over all he was doing' (v. 43b) that He tried to hammer into His disciples once more the fact of His suffering (v. 44).[15] So Luke injects irony into his story, careful to tie Jesus' stellar victory (vv. 37-43a) with His apparent defeat (vv. 43b-44). And a combination of both human and divine 'factors' conspired to prevent them from 'getting' it (v. 45).

---

12. See Garland, p. 403.

13. Verse 41 poses the question of to whom Jesus refers in His lament over the 'faithless and perverse generation.' I think it refers primarily to the disciples. See W. F. Arndt, *The Gospel According to St. Luke* (St. Louis: Concordia, 1956), p. 266; and Joel B. Green, *The Gospel of Luke*, NICNT (Grand Rapids: Eerdmans, 1997), pp. 388-89.

14. Gooding, p. 176.

15. Garland, p. 399.

Here then is a whole block of material with three scenes (confession, mountain, miracle) that both begins (v. 22) and ends (v. 44) stressing Jesus' coming suffering. That was His supreme mission. He was to be a suffering Messiah. 'The Son of Man must suffer many things' (v. 22). *That* was the mission of Jesus the disciples needed to learn.

At this point the disciples were a good way off-base about Jesus' *identity*. They confessed Him as the Christ (Messiah), but primarily their own conception of Christ. In principle this situation reminds me of a story about Gil Hodges, the star first baseman for the Brooklyn Dodgers in the 1950s. The Dodgers were in Cincinnati playing a series against the local Reds. Cincinnati also had a star first baseman by the name of Ted Kluszewski. 'Klu' was an imposing hunk of protoplasm—huge arms and a hulking chest. Hodges himself cut an imposing figure but not as massive. Hodges and Kluszewski, though on different teams, were good friends. During some gap time in the Cincinnati series, Hodges and his wife went to a movie. As they were leaving the theatre, Hodges saw big 'Klu' sitting at the end of the back row—and in the dark as they walked out Hodges pinched him really hard on his cheek. The Hodges walked out into the lobby and there stands Ted Kluszewski! Gil Hodges asked, 'What are you doing *here*? I just saw you in the theatre and pinched your face.' Klu replied, 'What theatre? I wasn't in a theatre.' Hodges then realized he had pinched a stranger![16] That is the situation of the disciples in this narrative. They thought they had insight to Jesus' identity and were willing to confess it, and yet to a large extent this Messiah was a stranger to them. We, like them, as mentioned, can often shape Jesus by our own conceptions and find out we are dealing with a stranger. We must allow Jesus to define Himself.

The last verses of this segment show us that the disciples need to learn about **the fellowship of Jesus** (vv. 46-50), both in matters of status (vv. 46-48) and scope (vv. 49-50). The two occurrences of 'on the basis of/in my name' (vv. 48, 49) hold the two sections together. But the reader gets a contextual

---

16. Tom Clavin and Danny Peary, *Gil Hodges* (New York: New American Library, 2012), pp. 170-71.

shock when he reads of 'a debate among them' about which of the disciples might be the greatest (v. 46). Jesus had just told them again of His coming arrest (v. 44) and, oblivious to that, they are absorbed with their own prestige. Something like a wife who has suffered the death of her husband and right after his funeral a neighbor drops by to say, 'Since Dick won't be needing his lawn-mower anymore, would you sell it to me for a really good price?' All heart and sensitivity.

Yet one dare not demonize the disciples too viciously. This status-consciousness was part of the air they breathed in their first-century society:

> At all points, in worship, in the administration of justice, at meals, in all dealings, there constantly arose the question of who was the greater, and estimating the honour due to each was a task which had to be constantly fulfilled and which was felt to be very important.[17]

But Jesus countered this mentality with a visual aid. He took a child and set it at His side with the explanation, 'Whoever receives this child in my name receives *me* ...' (v. 48a). 'In my name' means 'for my sake' or 'as my disciple.'[18] Receiving anyone, no matter how lowly, who is linked to Jesus is tantamount to receiving Jesus Himself. This means then, as verse 48c explains, that 'the one who is least among you all, he is great.' You cannot find in the fellowship of Jesus any no-counts; we must never think that any one of Jesus' disciples, however obscure, does not matter. Here's a needed corrective to entrenched attitudes in some churches.

Then there is the case of the mysterious exorcist, this inconvenient fellow who was casting out demons in Jesus' name. John said, 'We tried to prevent him,' because, he explained, 'he does not follow with us' (v. 49). We only have a two-verse clip here; we don't know details and have no additional information. But Leon Morris seems to have it right: 'The man who opposes demons in Jesus' name is to

---

17. A. Schlatter in TDNT, 4:532.

18. Max Zerwick and Mary Grosvenor, *A Grammatical Analysis of the Greek New Testament*, 4th ed. (Rome: Pontifical Biblical Institute, 1993), p. 216.

be welcomed, not opposed. He is on the right side.'[19] These verses are not teaching us a soupy, sentimental ecumenism but trying to prevent a jealous, narrow provincialism.

These two segments (vv. 46-48, 49-50) serve as an inoculation against pride and a standing reminder that the fellowship of Jesus has no need of hot-shots.

19. Leon Morris, *The Gospel According to St. Luke*, TNTC (Grand Rapids: Eerdmans, 1974), p. 177.

23

A Crucial Turn

(Luke 9:51-62)

The adjective 'crucial' in our heading is crucial, for the word is derived from the Latin 'crux,' cross. Here (at 9:51) is the hinge of Luke's gospel; here Jesus turns to go to Jerusalem and the cross. All that follows must be viewed in that light. Approximately a third of the way through the gospel the shadow of the cross falls across the page. Most all agree that 9:51 begins a new section of the third gospel but dispute where the segment ends. Some opt for 19:10, others for 19:28, still others for 19:44 or 48. If we take the last option, then this block of material begins with a reprieve of mercy for Samaritans (9:52-56) and ends with a threat of judgment on Jerusalem (19:41-44). The whole segment is sometimes called a journey or travel narrative (there are periodic reminders of the destination; see 13:22, 33; 17:11; 18:31; 19:11, 28), but Luke does not depict a step-by-step geographical progression. Note, for example, that in 10:38-42 Jesus seems to be in Bethany near Jerusalem and yet in 17:11 He is up north between Samaria and Galilee. The journey then is an overall rubric (we are not to forget that everything is geared toward what will happen in Jerusalem), but the textual material is not laid out in some tight, systematic way. The reader may note a shift of emphasis from the preceding material. In 9:51ff. there are fewer miracles (4) and more teaching (e.g., 17 parables).[1] Fifteen of those parables are peculiar to Luke; in fact, 44% of the material in 9:51–19:44 is found only in Luke.[2]

We can order the teaching of our text around three key words. The first is **commitment** (v. 51): 'Now when the days were reaching fulfillment for his departure, he set (his) face to go to Jerusalem.' That there are days 'reaching fulfillment' implies that there is an ordered divine plan involved. Jesus' 'departure' is likely equivalent to His 'exodus' in verse 31. The word used here (*analēmpsis*) can refer to death (as in the pseudepigraphal Psalms of Solomon 4:18) but also means 'taking up' or 'ascension.' The verb form is used three times in LXX of 2 Kings 2:9-11 of Elijah's departure—being 'taken up' heavenward. The term here in verse 51 then likely embraces Jesus' death, resurrection, and ascension in its scope. The first portion of His 'departure,' however, is His suffering and death, and that is the focus of His commitment here.

Luke—deliberately, I think—uses a fascinating expression to indicate Jesus' tenacious resolve. 'He set (his) face to go to Jerusalem.' Commentaries will usually note the expression in OT texts, sometimes including Isaiah 50:7 among them, but usually only indicating that the language is a way of expressing firm resolution.[3] But I think Luke intends us to read 9:51 especially in light of Isaiah 50:7. There the expression occurs in part of a speech by the Servant of Yahweh (Isaiah 50:4-11 is typically called the third 'servant song'); He says, 'Therefore I have set my face as a flint.' In this context this 'Servant' has faced unexplained suffering:

> The Lord Yahweh has opened my ear,
>   and I, I did not rebel;
>   I did not turn away.
>   I gave my back to smiters
>   and my cheeks to those plucking out my beard;
>   I did not hide my face from scorn and spit (Isa. 50:5-6).

---

1. Alan J. Thompson, *Luke*, EGGNT (Nashville: Broadman & Holman, 2016), pp. 163.

2. D. L. Bock, DJG, 1st ed., p. 501.

3. James Edwards gives a bit more attention to the Isaiah 50 context than most (*The Gospel According to Luke*, PNTC [Grand Rapids: Eerdmans, 2015], p. 297).

Yet He not only endures severe suffering but does so with irrepressible faith, as He says in verse 7:

> But the Lord Yahweh helps me;
> therefore I am not disgraced;
> therefore I have set my face as a flint;
> and I know that I will not be put to shame.

Why does He 'set his face as a flint'? Clearly, to face vicious suffering in store for Him. But more than that—the verse shows He 'sets his face' precisely *because* He has complete confidence that Yahweh will carry Him through the suffering and vindicate Him.[4]

Hence I don't think Luke uses this expression as a mere literary idiom but that he expects those who know their Bibles to catch that he is alluding to Isaiah 50 and the words of the 'suffering servant' there. And remember: in view of Isaiah 50, when He 'sets his face to go to Jerusalem' He is not only bracing Himself to endure the suffering ahead, but also 'setting his face' is the result of His tenacious conviction that 'the Lord Yahweh helps me' (Isa. 50:7a, 9a). So Jesus turns toward Jerusalem, where He will be victimized *and* vindicated. That is His commitment.

Sometimes His servants must make a similar commitment. Thomas Bilney was part of that Cambridge circle that instigated the English Reformation. On trial before Bishop Tunstall in 1528, he was induced to recant and elude the stake. Because of this he plunged into despair and such misery of conscience that he was inconsolable. He had been wrong to 'save his life.' Light at last dawned, he saw his way clearly, and he nearly yearned for the martyr's stake. So late one night in 1531 Bilney called his friends around him, reminded them of how he had fallen, then said: 'You shall see me no more .... Do not stay me: my decision is formed, and I shall carry it out. My face is set to go to Jerusalem.'[5] And on 19th August that

---

4. Isaiah 50:4-11 provides three pictures of the Servant—as (1) the disciple skilled in God's word, v. 4; (2) the sufferer submissive to God's will, vv. 5-6; and (3) the believer sure of God's help, vv. 7-9.

5. J. H. Merle d'Aubigne, *The Reformation in England*, ed. S. M. Houghton, 2 vols. (Edinburgh: Banner of Truth, 1962), 1:468.

year Bilney was led out to the 'Lollards' Pit,' where he went to his 'Jerusalem,' reciting the 143rd Psalm.

Secondly, we meet **correction** in verses 52-56. If we translate literally, the 'face' language continues in verses 52 and 53. He 'sent messengers before his face' (v. 52) to make arrangements (perhaps for food and lodging) for Jesus' entourage. But the Samaritan village in question rejected the overture, because 'his face was going to Jerusalem' (v. 53). Samaritans with their non-kosher temple on Mt. Gerizim were in no mood to be hospitable to Jews going to their temple in Jerusalem. This response rankles James and John; they ask Jesus if He would give the green light for them to 'bring down fire from heaven and destroy them' (v. 54). Jesus turns round and 'rebuked' them (v. 55) and they are off to another village (v. 56).[6] End of episode.

Two matters need clarified. One is the allusion to Elijah's activity. No matter what textual reading one follows in verse 54, James and John are clearly alluding to 2 Kings 1:9-18, in which Ahaziah, king of Israel, sent three posses of fifty men each (+ captains) to apprehend Elijah, who had prophesied Ahaziah's death. The first two contingents were destroyed. Elijah had told them that if he was really a man of God as the captain had said, 'Let fire come down from heaven and consume you and your fifty' (2 Kings 1:10). And the fire came. Some read this text superficially and accuse Elijah of harshness, in contrast to Jesus' restraint and mercy. But that misreads 2 Kings 1. Why did Ahaziah send posse after posse after Elijah? Not to invite him to dinner or for a friendly conversation. He intended to silence him—it's called execution. With his back to the wall and with no human defenders Elijah, one could say, asked God Himself to defend him via fire from above. It was a matter of self-defense and God approved Elijah's 'request.' Yahweh was protecting His defenseless servant. So talk of Elijah's harshness or vindictiveness misunderstands, distorts, and skews the OT narrative.

That's one matter. The other is that commentators and Christians (sometimes the two are identical) should stop to

---

6. Some manuscripts have additional clauses in verses 54-55 (check the footnotes in most English versions). The text seems abrupt without them, but they are not in the earliest manuscripts; so the 'abrupt' version is likely original.

think before condemning James and John as though they are a couple of non-ecumenical, trigger-happy dolts. I'm not claiming they were right here. Jesus, after all, rebuked them. But sit down with verse 54 again. What are James and John fired up about? The honor of Jesus. He had been rejected and dishonored and it bothered them terribly. Are we in our bland, tame world with Niceness as its supreme deity ever upset over Jesus being dishonored? Does that ever distress us? Perhaps we should let James and John be our teachers before we bad-mouth them for their misguided zeal.

The shorter text of verse 55 simply says that Jesus 'rebuked them.' Behind that rebuke was likely the thought that though there will be a judgment, the present time was a day of salvation (4:18-19)—even for Samaritans. And so it would prove to be, as Luke shows us in his second volume (Acts 8:4-8, 14-17). But there's a principle in this 'correction' segment that may be of use to us: one may have hold of a right insight (the honor of Jesus) and yet wrongly inject it or wrongly apply it in certain circumstances. I state it as a bare principle, but, with careful thought, we may find it has multiple (and maybe uncomfortable) applications.

Finally, I think **clarity** best sums up verses 57-62. Here Jesus makes it crystal clear what following Him will involve. And don't forget the context Luke supplies—all this discipleship must be seen in light of the cross (9:51).

The first volunteer claims he will follow Jesus wherever He goes.[7] Jesus counters with 'Foxes have holes and birds of the sky have roosts, but the Son of Man does not have anywhere he can lay his head' (v. 58). Jesus seems to be addressing his naivete. As if to say, You had better think carefully about that 'wherever' you mentioned. We have no reason to think that Jesus is being severe, much less harsh with this fellow; He is simply wanting him to consider carefully the difficulties that come with following Jesus. In fact, there's a certain kindness in this. The naïve candidate runs the risk of disillusionment with Jesus should he run into heavy weather he had not expected. The 'brake' that Jesus puts on his enthusiasm seeks to help him avoid such.

---

7. According to Matthew 8:19, this fellow was a teacher of the law.

Then Jesus Himself calls another fellow (v. 59a). His response is, 'Lord, allow me first to go off and bury my father' (v. 59b). (We must always beware of that word 'first'). Jesus retorts with, 'Leave the dead to bury their own dead, but you [emphatic] go off and proclaim the kingdom of God' (v. 60). Most take Jesus to mean, Let the spiritually dead bury the physically dead. It may mean that there are others in the family connection who can handle that duty. Burial of family was a supreme filial duty in Judaism.[8] But Jesus had a higher priority in mind for this man (see 10:1).

There is some debate over exactly what this man was asking. I don't think his father had yet died. In Israel dead people were usually buried immediately. So if the father had just died, this fellow would hardly have been around where Jesus would be talking to him. Hence I agree with those who assume that the man wanted to wait until his father died (perhaps it was obvious that he was nearing his end) and he could perform his duty before he followed Jesus. This, however, could involve considerable delay.[9] In any event, the man wanted to delay, and Jesus pressed on him the priority and urgency of proclaiming the kingdom. We too have to watch that our loyalties do not become our idolatries.

A third man volunteers, but he is also a 'but-first-er' (v. 61), 'But first allow me to bid good-bye to those in my house.' Jesus' reply in verse 62 assumes the man has a divided heart. The tenses of the verb forms help bring this out. No one, Jesus says, who has once put his hand on the plow and yet keeps glancing back is fit for the kingdom of God. He has made a commitment and yet he hasn't. His affections are still back there. The image may be of what a disaster one makes of plowing if, instead of keeping his eyes fixed on the end of the

8. See, e.g., Leon Morris, *The Gospel According to St. Luke*, TNTC (Grand Rapids: Eerdmans, 1974), p. 180, and E. Earle Ellis, *The Gospel of Luke*, NCB, rev. ed. (London: Oliphants, 1974), p. 153, or ZIBBC, 1:409.

9. See W. F. Arndt, *The Gospel According to St. Luke* (St. Louis: Concordia, 1956), p. 277. Some think this son might have been thinking of 'secondary burial.' 'In first-century Palestine, secondary burial was commonly practiced; when this "father" is dead, he will be buried in the cave. After one year, his bones will be collected and placed with the bones of his ancestors. It is possible that the request of this son is to wait for another year before following Jesus' (W. L. Liefeld and David W. Pao, 'Luke,' in EBC, rev. ed., 10:190). This option seems a bit more speculative.

field, he keeps looking back to see how he is doing. (The same is true when driving a row-tractor while cultivating young corn plants on a Kansas farm.) Here Jesus is warning of the danger of a divided heart.[10] Jesus deals seriously with these three men because Jerusalem discipleship (v. 51) is serious business. He addresses matters of naivete and priority and hesitancy. And don't miss what Luke does *not* tell you. As some (e.g., Geldenhuys) have pointed out, he does not tell you how these men responded to Jesus' responses. Had he done so, you, the reader, could have told yourself, 'Well, I see how that turned out.' But Luke is too smart for that. If he doesn't tell you their final responses, then you are still on the hook. You do not know how it turned out and you must then ponder: Well, how would *I* have responded to that?

---

10. The account of this third candidate is sometimes compared to Elisha in 1 Kings 19:20, where Elisha asked Elijah to let him kiss his father and mother (break his home ties) and then he would follow Elijah. And Elijah permitted it. Some then say that this man in Luke 9 is being called, due to the urgency of kingdom service, to make a 'higher' response than Elisha. But, as often, this misreads the OT text. Allow me to quote myself. 'Sometimes Elisha has received less than favorable reviews because people allow Luke 9:61-62 to color their reading of our passage. Because of the similar trappings and coloring of the two texts one wonders if interpreters don't view the volunteer of Luke 9:61-62 as Elisha's alter ego and therefore impute to Elisha an inferior commitment. The fellow in Luke 9 is far different from Elisha. Jesus' comment in verse 62 pictures one who has resolutely taken up a task (the plow) only to be continually looking back. That is, he has a divided mind. Luke 9:61 has only a formal similarity to 1 Kings 19:20. In Luke 9 saying good-bye is an obstacle to kingdom commitment, whereas in 1 Kings 19 it functions as the entry into kingdom service. Elisha goes back to *sever* his connections, not to delay his commitment. He does not return to hold back but to cut loose' (*1 Kings: The Wisdom and the Folly* [Ross-shire: Christian Focus, 2002], pp. 274-75).

24

Working the Harvest
(Luke 10:1-24)

During wheat harvest in those states which form the US plains, groups of harvesters will work their way north from Texas and eventually to North Dakota, cutting wheat for farmers who contract with them. An outfit will bring its trucks and combines and men and, for so much, harvest a farmer's wheat, then move on to another site. I recall college students getting jobs with such groups, which they would dub 'working the harvest' or 'following the harvest.' Here in Luke 10 Jesus is sending out workers into a 'harvest' (v. 2). He sends them by twos to prepare the way, as in 9:52, for his visits to various towns and locales (v. 1).[1] But how many were there? Manuscripts are divided—some say seventy-two, others seventy, and these choices are reflected in our English translations.[2] Is there some symbolism in the numeral, perhaps reflecting the seventy gentile nations in Genesis 10? Suffice to say, I think 'seventy-two' is to be preferred, and I'm skeptical about symbolism.

---

1. The sequence from chapter 9 is chronological but not tightly so ('Now after these things,' v. 1a). Conceivably, in 9:59-60 Jesus may have been recruiting for His crew of 70/72. Sending these men by twos 'before his face' (lit., 10:1) reflects the same 'face' language Luke used in 9:51, 52, 53 ('set his face,' 'sent ... before his face,' and 'his face was going to Jerusalem'). When Luke specifies the Lord appointed seventy-two 'others,' he's so much as saying: I know I told of Jesus sending out the twelve on such a mission [9:1-6], but this is a different occasion.

2. Read all about it in Darrell L. Bock, *Luke 9:51-24:53*, BECNT (Grand Rapids: Baker, 1996), pp. 994, 1014-16.

Scholars sometimes love to play with numbers, e.g., Is there some hidden significance in the 153 fish in John 21? I doubt it; I tend to think they simply counted them and that's how many there were. So with the seventy-two here; I doubt the number is symbolic—it's just how many there were.

Jesus, then, sets out **His stipulations for servants** (vv. 2-12), how they are to conduct themselves on their mission. He begins by citing the need: 'The harvest is immense, but the workers are few' (v. 2a). The harvest imagery likely carries the idea of gathering His people into the kingdom, secure from judgment (cf. Matt. 13:29-30). What to do in face of this need? Jesus' simplicity is striking: 'Pray therefore the Lord of the harvest that he thrust out workers into his harvest' (v. 2b). So 'naïve.' Ask God to reverse the trend. Jesus skips over our pet solutions: long-range planning, management by objectives, producing vision statements. Jesus also implies there is a definite urgency about the present 'harvest' situation (vv. 3-4). They are not to carry money bag or tote-bag, nor sandals—I assume Jesus means an extra pair. Nor are they to fritter away time in greetings along the road. This last sounds anti-social, but in the Near East greetings could be quite involved and consume substantial time.[3] Even in the west we know this problem. If you are in a hurry for an appointment and bump into an acquaintance you've not seen in a while, you inwardly cringe, for you know you'll be asked about your health and your family and their locations and be expected to reciprocate with the inquiries. Because of this, if you have opportunity, you duck down another hallway or wherever and, like the Magi, go out another way.

Jesus' 'travel light' orders may imply more than urgency. David Gooding has suggested what the 'more' may have been:

> They were to carry no cash, spare clothes or provisions. The effect would be to force the townspeople to a decision as to what they should do with them …. [I]f the people were faced with penniless, destitute men claiming to be Messiah's own ambassadors, they would be forced to decide whether they would receive and entertain them as such, or reject them.[4]

---

3. TDNT, 1:498-99.

4. *According to Luke* (1987; reprint ed., Coleraine, N. Ireland: Myrtlefield Trust, 2013), p. 204.

Jesus goes on to specify what His emissaries' demeanor should be (vv. 5-8). Should they be welcomed in a home, they are to stay in that same home 'eating and drinking what they provide' (v. 7b). No need to blush over that—kingdom work deserves material provision (v. 7c), but they are not to 'move around from house to house' (v. 7d). Why might some want to do that? Oh, they might hear the cuisine is better in a more well-provided home. But Christ's men are to be content with what they eat and drink in the first home that receives them. If they go lobbying around to find the best table and the best 'digs' in the community, not only are they insulting their original host but clearly showing that their conveniences matter far more to them than proclaiming Christ.[5] Christ's servants must demonstrate their genuineness and integrity by the way they conduct themselves when 'on mission.' Once during the American Revolution, the Marquis de Lafayette favorably impressed a group of Oneida Indians. He wrote to General Washington, referring to them as 'scalping gentlemen.'[6] The phrase is a problem. They could be gentlemen if they were not scalpers, or they could be scalpers but not gentlemen. But scalping destroys any 'gentlemen' status they had. So too, anyone slithering around an Israelite village and scoping out the homes with the best bed and board is no servant of Christ.

Then Jesus speaks of their proclamation (vv. 9-12). They are to 'heal the sick' and then say to the given community, 'The kingdom of God has come near you' (v. 9; see also v. 11). I take this to mean 'to come near in the sense of having arrived.' The kingdom of God was already on the scene in whatever particular town or village it was. In what sense? In the healings that the seventy-two were doing (v. 9a); those were signs and indicators of the presence of the kingdom. And then the kingdom has come near in that Jesus Himself is coming. The kingdom is present because the king himself is here. You can enter into all kinds of discussions on the kingdom of God, but you need to face that the kingdom of

---

5. The early church faced a similar problem with various visiting teachers (see Didache para. 11).

6. Thomas Fleming, *Washington's Secret War* (New York: Collins, 2005), p. 291.

God means that you have to deal with the person of Jesus. So the kingdom arrives not in a complete or consummated sense but in a real sense, in the works of Jesus' power and in the presence of Jesus' person.

Jesus makes clear that His servants are not merely playing at Sunday School. It may be that some towns will 'not receive' them and give the stiff arm to their mission (v. 10a). In such cases the seventy-two were to act out a 'repudiation procedure' (vv. 10b-11), wiping off town dirt from their feet. As if to say: We leave even your dust to face judgment and we ourselves are free of responsibility for you.[7] That town will pass notoriously wicked Sodom (Gen. 19; Deut. 29:23; Ezek. 16:48-50) on the 'severity index' for judgment day (v. 12). Don't miss the kindness in the candor of Jesus. He clearly tells them that they may not be welcomed at every place. What a gracious Master who kindly prepares us for what may be coming our way (John 16:4)!

Secondly, Jesus speaks of **the peril of privilege** (vv. 13-16). He had just laid it down that Sodom would face a more 'tolerable' judgment at the last day than a town that rejected the testimony of His seventy-two servants (v. 12). Verse 16 supplies the reason for that: the seventy-two are Jesus' own representatives— to reject their witness is to reject Him and to reject Him is to reject the One who sent Him. The '72 mission' then is not an exercise in religious poll-taking. The healings they do in Jesus' name are not mere fascinating anecdotes to tell grandchildren. They are not like an 18-inch snowfall in Pennsylvania in the last of April—utterly amazing but of little consequence. No, this mission of pre-Jerusalem healing and preaching imposes a massive responsibility on the towns visited.

In this connection Jesus utters 'woes' on towns that have already extensively enjoyed His ministry and largely failed to embrace Him. He cites Chorazin[8] and Bethsaida (v. 13). All

---

7. ZIBBC, 1:400.

8. This mention of Chorazin should stop us in our tracks. William Barclay offers a very perceptive comment: 'It is implied that Jesus did many mighty works there. In the gospel history as we have it Chorazin is never even mentioned, and we do not know one thing that Jesus did or one word that Jesus spoke there. Nothing could show so vividly how much we do not know about the life of Jesus' (*The Gospel of Luke*, Daily Study Bible [Philadelphia: Westminster, 1956], p. 135). All of which means no one should be so cautious and humble as New Testament critics.

three of the towns Jesus notes in verses 13 and 15 are on or near the north shore of the Sea of Galilee, Chorazin perhaps two miles north of Capernaum. Jesus asserts that had the mighty works He did in Chorazin and Bethsaida been done in Tyre and Sidon, they would have 'repented long ago sitting in sackcloth and ashes.' Not that Tyre and Sidon get a pass on judgment day, but it will be less severe for them than for these two Galilean towns (v. 14). Tyre and Sidon were pagan cities. Isaiah (ch. 23) and especially Ezekiel (chs. 26-28) reamed them out and pronounced ruin on their godless, arrogant, commercial mega-power. Yet judgment will be more tolerable for them than for these indifferent Israelite towns. It ought to be unnerving. Similarly, Capernaum's lot will not be heaven but Hades (v. 15).[9]

We will find this peril-of-privilege theme surfacing often. For now J. C. Ryle's comment must suffice:

> [These declarations] teach us that all will be judged according to their spiritual light, and that from those who have enjoyed most religious privileges, most will be required. They teach us the exceeding hardness and unbelief of the human heart. It was possible to hear Christ preach, and to see Christ's miracles, and yet to remain unconverted.[10]

And, if so, we may wish to find our way into Tyre and Sidon— or Sodom.

Thirdly, Jesus presses home **the matter that matters** (vv. 18-20). Note how Luke leads into this section. There is a 'narrative gap.' Luke omits any description of the disciples' mission. He only tells of their return from it—and delight in it: 'Lord, even the demons are submissive to us in your name!' (v. 17b). Jesus' response nails down the significance of their work: 'I was watching Satan, like lightning, fall from heaven' (v. 18). As the seventy-two cast out demons in Jesus' name they were bringing defeat upon Satan. Jesus is not saying

---

9. On Capernaum, see Cyndi Parker, 'Millstones in Capernaum,' in *Lexham Geographic Commentary on the Gospels*, ed. Barry J. Beitzel (Bellingham, WA: Lexham, 2017), pp. 309-310. It was quite a town.

10. J. C. Ryle, *Expository Thoughts on the Gospels: St. Luke*, 2 vols. (New York: Baker & Taylor, 1858), 1:354.

this is Satan's definitive or final defeat, for, as Bock says, those aspects are associated with Jesus' death and return (John 12:31-32; Col. 2:14-15; Rev. 12:10-12; 20:1-3, 10).[11] But, if it is not definitive, it is definite; it is a real defeat, one, we might say, of an ongoing series. I think we sometimes slide over part of Yahweh's curse on the Serpent in Genesis 3:14-15. We tend to gravitate to the last of verse 15, which speaks of the Victorious Man (seed of the woman) fatally bruising the Serpent's head. But we neglect the metaphorical language of defeat in verse 14b: 'upon your belly you will go and dust you will eat *all the days of your life.*' This implies that the Serpent, the enemy, will experience ongoing reverses, defeats, and setbacks all along. Perhaps Luke 10:18 fits in there.

Jesus then adds a staggering assurance of His servants' invincibility; He tells them He's given them authority 'to trample on snakes and scorpions, and over all the power of the enemy, and nothing will ever harm you' (v. 19). I don't think this is a promise of immunity. It doesn't mean a James won't be executed by Herod Agrippa (Acts 12:1-2) or a Paul won't be stoned within an inch of his life at Lystra (Acts 14:19). But the enemy can do them no final harm. Yet the keynote Jesus wants to strike comes in verse 20. Their primary joy should not be in the power Jesus gave them nor in the success of their mission but in knowing their 'names are written down in heaven.' Their thrill should not be over power but over grace. So easy for us to forget that there is something greater.

It was my privilege the last few years to be the Sunday evening preacher at First Presbyterian Church, Columbia, South Carolina. I didn't have other responsibilities—simply Sunday evening preaching. It was a 'job' others would kill for! And the specially wonderful thing about it was that those who came on Sunday night were those who really wanted to hear the Bible explained and applied. I have always found preaching, both in preparation and execution, a bit of low-grade torture, but an expectant congregation can mitigate that to a marked degree. Hence it was usually a pleasant affair to finish up a Sunday evening service there. But that was not the best. After a service and greeting some people, I would go up to the pastors' room, get rid of the mobile mic, collect my materials, and make my way back down to the sanctuary. My wife would be there. She might be talking with someone, or, if most were gone, just waiting for me. But *she* was there. And, if you'll pardon it, that was more than even preaching to a receptive congregation. Jesus' point in verse 20 is something like that. Having assurance of your place in glory is much greater than enjoying stellar success in ministry. That's the matter that matters.

Finally, our passage highlights **the joy of Jesus** (vv. 21-24). As the seventy-two return with joy (cf. vv. 17, 20), Jesus also erupts in ecstatic praise. Verse 21 is a remarkable statement: 'He rejoiced in the Holy Spirit and said, "I praise you, Father, Lord of heaven and earth, that you have hidden these things from wise and understanding (folks) and have revealed them to infants; yes, Father, because you were pleased to do it this way."' Jesus offers praise for the Father's methodology. For He works, one might say, contrary to conventional expectations, for He hides 'these things' from those thought to be informed and enlightened and reveals them to the no-counts of this age. 'These things' are most likely linked with verse 20, having one's place assured in glory.[12] The best commentary here may be 1 Corinthians 1:26-31. Jesus' praise may provide a pattern for our own. How often, for example, in reading biblical narratives, we see how God acted in some unique manner, in one of those 'I'd-never-thought-of-doing-it-like-that' ways. And the story almost grabs us by the lapels to say, 'Don't you need to offer praise for that?'

Then Jesus goes on to make an assertion of His own authority. It takes little imagination to see His attitude of praise carrying over in the words of verse 22: 'All things have been handed over to me by my Father' (v. 22a). That should elicit a gulp not a yawn; it's on the level of Colossians 1:16-17 or Matthew 28:18. Then Jesus goes on to speak of the one-of-a-kind relationship between the Father and the Son. Let me get at it by the back door. There's a horrible hymn that sometimes still gets played in churches and at funerals; it's called 'In

---

12. Alan J. Thompson, *Luke*, EGGNT (Nashville: Broadman & Holman, 2016), p. 173; for a bit different 'take,' see Robert H. Stein, *Luke*, NAC (Nashville: Broadman, 1992), p. 312.

the Garden.' In the refrain it speaks of the believer (the one singing presumably) and the Lord enjoying fellowship in the garden—'and the joy we share as we tarry there, none other has ever known.' I know there's such a thing as poetic license in hymns, but that makes one sing a palpable falsehood. No one else has ever had fellowship or joy with Jesus like you have had? If two people are singing that refrain at the same time, at least one of them has to be lying. If a whole congregation sings that hymn, all but one (and probably he or she as well) has to be fibbing! But here's the point: Jesus *can* say that of the Father-Son relation. There is an intimate one-of-a-kind relationship in that case—'And no one knows who the Son is except the Father, and who the Father is except the Son' (v. 22b). What they have together 'none other has ever known.' And yet .... And yet there is a colossal conjunction on the end of Jesus' statement: 'AND to whomever the Son wants to reveal him' (v. 22c). So, only the Son and no other knows 'who the Father is,' but should the Son will to reveal the Father to me then I too might know (not like the Son does, but in a real way) the Father. Don't miss, however, the note of authority in 'to whomever the Son *wants* to reveal him.' It rests on Jesus' decision because, well, 'all things have been handed over to [him].' Normally, we may not mind Jesus having authority, but there's a rebel streak in the human spirit that chafes at His having that much.

There's a story about Abraham Lincoln dealing with a dispute in a cabinet meeting. At the end of the disagreement (in which he had been 'outvoted') he announced, 'Seven nays, one aye; the ayes have it.'[13] He could do math that way. He was the President. He, after all, had the authority. And so does Jesus. My knowing the Father ultimately rests on *His* decision. That may rankle some, but 'infants' (v. 21) just bow and worship.

_____

13. Seymour Morris, Jr., *American History Revised* (New York: Broadway Books, 2010), p. 232.

25

The Good Samaritan is Bad News
(Luke 10:25-37)

Any reader of Agatha Christie's murder mysteries periodically runs into a scenario in which the local investigators
assess the evidence and conclude who was 'obviously' the
culprit or that the death was 'clearly' a suicide and not a
murder. But that sort of certainty seldom satisfies Christie's
super-sleuth, Hercule Poirot, who divines that his 'little gray
cells' will find it far more complicated. And that may be
a parable about this parable. Easy for Bible readers to be
a little too sure about the 'good Samaritan' story. Easy to
think it's mainly pushing 'boy-scout philanthropy' (cf. Ellis)
or simply pressing us to be merciful and generous to those
in need. Hence the *immediate* context is important: we don't
begin with verse 29 or 30 but with verse 25. To oversimplify,
the issue is not the identity of the neighbor but the matter
of eternal life.

However, we should note the *larger* context as well. Luke
begins with a phrase traditionally translated 'And behold ...'
(*kai idou*; 26 times in Luke, according to Bock). It's a bit of a
loose connective here; we don't know if this encounter with
the 'law-expert' took place soon after what precedes or not.
Maybe some time after, but Luke seems to have placed it
here for his own reasons. He seems to be holding up the law-
expert as a sample of those who are 'wise and understanding'
in verse 21 and then, by contrast, depicting Mary in verses

38-42 (espec. v. 39) as one of the 'infants' or 'little children' who has been given light from above. Though verses 25-37 and 38-42 may seem unconnected at first glance, Luke has them serving as 'cases in point' to verses 21-22. The 'good Samaritan' is not a beautiful story teaching the duty of social service (though that is not denied) but bad news. We must approach the parable in light of the theologian's question in verse 25 and keep that in view at every point. Let's follow him through the story.

We stick then with verse 25 and notice **the matter that concerns him**: 'And indeed, a law-expert stood up, putting him to the test and saying, "Teacher, what must I do to inherit eternal life?"' That is his apparent concern—eternal life, the life of the age to come. He's asking, 'What must I do to share in the resurrection of the righteous at the end?'[1] That's a vital and commendable focus. He's not talking about the latest lending rates or whether his auto insurance includes 'accident forgiveness' or about the latest Hollywood starlet who is pregnant out of wedlock and has the media drooling.

And yet. Yet this apparent concern may not be a real concern. His premier intent seems to be 'putting (Jesus) to the test.' He seems then more concerned with critiquing Jesus than having eternal life. Eternal life is not a passion of his soul but a topic for debate; he is not wanting to satisfy a crying need but to engage in a battle of wits. Eternal life is a fine concern and some have been in a white heat over it. Think of the pilgrim before he became a pilgrim in Bunyan's classic. A huge burden on his back, a horrid fear of judgment in his mind, he obeys Evangelist's command to flee toward the light he sees across a wide field. But his wife and children see him going and cry for him to return, but he stuffs his fingers in his ears and runs on with the cry, 'Life! Life! Eternal life!' But many are not driven like that. Richard Bewes writes of once leading a mission at the University of Durham and speaking there with a cynical theologian. The fellow was an atheist. Richard asked him, 'So why theology for you?' Indeed, why mess with theology when you deny there's a

1. Darrell L. Bock, *Luke 9:51-24:53*, BECNT (Grand Rapids: Baker, 1996), p. 1023.

theos! His answer was, 'It amuses me.'[2] It almost nauseates one to read that. Our law-expert in the text does not share the latter's baggage but he seems close in approach—curiosity drives him more than urgency. The law-expert had the right question with the wrong motive. Let's even grant that he may have been sincere to a certain extent; but he was not desperate. Something's wrong if you only come to Jesus curiously but not desperately.

Secondly, notice **the doctrine that comforts him** in verses 26-29. To the law-expert's question Jesus responds with a question: 'What has been written in the law?' (v. 26). That is, what does the Bible say? His answer comes readily: 'You shall love the Lord your God with all your heart and with all your being and with all your strength and with all your mind—and your neighbor as yourself' (v. 27). He quotes Deuteronomy 6:5 and Leviticus 19:18.[3] He does not seem unduly disturbed by his quotation.

But there may be more here than he was aware. In verse 28 Jesus tells him, 'You've answered correctly; keep on doing this and you will live.' Who knows exactly how this was said in Aramaic, but assuming Luke's Greek faithfully reflects Jesus' meaning, the present tense verb (*poiei*) is telling, for it carries the connotation of ongoing, continuous, undeviating obedience.[4] Jesus simply leaves it there. He does not comment on whether it is possible, only necessary.

We must stop a moment on verse 29, which tells us this man wanted to 'justify himself' and so asked Jesus, 'Who is my neighbor?' Just what was he after in this 'justifying' of himself? There are two primary possibilities: (1) Perhaps he realized he needed to justify his sub-par performance, especially on the loving-neighbor provision, and may have thought he could do so if Jesus would helpfully limit the scope of 'neighbor'; as if to say, 'Let's define this and make

---

2. Richard Bewes, *Words that Circled the World* (Ross-shire: Christian Focus, 2002), p. 145.

3. On these two texts in Judaism, see D. W. Pao and E. J. Schnabel, 'Luke,' in *Commentary on the New Testament Use of the Old Testament*, ed. G. K. Beale and D. A. Carson (Grand Rapids: Baker, 2007), pp. 320-21.

4. See A. T. Robertson, *Word Pictures in the New Testament*, 6 vols. (Nashville: Broadman, 1930), 2:152.

it more manageable'; or (2) perhaps 'justify' is used in a social sense, like 'saving face'; to let the whole thing drop with Jesus' answer in verse 28 makes it look too simple; so it may be as if he is saying, 'We need to talk about this some more, we need more clarification and precision about this "neighbor" matter—it's not so simple as it sounds.'

But verse 27 is a problem. The law-expert didn't seem very bothered by it, but we should also be bothered that many of us are not bothered by it. A superficial 'take' on verse 27 might spout nonsense like this: 'Why, isn't this after all the essence of true religion? Such beautiful words and lofty sentiments—not a bunch of complicated doctrines but love.' So easy to think this is a congenial 'creed.' But what is the real situation? We may smile benignly at these words … as long as we never hear Jesus' *'keep on* doing ….' Even as Christian believers and as Christ's servants these words can be no comfort to us.

I remember a prized friend telling me of his ordination exam before his presbytery at the outset of his ministry. Naturally, they examined him on all kinds of doctrinal issues, but, every once in a while, they would sneak in a very 'practical' matter. Someone asked him of his relation to or attitude toward the Lord. And in all sincerity, as he supposed, he answered, 'I love him with all my heart and all my soul and all my strength.' My friend told me that there was a certain theology professor (whom we both knew) visiting presbytery that day. Sometime during the day he spoke to my friend and told him that he had 'prevaricated' before the presbytery that morning! He was not being nasty; he simply wanted my friend to realize that he had probably told a 'whopper' when he had averred how he loved the Lord with all his heart, etc. Can any of us truly claim to love God with heart, soul, strength and mind completely (note the repeated 'alls') and continually? As a Christian, is your will constantly bent on obedience to Him, your mind focused on adoration of Him, your emotions always stirred with warm affections for Him? Not for ten minutes at a time. And let's not even speak of the scads of unworthy motives that come into play in loving our neighbor. How abysmally deceived we are if we think verse 27 is somehow our solution. There was once a couple who were very kind to my step-grandmother (the only grandma I ever knew) and, I believe, were regulars at their Episcopalian Church. On one occasion the husband let go with one of those worldview statements, 'Well, I just do the best I can.' To which my grandmother retorted, 'But, John, you can't do your best.' Our law-expert had not yet seen that—his 'doctrine' still comforted him.

Finally, we come to what is usually called the parable, **the story that reveals him** (vv. 30-37). Here Jesus helps the law-expert to see himself. As the story proceeds the audience would likely form certain expectations. The priest and the Levite are the religious all-stars of Judaism and yet when they see the battered fellow, they both 'went by on the other side' (vv. 31, 32). It may be they thought he was dead, in which case they would contract ritual uncleanness by touching a corpse. Apparently the Pharisees thought one contracted such impurity 'if even one's shadow touched the corpse.'[5] So they preferred the 'other side.' But it really shouldn't have been a problem. Both the priest and the Levite were going *down* (vv. 31, 32) the road to Jericho, not up to Jerusalem. Whatever their temple duties had been, they were finished for now and they were headed home. If they contract uncleanness, there would be plenty of time to deal with it.

The 'kicker' comes in verse 33. If both a priest and a Levite strike out, the worst the audience might expect would be to hear that a Jewish layman proves the hero. Alas, no—a certain Samaritan (v. 33), a Samaritan who shows compassion (vv. 33-34a), provides care (v. 34b), and absorbs costs (v. 35). Jesus doubtless irked His hearers by flying in the face of their customary attitudes.

Some Jews were willing to eat with Samaritans ..., but many were not because of ritual defilement. Samaritans were thought to convey uncleanness by what they lay, sat, or rode on, as well as by their saliva or urine. Samaritan women, like Gentiles, were considered to be in a continual state of ritual uncleanness:

---

5. Craig Keener, *The IVP Bible Background Commentary: New Testament* (Downers Grove, IL: InterVarsity, 1993), p. 218.

'The daughters of the Samaritans are [deemed unclean as] menstruants from the cradle ....'[6]

I suppose Jesus made a risky move placing a Samaritan in so positive a light. Kenneth Bailey has said that in twenty years in the Middle East he has not had the courage to tell a story to Palestinians about a noble Israeli, nor a story about a noble Turk to Armenians! But here is a Samaritan who, in contrast to the most religious Jews, shows mercy to a mangled fellow—probably assumed to be a Jew.

The symbolism is clear. The priest and the Levite personify, as does the law-expert himself, Judaism. Not every individual Jew but Judaism at the time. They depict the deficiencies of Judaism—that for all its sacrifices, prayers, devotions, fastings, and ceremonies, it can still be, on the whole, cold and formal and lifeless and dead. By the parable Jesus says: *If loving your neighbor as yourself has anything to do with life eternal, it is clear that you* [the priest/Levite types as representatives of Judaism] *do not have life, for you do not love.* The flip side is: This Samaritan whom you regard as the scum of the earth and the manure pile of God's creation will go into the kingdom of God before you.

Who can imagine the biting blow this story must have inflicted? This dirty, rotten, no-good Samaritan does not stand first of all as an example for our theologian (though see v. 37) but as his *critic*. The theologian who had been pressing Jesus with his question should see only too clearly that in the priest and the Levite of the story Jesus had been drawing his own portrait. Howard Marshall is right:

> Jesus does not supply information as to whom one should help; failure to keep the commandment springs not from lack of information but from lack of love. It was not fresh knowledge that the lawyer needed, but a new heart—in plain English, conversion.[7]

---

6. A. J. Köstenberger in ZIBBC, 2:44. See further, Kenneth Bailey, *Poet & Peasant* and *Through Peasant Eyes*, combined ed. (Grand Rapids: Eerdmans, 1980), p. 48; apparently a daily synagogue prayer asked that the Samaritans might not be partakers of eternal life.

7. I. Howard Marshall, 'Luke,' in *New Bible Commentary*, 4th ed. (Leicester: Inter-Varsity, 1994), p. 998.

Let's be sure we pick up the emphasis of Jesus. We can miss it, because we tend to get all sentimental over the 'good Samaritan'; what a nice thing he did, what a brave thing, what a generous thing; and we get all filled with gooey thoughts over neighborliness. And we miss what Jesus is saying by this parable to his questioner: You do not have life! We forget that the story was not first of all told to give us an example to follow but to expose our lovelessness and lead us to repentance. The first note of the parable is not: here is what you should do, but: here is what you do *not* do. The 'good Samaritan' does not preach to us our duty but reveals that we have not met that duty.

I suppose some may get upset over the manner of Jesus. But He simply takes His questioner from where he is. He asks, 'Who is my neighbor?' Well, let me tell you a story. Hear the story. Do you see the story? Do you see how it exposes you? Jesus concentrates on showing him that judging himself by his own doctrine (v. 27), he does not have life, that he is very lost. The pattern seems clear: If you had life, you would love; but if, like the priest and Levite, you do not love, then you must not have life. Some may complain that there is no word of grace in this. But what use is there in urging God's grace on someone who doesn't think he needs it? This man must first come to total despair over himself. That's where the gospel begins. Not with the good news but with the bad news. And the good Samaritan is bad news.

26

A Woman's Place Is ...

(Luke 10:38-42)

Virile feminists of our own day would probably hate Martha if they read about her, because she seemed to think that a woman's place was in the kitchen. But Jesus didn't hate her, even though He had to oppose her. His 'Martha, Martha' (v. 41) is full of tenderness and appreciation. What matters is that three times this text calls Jesus 'Lord' (twice by Luke, vv. 39, 41; once by Martha, v. 40). Rather a large dose within a short text. This is the major point: '[Jesus] is "the Lord," teaching the "word" of life to a family.'[1]

We can begin by calling attention to what we may call **the Lord's folly** (vv. 38-39). Luke opens with 'Now while they were going along he himself entered a certain village' (38a). Very general. And Luke picks up the 'journey' idea (see 9:57), hinting that Jesus is still on His way to Jerusalem. We know, however, from John 11 that this family lived in Bethany very close to Jerusalem. Did this episode take place around the time of the John 11 events, perhaps quite late in Jesus' public ministry? Don't know. Luke doesn't say. He may well have brought the incident forward and placed it here, clearly without specific chronological or geographical

---

1. E. Earle Ellis, *The Gospel of Luke*, NCB, rev. ed. (London: Oliphants, 1974), p. 161. This should keep us from psychological interpretations that go on about how we really need both our Martha- and Mary-types in the church. You may find something like that in another text somewhere but don't try to drag it out of this one.

indicators, because he had his own purpose in telling the story at this point.

What then is Luke up to? He tells this story here because he wants you to see Mary in contrast to the law-expert/theologian in verses 25ff.[2] There is a man testing Jesus (25) and seeking to justify himself (29), and here is a woman drinking in Jesus' teaching (39). These two are samples of those Jesus mentions in His praise to the Father in verse 21: the law expert is one of the 'wise and understanding' from whom truth was hidden, while Mary is one of the 'infants' (or little children) to whom it is revealed. And why does Jesus do so? Because the Son 'wants to reveal' the Father to her (v. 22c). It is the Lord's sovereign choice to reveal His word to a woman in a certain village on His way to Jerusalem. It's Jesus' little bit of 'foolishness.' We read about the same thing later in 1 Corinthians 1:26-31.

Jesus' 'folly' appears also in His willingness to teach a woman. Ellis provides a balanced view:

> The extraordinary feature is that the pupil is a woman. Judaism did not forbid women to be instructed in the Torah.... But it was very unusual for a rabbi to lower himself to this.[3]

This assessment reminds me of traveling on a train with my mother when I was about five. A few seats ahead of us was another mother with her son, a bit younger than I. But this woman periodically smoked a cigarette. That seemed strange to me. At that time and in our social orbit, I knew many men who smoked but no women who did so. This lady, then, became for me 'the woman who smoked.' So with teaching women in the first century: not that it never occurred but was markedly rare at the time. Yet the text also implies that Mary made a quiet decision to be taught. Some (e.g., Bock, Fitzmyer) hold that the participle in verse 39 is reflexive; so

2. Why Fitzmyer calls it 'an episode, unrelated to the preceding passages' is beyond me; *The Gospel According to Luke (X-XXIV)*, AB (Garden City, NY: Doubleday, 1985), pp. 891.

3. Ellis, 162. On the position of women during the time of Jesus' ministry, see J. Jeremias, *Jerusalem in the Time of Jesus* (1969; reprint ed., Peabody, MA: Hendrickson, 2016), pp. 373-75. Cf. also A. Oepke, TDNT, 1:781-82.

we can translate, 'having sat herself down beside the Lord's feet, she was listening to his word.' She must have sensed that her attention would be welcomed.

Teaching a woman. That too is a part of the picture of Jesus' 'folly.' Imagine—Jesus does something differently. After a while we get somewhat used to seeing that. But isn't that in itself so *refreshing*? So easy for us to use our expectations as the field for what Jesus may or may not do. And so often He smashes our boring boundaries and confining conceptions about how He should or should not operate. He is just so terribly *interesting*.

Jesus then deals with Martha, and here we see **the Lord's correction** (vv. 40-42a). Martha, Luke tells us, 'was being pulled this way and that over a lot of serving' (v. 40a). She was intent on having a decent dinner. It only takes one casserole to boil over perhaps for her to get hot herself. So 'she came up (to him) and said, "Lord, doesn't it matter to you that my sister has left me to serve alone? So tell her to give me a hand"' (v. 40b). One sort of has to deal with that. Martha is not only exasperated at her sister but, as Schlatter says, she is annoyed at the conduct of Jesus.[4] Why is He dedicating Himself to Mary, absorbing her attention? Can't He see the dither Martha is in? To a large degree, it's Jesus' fault. Jesus is imparting His word to Mary, but Martha gives her word to Jesus!

Now a bit of clarification in all this fuss and fury. Don't get Martha wrong. She didn't think Mary should *never* listen to Jesus' teaching. She didn't think Jesus should *refrain* from teaching in her home. She's no secular humanist. She simply believes there are times when listening to the word of Jesus should take second place to the pressing needs of the moment. The Lord graciously corrects her: 'You are worried and distracted over many things; but (only) one thing is necessary' (vv. 41b-42a). The juxtaposition of words in the Greek text is telling. The last word of verse 41 is *polla* ('many things') and the very first word of verse 42 is *henos* ('one thing'). I don't think Jesus is referring to only one dish being

4. Adolf Schlatter, *Die Evangelien nach Markus und Lukas*, Erlauterungen zum Neuen Testament (Stuttgart: Calwer, 1961), pp. 272-73.

needed for dinner; He's referring to the 'good portion' (42b) Mary has chosen. 'Only one thing is needed, which Mary has: the open ear for his word.'[5] I suppose the big point is that true service for Christ does not consist in what we in our busyness can give Jesus but in receiving what He delights to give us, namely, His word, which we should greedily covet. Earle Ellis has summed it up well:

> Jesus rebukes Martha for diverting Mary from his word to less essential tasks. The issue is not two kinds of Christian service but religious busyness which distracts the Christian—preacher or layman—from the word of Christ upon which all effective service rests.[6]

There's a specific application here for Christian pastors. How often one bumps into that expression in book advertisements or plugs for ministry resources that it is just what the 'busy pastor' needs. It's accessible or brief or dumb-downed or whatever. The 'busy pastor' obviously doesn't have time to ponder or think or read (or listen), because he is, well, a 'busy pastor.' Believe me, I know something of the load a pastor carries. But I repudiate the busy-pastor model. I don't think there should be any busy pastors. Ministerial busyness may fulfill our egos but it empties the soul. Many of us need to join Mary at Jesus' feet if we are to be equipped for our labor (2 Tim. 3:17).

Lastly, in this passage we hear **the Lord's assurance** (v. 42b). As usual, Luke doesn't tell us how the whole dilemma was resolved. How did Martha respond? How did the whole affair play out? No need for that. Rather Jesus has the last word; it is that Mary 'has chosen the good portion, which will not be taken away from her.' What a marvelous assurance of the 'stickability' of Jesus' word. What you receive will remain with you and stand by you.

How often the Lord's servants have found it so. Professor John Murray of Westminster Seminary received word of his father's death and shortly afterward wrote a letter to his own

---

5. Schlatter, p. 273.
6. Ellis, p. 162.

pastor. It was January 1942. Such a grateful if sorrowful letter it was. He notes that his sister had written that their father had been for two days near his death 'in the 51ˢᵗ psalm and repeated it again and again from the beginning to the end in Gaelic,' which was his mother tongue.[7] Jesus' word simply doesn't leave His people but sustains them to the end. I think also of a parishioner (and friend) who had been diagnosed with maladies which clearly meant his years were close to their end. We were able to talk of what assurance he had. I read in my visit that day from John 6, focusing on verse 37. He asked me to write it out for him. I had a blank 'sticky note' inside the flap of my testament and wrote out the whole verse on it. He folded it and put it in his wallet. He was gripped by Jesus' word, and he went into the following months holding Jesus' word—or being held by it—'And the one who comes to me I will never, ever cast out.'

---

7. Iain H. Murray, 'Life of John Murray,' in *Collected Writings of John Murray*, vol. 3 (Edinburgh: Banner of Truth, 1982), p. 82.

27

The School of Prayer
(Luke 11:1-13)

Luke 11 doesn't seem to have a 'tight' connection with what precedes; Luke begins it with his common 'And it happened ....' It's another journey-to-Jerusalem scenario Luke wants us to ponder. I suppose one could see a link with 10:38-42 under a rubric like 'proper devotion' (hearing the word and now prayer), but I tend to think 11:1-13 may have a more direct link with what follows (more on that in the next section). At any rate, the focus is prayer and that is Jesus' 'fault,' because He had been praying and that stirs the desire of His disciples.

It is easy to pass over verses 1-2a as mere background, but I think that would be a mistake, for it's here that we see **the wisdom Jesus shows in addressing our needs.** Jesus' practice of prayer awakens some sense of need in the matter of prayer: 'Lord, teach us to pray, just as John also taught his disciples.' Shouldn't we bless this disciple for making this request? Look what we've gotten from it.[1] How much seems to rest on a simple, incidental request! But note: Jesus didn't simply

---

1. Gallons of ink have been spilled over whether the prayer in Luke or in Matthew (Matt. 6:9-13) is more original or if they both derive from a common source and so on; I don't intend to add my half-pint. It seems to me that the setting in Luke has a very natural and 'original' feel about it. However, it would be near non-sensical to assume Jesus never repeated similar themes or content, so it would be perfectly proper to expect this instruction to appear in an overall kingdom manifesto like that given His disciples in Matthew 5–7.

foist this teaching on them. He didn't say: 'You men need a guide for prayer; here is one you can use.' No, it came about 'naturally.' He waited, we might say, until someone *asked* Him. Isn't this His way still? Doesn't He often allow us to feel and sense our need before He moves to fulfill it? The pattern is as old as Genesis. Yahweh didn't simply dump the famous first female in front of the man and announce, 'Here—you need this.' Rather He put him through a process of assessing animate creation and thereby internally realizing that the whole menagerie had no helper 'corresponding to him.' It was then that Yahweh 'built' the woman (Gen. 2:22) and the man was thrilled. I am not saying that our Lord invariably acts this way but that He often does—because He is wise.

Let us also stop long enough to observe **the privilege Jesus extends in the address of prayer** (v. 2a). 'When you pray, say "Father …."' I remember Dr Walter Liefeld beginning a seminary chapel message on the Lord's prayer by saying, 'Prayer is the expression of a relationship.' And so it is—a relationship that Jesus grants because 'no one knows … who the Father is except the Son—and the one to whom the Son wants to reveal him' (10:22). So this prayer is not for the public but for disciples, those to whom Jesus has made the Father known. They are granted the privilege of calling on God as 'Father.'[2]

This address has a certain *simplicity* about it. I do not need to supercharge my address to God with ornate and overloaded epithets. Then this address implies a certain *adequacy*, for clearly God must be all that a father should be. Hence He is protector and provider, a universe removed from 'father as inept bungler' depicted in American TV sitcoms.

---

2. Jesus' use of 'Abba' likely lies behind this use of 'Father' (cf. Mark 14:36; a use that apparently persisted in the early church, cf. Rom. 8:15; Gal. 4:6). 'Abba' is the Aramaic word for 'father' commonly used within the family circle. One still hears sermons claiming that Abba was a little child's term for its father and is therefore equivalent to 'Daddy.' But it's not. Abba was also what grown-up or adult children called their father—it was simply the family circle term for 'father.' It was also rare to find God addressed as 'Father' in prayer in pre-Christian Judaism. There is some evidence for it (cf. Sirach 23:1, 4; 51:10; Wis. of Sol. 14:3; 3 Macc. 6:4, 8) but the practice was not prevalent or characteristic. In 'Father' Jesus gave new freedom and freshness to our prayer. On these matters, see DJG, 1st ed., pp. 618-19; DJG, 2nd ed., pp. 685-86; also J. A. Fitzmyer, *The Gospel According to Luke (X-XXIV)*, AB (Garden City, NY: Doubleday, 1985), pp. 902-3; Robert H. Stein, *Luke*, NAC (Nashville: Broadman, 1992), p. 324.

Nor is He an abusive tyrant, a scourge endured by many children in our day. But, above all, 'Father' strikes the note of *intimacy*. A disciple should never cease to wonder at this, especially when, as Jesus says, the Father is 'Lord of heaven and earth' (10:21).

William Barclay has nicely captured the sense of intimate relationship here. He writes of an old Roman story of how a Roman emperor came back to Rome in triumph. He was marching his troops through the streets along with a number of prisoners. The streets were lined with cheering people, and legionaries were stationed at streets' edge to keep people in place. At one spot along the route was a platform where the empress and her family were sitting to watch the emperor go by amid all the acclaim. On that platform with his mother was a wee lad, the emperor's youngest son. As the emperor's chariot came near, the little fellow jumped off the platform, wriggled through the crowd, and tried to dart between the legs of a legionary and run out to greet his father's chariot. The soldier stooped down and scooped him up in his arms. 'You can't do that, boy,' he said, and added, 'Don't you know who that is in the chariot? That's the emperor. You can't run out to his chariot.' But the lad laughed in his face. 'He may be your emperor,' was his retort, 'but he's my father.'[3] That is the marvel—and a Christian never quite recovers from it.[4]

Next, consider **the paradigm Jesus gives for the shape of our prayers** (vv. 2-4). Here we find the petitions of the Lord's—or rather, disciples'—prayer. And Jesus instructs us to pray first for *God's preeminence*: 'Let your name be held sacred; let your kingdom come' (v. 2). Ezekiel 36 is essential for understanding this dual petition, especially the first segment. In Ezekiel 36:23 Yahweh speaks of how His name will be held sacred or holy:

3. William Barclay, *The Gospel of Matthew: Volume 1*, Daily Study Bible (Philadelphia: Westminster, 1958), pp. 202-03.

4. Sadly, addressing God as 'Father' seems to have been repudiated in some circles of the western church. It is apparently thought to be a vestige of 'paternalism,' and I suppose the propaganda of militant feminism has played its part. I have been in a setting where addressing God as 'Father' is studiously avoided. Prayers begin, 'Holy One,' or 'Eternal One,' but 'Father' is consigned to the liturgical ash-heap. Jesus has revealed God to us as 'Father,' but some in the church in their arrogance and hubris are saying, 'No thanks; we think we know better.'

And I shall show how holy my great name is, which has been
profaned among the nations, which you have profaned among
them, and the nations shall know that I am Yahweh (says the
Lord Yahweh), when I show how holy I am among you before
their eyes.

In the preceding context Yahweh had said Israel had defiled
their land with bloodshed and idolatry, and so Yahweh had
'scattered' them among the nations (36:17-19). However,
when they turned up as exiles in other lands, those nations
said, 'These are the people of Yahweh, and yet they have
gone out of his land' (36:20). Yahweh had to judge Israel
for her infidelity and yet when He did so, it made for a
'media problem.' It looked like Yahweh must not be able to
protect and defend His people. So the nations would say that
whatever kind of God Yahweh was, He must be a real sub-
god or He would've defended His people from capture and
exile. Yahweh, then, got what one would call an international
black eye. He had to judge His people yet when He did so, it
was a blotch on His reputation. In this way Israel profaned
His name. Yet in this very context Yahweh says He is going
to reverse all this; He will show how holy His great name is,
and will do so by thoroughly restoring Israel. He will give
them a new tenure by restoring them to the land (36:24, 28-30,
33-36), a new purity (36:25, 29), a new disposition (36:26-27)—
and even a new sadness (36:31-32, of genuine loathing over
their sin) and a new privilege (36:37-38). When Yahweh's
restoration scheme comes about the peoples around will be
clearly impressed (cf. 36:34-36) and Yahweh's reputation will
no longer be 'profaned.' He will have shown how holy His
great name is.

I am convinced that is the proper background for the first
petition in this prayer. 'Let your name be held holy.' We are
praying that God's Name-Sanctification Program will take
place and that He will bring about the final restoration of
His people. The petition does not exclude other 'honorings'
of God, but it prays primarily for a 'last thing' thing.

The parallel petition, 'Your kingdom come,' supports this
view. Yes, the kingdom in one sense had already come in the
presence and work of Jesus (cf. Luke 11:20; 17:20-21). But by

asking that God's kingdom 'come,' we are assuming that it is yet to come in its fullness, in all its power and glory—and that is what we especially pray for in this prayer. It's not in prophecy conferences that we salivate over last things, but in our prayers. We need to hear that God's preeminence must be, well, preeminent in our prayer. God's interests come first. This is the antidote our self-absorption needs. Think of the times you might be sitting in a restaurant and in comes a young couple who are dating. They, one presumes, have all sorts of things they want to talk about. But no. They are scarcely seated before the iPhones are out and they are punching around, checking for messages. They may be together, but they're each in his/her own world. To think of someone else seems unthinkable. Jesus teaches otherwise.

Jesus, however, does not use the priority of God's name and kingdom to squash our own needs. He goes on to urge us to pray for *God's provision* (v. 3), *God's pardon* (v. 4a), and *God's protection* (v. 4b). We pray for provision because we are dependent; we pray for pardon because we are guilty; we pray for protection because we are fragile.

Scholars may wrangle over what sort of bread we are praying for. Does *epiousios* (v. 3) mean 'daily' or 'for the coming day' or 'necessary'? We needn't solve the conundrum. I would translate, 'Keep on giving us the bread we need day by day.' Even if we live in a 'sophisticated' society with a well-stocked grocery near-by and have a job so that we can purchase there—who do you think enables the economy to produce the food and who gave you your job to pay for the stuff? As Jesus' disciples we are always totally dependent on our Father. The text in the manna story, 'they gathered it morning by morning' (Exod. 16:21), is still the story of our life.

When Jesus tells us to pray, 'And forgive us our sins' (v. 4a), He knocks on the head any sort of Christian perfectionism. He is assuming that disciples will need forgiveness and need to pray for it. So Jesus implies that the Christian life will be one of continual repentance. When we are to add, 'For we also are forgiving each one indebted to us,' we are not urging such conduct as a meritorious basis for our forgiveness. Instead we are essentially saying that we are sinners but not hypocritical sinners. We do not beg God's forgiveness while ourselves withholding it from others (cf. Matt. 18:21-35). This petition assures us that we will never run out of prayer material, for our sins will supply us with plenty to mourn and pray over. Nor does Jesus want us having inflated views of our own strength. Rather we are to pray, 'Do not bring us into temptation' (v. 4c). I don't think Jesus is referring to any general 'testing' but to 'temptation' to evil or apostasy or failure of faith. Note the parallel in Matthew's account adds, 'But rescue us from the evil one' (Matt. 6:13b). Hence we recognize our weakness and pray that we will not be found in situations where we might deny or fail or turn from our Lord. It's a petition driven by fear, fear both of the assaults of Satan and our own flip-floppiness. Sometimes if you order a book via an internet site, a notice may come up like, 'People who bought the volume you ordered also purchased ...'—and there are two or three other books highlighted for you to consider. So we might say that disciples who pray this petition also sing,

> Prone to wander, Lord, I feel it,
> prone to leave the God I love ....[5]

They are acutely aware of their own weakness and so appeal to their Defender.

What difference, then, should Jesus' 'prayer paradigm' make for us as His disciples? First, it should give us deep assurance in prayer. No one has said it better than John Calvin:

> For he prescribed a form for us in which he set forth as in a table all that he allows us to seek of him, all that is of benefit to us, all that we need ask. From this kindness of his we receive great fruit of consolation: that we know we are requesting nothing absurd, nothing strange or unseemly—in short, nothing unacceptable to him—since we are asking almost in his own words.[6]

What a kindness then! The Lord, as it were, gives us the very words He wants to hear. How can we help but be heard?

---

5. From the third stanza of Robert Robinson's hymn, 'Come, Thou Fount of Every Blessing.'

6. Calvin, *Institutes*, III: XX: 34 (Battles' translation).

Secondly, the prayer leaves us with abiding wonder, for there is a certain tension in the prayer. We are on the one hand sinners needing forgiveness and possibly poor risks for facing temptation and yet ... we are to come to our Father. It's the sort of paradox captured in one of J. S. B. Monsell's (1811–75) hymns:

> Too vile to venture near Thy throne,
> Too poor to turn away,
> Depending on Thy help alone,
> Lord, teach us how to pray.[7]

We must not walk away from Jesus' instruction on prayer without noting **the encouragement Jesus includes for the practice of prayer** (vv. 5-13).

The first segment of this section consists of verses 5-10, and its primary difficulty occurs in verses 5-8 in the scenario Jesus depicts. It's important to realize that verses 5-7 hang together as all one question. Jesus' comment on that situation will follow in verse 8.

There's a wisp of humor in verses 5-7 as Jesus describes a can-you-imagine-this situation. Which one of you, Jesus says, may have a friend and you go to him at midnight (!) and say, 'Friend, lend me three loaves of bread,' for, he says, I'm in a real pickle. A traveling friend of mine has arrived at my place and I don't have a thing to set in front of him. And, Jesus says, imagine that fellow in the house answering his nocturnal friend, 'Stop bothering me! The door's already shut and the children are with me in bed; I can't get up and give anything to you.' Jesus says, Can you imagine that happening? Especially that grouchy response? (v. 7). Jesus' footnote in verse 8 implies, 'Of course not!' He seems to say, 'Well, he might not answer his request because the fellow is a friend, but he will get up and give him as much as he needs because of his *anaideia*.'

There is the rub. What does *anaideia* mean? A prevalent view takes it as 'persistence.' Sometimes one may hear expositors speak of the petitioner hammering on the door and

---

7. In *Christian Hymns* (1977), No. 394.

continuing to holler at his sequestered friend. But the word doesn't mean 'persistence' and there is no hammering or hollering in Jesus' scenario. Others draw on a Middle Eastern background. They take the word as 'a desire to avoid shame.' The idea is that a village would be very concerned about its own honor. The man within would never refuse such an inconvenient friend because he wants to avoid the shame of having his village viewed as inhospitable. But the word does not mean 'a desire to avoid shame' but 'shamelessness,' and the shamelessness belongs to the man making the request.[8]

But if *anaideia* means 'shamelessness,' what do we mean by that here? We must begin by saying that *anaideia* is not a nice word. Klyne Snodgrass has checked out over 250 uses of the word outside the NT—all of them are negative.[9] It refers to outrageous, offensive behavior. Note ESV's 'impudence' here. No shame puts brakes on the behavior of a 'shameless' fellow. So he will go rouse a friend at midnight to borrow bread. His shamelessness appears as rudeness, or nerve, gall, or chutzpah. Jesus then seems to say in verse 8 that friendship is not what moves the man inside but rather the fellow's utterly off-the-charts behavior. I would translate *anaideia* here 'audacity.'

Taking verses 5-8 together they appear to be teaching that having a proper *anaideia* (shamelessness, audacity) means we will bring our most dead-end, embarrassing, insoluble sorts of requests and needs to the Father. No shame or hesitancy holds us back. And to this Jesus adds the encouragement of verses 9-10: So ask, seek, knock—don't be in any way tentative or reluctant to place what seem way-out requests before your Father.[10] Jesus may well intend a how-much-more argument here. That is clearly the case in verses 11-13. It may be so in verses 9-10, drawing a contrast between a crabby friend at

---

8. On this matter, see Alan J. Thompson, *Luke*, EGGNT (Nashville: Broadman & Holman, 2016), pp. 184-85.

9. I don't think one can find a finer, more helpful discussion of this passage than in Snodgrass' *Stories with Intent* (Grand Rapids: Eerdmans, 2008), pp. 437-49.

10. Our 'shamelessness' does not mean we are to be obnoxious but uninhibited in our prayers. Additional note: those who take the 'persistence' view in verse 8 may stress the present tense of the verbs in verse 9 as supporting that view ('Keep on asking,' etc.). However, the stress in the verb forms may not be so much on continuity but actuality—asking, seeking, knocking is precisely what you must do.

midnight and a willing heavenly Father. Can you imagine God saying, 'Oh, don't bother me with that! I've enough of your troubles! Can't you see I need some rest from these piddly types of interruptions over your trivial concerns? No, no, the door is locked, the angels are quiet, and the turmoil in the Middle East isn't totally out of control.'

Do not pass up Jesus' encouragement in verse 10: 'For everyone who asks receives ...,' etc. There's that wonderful little word *pas*, 'everyone.' Jesus does not reserve this assurance to some elite class or super group, not to some bunch of Christian commandos or even 'prayer warriors,' but to each one of His disciples, whether Mac the plumber or George the stockbroker, Heather the successful internist or Sophie the faithful laundry woman. We pray, Jesus tells us, knowing the willingness of God to be 'disturbed.' God the Father really is your Friend at every midnight.

Then Jesus adds another assurance: 'Now who among you as a father shall have (his) son ask for a fish, and instead of a fish, he shall give him a snake? Or again, he will ask for an egg, (and) he will give him a scorpion?' (vv. 11-12). Jesus brings up another of those now-you-know-no-one-would-ever-do-anything-like-this affairs. Jesus means to underscore the consistency and 'trustability' of God. If even sinful fathers, for all their short-sightedness, meanness, and selfishness, can get it right and don't play cruel games with their kids, how much more you can rely on your Father in heaven.[11] The supreme gift we can ask for is the Holy Spirit (v. 13). This is not merely longing for the gift at Pentecost (Acts 2) but seeking increasing measures of Him in their lives—for discernment in perplexity, for power for endurance, for utterance under pressure and persecution (cf. 12:11-12; and Eph. 1:17; 3:16). But the big point is: Your Father will consistently do you good from heaven. And we may have problems believing this.

When I was a boy our family was visiting my grandmother. And my great uncle came back from western Kansas to see us there in southeastern Kansas. He offered me a whole one-

---

11. The way Jesus simply assumes even His disciples' natural, sinful nature is all the more telling in that it comes up merely as an aside: 'If you then being evil ...' (v. 13a). No doubt about how He assesses our nature.

dollar bill (equal, I suppose, to five to ten dollars today). But I refused to take it much as I loved filthy lucre. That's because I didn't trust Uncle Howard. He was a joker. He once gave my father a drink of water; it was in a glass that leaked when one tilted it to drink, and so my dad got a damp shirt out of it. That was Uncle Howard. So, although he was sincere with his dollar (I was later told), I would have no truck with it. Sometimes we have our own 'Uncle Howard' views of God. We have our own Christian superstitions. We hear about someone that prayed for patience and God sent them trials in order to learn it. And we think, 'Yes, God has a tricky way of working.' But Jesus is telling us that God is not devious, that He will not give you the shaft, that you can trust His goodness.

Jesus is telling us that we can rely on God to answer our prayers appropriately. If His child asks for a fish, will God hand him a serpent? If he asks for an egg, will He give him a scorpion and say it was only a 'yoke'? Perhaps we can extend Jesus' teaching here. Would He not also say: And if His son asks for a serpent, He will not give him a serpent. You then can pray securely. Your Father won't double-cross you. He doesn't analyze the grammar and requests in your prayers looking for loopholes in order to play pranks on you. You can come to pray assuming the willingness of God (vv. 5-10) and the trustworthiness of God (vv. 11-13).

28

The Problem with 'This Generation'
(Luke 11:14-54)

Luke may intend for us to see a contrast between verses 1-13 and the huge chunk of text that begins here (vv. 14-54). In verses 1-13 we see those who seek fellowship with the Father in prayer, while in this section we meet Israelites who explain away Jesus' works or push Him for signs (vv. 14-23). The rest of the chapter continues in this vein, for it deals with 'this generation' in its resistance and unbelief. One might say, then, that one meets two 'Israels' here (vv. 1-13 versus vv. 14-54). In this latter section Luke highlights Israel's hard-heartedness and hypocrisy, a theme he will underscore in chapters 13 and 14 as well.

Luke obviously introduces a new scene at verse 14 but is rather informal, almost lackadaisical, about it. He simply begins with 'And' (*kai*) and goes on to tell of Jesus casting out a demon that had made a man mute. Jesus casts out the demon, the man speaks, the crowds are astounded, but some have another 'explanation'—and that leads into **the dispute over Jesus' power** (vv. 14-28).

Some at the scene asserted, 'It's by Beelzebul, the ruler of demons, that he casts out demons' (v. 15).[1] There were

---

1. As a rule I do not touch on the parallel accounts of such incidents in Matthew and/or Mark. In this case, Matthew 12:22-30 and Mark 3:22-27. Such comparisons and debate over them are the proper province of larger commentaries. See, e.g., Darrell L. Bock, *Luke 9:51-24:53*, BECNT (Grand Rapids: Baker, 1996), pp. 1067-71.

still others who kept pressing Him for a 'sign from heaven' (v. 16).[2] Jesus answers their Beelzebul-charge in verses 17-18. Without irreverence perhaps we could colloquialize Jesus' retort, as if He says: 'Yes, sure, that makes so much sense, doesn't it—that Satan would bash his own kingdom and works to bits. Is that something any self-respecting, clear-thinking demon would do? Satan is evil, but he's not a moron.' Their argument, He says, is logically absurd.[3] He then sets out the alternative: 'But if it's by the finger of God that I cast out demons, then the kingdom of God has come upon you' (v. 20), with the implication: and you'll have to deal with that. By 'the finger of God' Jesus means 'only by God's power and nothing else.' Expositors often refer to the use of the phrase in Exodus 8:19 (English text), the account of the third 'plague' against Egypt. Pharaoh's magicians had somehow duplicated the blood and frog plagues (Exod. 7:22; 8:7), but when it came to the gnats or mosquitoes, or whatever they were, in the third plague their power tanked. They had to shrug at Pharaoh and confess, 'This is the finger of God,' i.e., This is purely and utterly supernatural—no other explanation.[4] Hence Jesus claims that He casts out demons solely and clearly by God's power and that means the kingdom of God 'has come upon you' (v. 20). Not that it has 'come near' but has 'come upon,' has 'arrived.' In Jesus' mighty work God's kingdom has already put in its appearance and in Jesus He is already overthrowing Satan's regime on this very Tuesday (or whatever day it was). They must not dodge the evidence of 'the finger of God' by dredging up this nonsense about Beelzebul. Even Egyptian magicians were smarter than that.

However, such discussions in a primarily expository work will only bog us down. For the same reason I have not tried to filter through the relation of verses 37-54 with Matthew 23. On Beelzebul, cf. D. A. Carson, 'Matthew,' EBC, rev. ed., 13 vols. (Grand Rapids: Zondervan, 2010), 9:294.

2. Casting out a mute demon doesn't satisfy such folks; they always have to have more. There is never enough evidence for such people; they are the sort that will even want signs that the signs are really signs.

3. In verse 19 Jesus adds another consideration: apparently there are other Jewish exorcists ('your sons')—are they going to tar them with the same Beelzebul-brush as well?

4. Cf. the remarks of Bruce Wells, 'Exodus,' ZIBBC (OT ed.), 1:195-96.

Jesus gave a snapshot of what is actually occurring in His anti-demon work in verses 21-22. Here is a 'strong man,' armed to the teeth, defending all his turf and while he's doing so his possessions are secure (lit., 'in peace,' v. 21). But what if a 'stronger' man comes and overpowers him, strips him of his armor and deals out the spoils to others (v. 22)? Jesus is the 'stronger man' who is trouncing Satan and his stronghold as He casts out demons. That is what is really happening.

When my oldest brother was a small boy and on vacation with my parents, he was told he was in no way to go near a certain very attractive near-by pond. He came back to the cottage sopping wet and, when asked to explain, said, 'I was standing by the pond, and I said, "Get thee behind me, Satan"—and he pushed me in!' A terribly lame explanation—like attributing Jesus' power to Beelzebul. People who resort to such desperate stratagems are clearly 'against' Him (v. 23).

Here in Luke's account Jesus goes on to make a further point regarding exorcisms (vv. 24-26). Simply because a demon is cast out of a man does not mean he is beyond danger from evil. Jesus depicts a restless, exorcized demon seeking something/someone to inhabit and, finding none, deciding to go back to its original victim, whom (in Jesus' description) the demon calls 'my house.' All is in complete order, but it is a vacuum. Nothing else, no one else has residence there. So the demon solicits a posse of its kind—only 'more evil' than itself—and brings the man under an extreme intensification of demonic bondage. No one, then, dare try to exist in some bland neutrality. A spiritual vacuum unfilled with commitment to Jesus (i.e., being 'with me,' and 'gathering with me,' v. 23) is leaving itself open to utter spiritual ruin. Perhaps one could say there is no one demons prize so much as one of their former 'apostates.'

At this point there is a response. A certain woman in the crowd bursts out with 'How blessed the womb that carried you and the breasts that you sucked!' (v. 27). It was a blessing on Jesus' mother but also on Jesus Himself. This woman's outburst tends to be downplayed by expositors. They go, in my opinion, too quickly to Jesus' response in verse 28 and thereby almost negate the woman's exclamation. But Jesus' words ('Rather how blessed are those hearing the word of

God and keeping it,' v. 28) are not putting down the woman's response but simply adding to it. Jesus is not saying, 'Not that, but this,' but, 'Yes that, but also this.'

Don't allow verse 28, then, to diminish this woman's cry in verse 27. It's a courageous cry—here was one in that crowd unashamed to be pro-Jesus. And, in the larger context, it is a response of faith that stands against the hostility of the 'Beelzebul' contingent (v. 15). In one sense, it must have been music to Jesus' ears. Jesus receives her 'blessing' and adds to it. In this context 'the word of God' (v. 28) equals the claim that Jesus is the 'stronger man' (v. 22), who decimates Satan's kingdom and calls people to be 'with him' (v. 23).

Secondly, verses 29-36 focus on **the sufficiency of Jesus' word**. In verse 29 Jesus answers the sign-seekers of verse 16 with 'This generation is an evil generation—it seeks a sign.' He says no sign will be given except 'the sign of Jonah' (v. 29b). There is some debate about whether the 'sign of Jonah' here in Luke is intended as equivalent to the parallel in Matthew 12:40 ('For just as Jonah was in the belly of the sea monster three days and three nights, so also the Son of Man will be in the heart of the earth three days and three nights'), a text that implies Jesus' resurrection. Whether or not that is the case, note that the stress in Luke is on the communication of truth. Jesus speaks of 'the queen of the south' (see 1 Kings 10:1-13) who will be raised and appear at the last judgment to condemn 'this generation.' She came from way down Yemen-way to hear 'the wisdom of Solomon' (God's truth through him) and, Jesus asserts, 'Something greater than Solomon is here' (v. 31). The 'something greater' is the kingdom of God already arrived and in their face in the work and preaching of Jesus (v. 20). Similarly, the men of Nineveh will condemn 'this generation' at the judgment 'because they repented at the preaching of Jonah, and indeed something greater than Jonah is here' (v. 32). The emphasis is on properly receiving truth, either the wisdom of Solomon, the preaching of Jonah—or the work and word of Jesus. The purpose of the truth brought through Jesus is to give light (v. 33), but the danger can lurk in the 'receiving apparatus' (vv. 34-36). If one's eye is 'single' (*haplous*, healthy), all will be focused and clear; but should the eye be 'evil,' then the whole body is dark and in darkness. One small item controls the whole. In that case, it's not that there isn't light, but that the 'looker' is in such sad shape that he can't see the light. That's the problem with 'this generation'; they see Jesus' work but chalk it up to Beelzebul, and they hear Jesus' word but won't receive it and yammer for spectacular signs. A gentile queen craves the wisdom Solomon imparts, a pagan city believes the threat Jonah proclaims, but the word of someone 'greater' than both is not received by 'this generation' in its darkness.

Once when we had a small Mazda station wagon, the brake light on the dashboard came on. Now I had been reared in a family that had bemoaned the trend among auto-makers of replacing actual gauges with dashboard warning lights. There were stories of such lights coming on when there was nothing amiss, and so such warning lights were dubbed 'idiot lights' in my circles. When my 'brake' light came on, I assumed that it indicated nothing but the malfunction of a dashboard light. What else? How to get it to go off? I reviewed the way the dashboard was installed, thinking I might take it apart, get behind the dash, and disconnect the 'stupid' light. That, obviously, was beyond my competence. So I left it alone. My in-laws came to visit and my father-in-law noticed the 'brake' light shining forth on the dashboard. He flipped up the hood (bonnet), opened the brake fluid reservoir, added a little brake fluid, and the light went off. The problem was not with the auto manufacturer but with my own thick-headedness and perversity. So here, there's plenty of light coming through the revelation in Jesus (v. 33), but if one's eye is 'evil' (v. 34b), he simply won't 'get' it.

Finally, in verses 37-54 Luke highlights **the fury over Jesus' severity**. It begins when a Pharisee invites Jesus for a meal. If Jesus eats with sinners (15:1-2), He also eats with Pharisees. The Pharisee registers surprise at Jesus' failure to conform to traditional ceremonial washing and Jesus launches into an attack on Pharisees and theologians and doesn't let up until verse 52. It was quite a lunch. We're only in the middle of Luke's gospel and already things are getting really nasty. The whole section follows an ordered structure:

Amazement, vv. 37-41
3 woes, vv. 42-44
Objection, v. 45
3 woes, vv. 46-52
Attack, vv. 53-54

It's a fascinating piece of 'improper' etiquette: Jesus goes on the attack against His host!

Back to the beginning. Jesus' host is surprised that Jesus does not go through with the traditional ceremonial washing prior to the meal (lit., 'he was not first baptized,' v. 38). This was not a matter of hygiene but of ritual.[5] Jesus responds (note Luke is careful to call Him 'the Lord'), 'Now you Pharisees cleanse the outside of the cup and of the dish, but your inside is full of greed and wickedness' (v. 39). Jesus left the cup/dish imagery behind in the second part of the verse, referring directly to the Pharisees—'*your* inside' (emphasis mine). Then, in a horrendous breach of good manners, Jesus launches into a series of 'woes' on the Pharisees, condemning their priority-reversing (v. 42), ego-driven (v. 43), defilement-producing (v. 44) religion. They went beyond tithing crops and livestock (cf., e.g., Lev. 27:30-33) and even tithed garden herbs, though it seems even Jewish tradition exempted rue from tithe. If so, Jesus may imply they are so scrupulous about tithing that they make a point about tithing what even their own rulings exempt from the tithe. For all that, they 'pass by' justice and love for God.[6] And Jesus condemned their affections—how they craved status and recognition, loved having their egos stroked whether in synagogue or marketplace (public greeting could be an elaborate affair). And, far from being exemplars of ritual purity, they were

---

5. For background, see David E. Garland, 'Mark,' ZIBBC, 1:245-50, and W. L. Lane, *The Gospel According to Mark*, NICNT (Grand Rapids: Eerdmans, 1974), pp. 245-47.

6. We are prone to 'deify' trivia. Cf. the Metropolitan Nikon's stipulation in the 1600s that believers were to cross themselves, not with two fingers, but rather using the first three fingers of the right hand. And a Russian Orthodox Christian who did not make the sign of the cross this way was a heretic and would be damned; see John D. Woodbridge and Frank A. James III, *Church History: From Pre-Reformation to the Present Day* (Grand Rapids: Zondervan, 2013), pp. 484-85. Or does damnation work in reverse—toward those who decree such absurdities?

actually infecting folks with moral uncleanness. Jesus compares Pharisees to unmarked tombs. Graves were sources of ritual defilement because of the corpses they held. If graves were unmarked, a Jew might come in contact with them and become 'defiled' without being aware of it. So these Pharisees were conduits of contamination to their unsuspecting fellows.

All this is more than one *nomikos* (v. 45) can stand. The term denotes a Torah- or law-expert (remember 10:25), one whom Earle Ellis dubs a 'theologian.' He tells Jesus that in his scathing remarks to the Pharisees he is also insulting the theologians. It's almost as if Jesus shot back, 'Yes, yes, that's right—I intend it to be so.' And He's off again, announcing more 'woes' on these scripture interpreters. He berates (1) the legalism they impose (v. 46); (2) the tradition they sustain (vv. 47-51); and (3) the knowledge they remove (v. 52). Their legalism consists of burdening down folks with 'burdens difficult to carry.' One thinks of the pile of oral tradition that these leaders heaped on God's commandments. Take the fourth commandment. How does one refrain from work on the sabbath? Well, what is work? In the Mishnah (*Shabbath* 7.2) there are thirty-nine kinds of work from sowing, plowing, reaping to making two loops, weaving two threads, separating two threads, tying a knot, or putting out a fire, and lighting a fire. These are burdens that go far beyond what Scripture requires, but, like a government bureaucracy, they never became lighter or less. It was as if the theologians were saying 'Be obedient and be crushed.'

In his second woe, I think Jesus is being semi-ironic: these Jewish leaders are building the tombs of the prophets (47a) which they likely regarded as a tribute to them. But Jesus turns this on its head, for, He says, 'Your fathers killed them,' so you must approve of what your fathers did (48a), 'because *they* killed them, but *you* build their tombs' (48b). That is, you are 'capping off' the work your fathers began, you are completing what they initiated; you maintain the 'killing tradition.' Nor would it be that long before in their own rage they themselves would do the killing (vv. 53-54).

The law-experts were to be skilled interpreters of Scripture leading people to a knowledge of God (v. 52):

'The key of knowledge' is the key that opens the treasures of knowledge; it is the right interpretation of Scripture. The scribes had taken this key away through their erroneous explanations of the OT, making it chiefly a book of rules and hence of work-righteousness, at the same time covering it with numberless additions of their own devising.[7]

So Jesus' third woe accuses the theologians of being roadblocks rather than pathways to the knowledge of God and to entering His kingdom. I think of my Latin II teacher in high school. Aside from his obnoxiousness, we spent little time with Latin grammar or translation, could spend almost whole class periods talking about anything besides Latin, and nothing moved him to enthusiasm over Latin except when he saw the superintendent of schools coming down the hallway. He should have led us along to increasing skill in Latin, in seeing the value of Latin. But there was none of that. His classes were largely a waste of time and he 'took away' any incentive or desire we might have had for Latin. He was 'teaching' Latin and yet 'destroying' Latin. We who are contemporary *nomikoi* in the church must be careful that we do not make Scripture so tedious or dull that people are turned away from the interesting God of which it speaks.

The explosion was not long in coming. Note verses 53-54:

> When he left there the scribes and the Pharisees began to get vicious, to have it in for him, and to goad him to speak about many things, (trying to) ambush him, to trap him in something he might say.

In a word, they were livid. This is the fury that Jesus' severity ignited. How could He talk like this? Is He not 'gentle and lowly in heart' (Matt. 11:29)? Yes, but He is not a wimp. He does not stand by and stroke the egos of men whose hypocrisy is damning themselves and other people. Some times require the blistering tirade not the soothing word, the hard rebuke rather than the subtle suggestion. When Hugh Latimer wrote to Henry VIII that the 'day is at hand when you

7. W. F. Arndt, *The Gospel According to St. Luke* (St. Louis: Concordia, 1956), pp. 310.

shall give account of your office, and of the blood that hath been shed with your sword,' he well knew he could literally lose his head for it.[8] But it needed to be said. And Jesus surely knew what this would cost Him. Verses 53-54 already cast the shadow of the cross.

These Pharisees and Bible interpreters stood in a most enviable position at the end of verse 52. It was the moment of their finest opportunity for repentance. Jesus had stripped them naked; they had but to acknowledge it and walk free.

Additional Note on 11:49-51
I want to focus on what Jesus means by 'this generation' (vv. 50, 51). He refers to the killing of God's servants from the murder of Abel in Genesis 4 to that of Zechariah in 2 Chronicles 24:20-22. Since Chronicles was the last book in the Hebrew canon, Jesus seems to be saying that such opposition and elimination of Yahweh's servants has gone on from the beginning to the end of the biblical record. Rejection of the Lord's servants has been ongoing.[9] When Jesus says that all the prophetic blood shed from the foundation of the world, from Abel to Zechariah, is to be required of 'this generation,' I do not think He is referring only to people who are His current contemporaries. Contextually, it seems that 'this generation' in verse 50 includes both the 'fathers' who killed the prophets and 'you,' the current Jewish leaders, who build their tombs (vv. 47-48). Here then 'this generation' seems like it encompasses people of any number of actual 'generations.' The parallel in Matthew 23:35 (in spite of the textual/historical conundrum) is even more explicit. There Jesus refers, it seems, to the same Zechariah of 2 Chronicles 24 and continues with 'whom you murdered between the temple and the altar.' He's speaking to the Jewish theologs in front of Him but He says 'you' murdered Zechariah. Obviously, they themselves did

---

8. J. H. Merle d'Aubigne, *The Reformation in England*, ed. S. M. Houghton, 2 vols. (Edinburgh: Banner of Truth, 1962), 1:459.

9. Second Chronicles 24:19, right before Zechariah's murder, is very much like verse 49 in our Luke text. Henry Alford calls Luke 11:49 simply an amplification or paraphrase of 2 Chronicles 24:19 (*The Greek Testament*, 4 vols. [reprint ed., Chicago: Moody, 1968], 1:560). So 'the wisdom of God' is essentially what 2 Chronicles 24:19 stated.

not actually do it (since they were born hundreds of years too late). But they are so joined and united with the prophet-hating thugs who kissed up to king Joash that the 800 B.C. murder they committed was one Jesus' current opponents 'joined in' as well. 'Whom you murdered.' 'This generation' (Matt. 23:36; Luke 11:50, 51), then, is lingo that refers to a Yahweh-opposing, word-of-God-rejecting kind of people. 'This generation' is not a time-indicator but a character-indicator. 'This generation' can take in many 'generations' that share the same unbelieving disposition.

Studies of the use of 'this generation' in the synoptic gospels confirm that the phrase has a pejorative sense, describing 'unbelieving, rejecting humanity, unresponsive to God and oblivious to the possibility of facing his judgment,'[10] a Jesus-hating, kingdom-opposing brood of people. 'This generation' alludes to the *type* of people rather than to the *time* of people. All this can prove important when one comes to Luke 21.

10. Neil D. Nelson, Jr., '"This Generation" in Matt 24:34: A Literary Critical Perspective,' *Journal of the Evangelical Theological Society* 38 (1995): pp. 369-85 (quote from p. 383). See also Susan M. Rieske, 'What Is the Meaning of "This Generation" in Matthew 23:36?,' *Bibliotheca Sacra* 165 (April-June 2008): pp. 209-26; and Herman Ridderbos, *The Coming of the Kingdom* (Philadelphia: Presbyterian and Reformed, 1969), pp. 496-502. Cf. also K. E. Guenter, '"This Generation" in the Trilogy of Matthew 24:34-35,' *Bibliotheca Sacra* 175 (April-June 2018): pp. 182-89; though I'm not convinced by Guenter's whole argument, he has a very telling discussion of 'this generation' in the OT.

29

Discipleship: A Fearful Calling
(Luke 12:1-12)

Chapter 12 begins in a hubbub, in a wild mix of the animosity of 11:53-54 and the popularity of 12:1a. Here Jesus switches audience and speaks primarily to His disciples (v. 1b).[1] Actually, as readers we are happy to be in chapter 12, at least initially, because the latter part of chapter 11 was so tense and intense that anything chapter 12 offers will seem like a relief. I think we could say this section deals with the fears of disciples, fear they should have and fear they shouldn't have.

Jesus tells us **we should be alert to a subtle fear** (vv. 1-3)—though, strictly speaking, it is a subtle matter that should produce fear. 'Be on your guard against the leaven of the Pharisees, which is hypocrisy' (v. 1). That might seem a bit difficult since in the first century the Pharisees seemed to be beavers of devotion. Christians today tend to assume that such hypocrisy would be blatant, crass, and obvious. But that assumption is mistaken. Notice Jesus speaks of 'the *leaven* of the Pharisees.' The tricky thing about leaven or yeast is that it works slowly and secretly and silently. You may

---

1. Bock sees discipleship as the primary theme of 12:1-48 (*Luke*, IVP New Testament Commentary [Downers Grove, IL: InterVarsity, 1994], 221); Alan Thompson, taking in 12:1-13:9, notes how predominant 'the constant reference to the final judgment' is in governing present priorities (*Luke*, EGGNT [Nashville: Broadman & Holman, 2016], p. 199).

see the final result of its work but the process is quiet and incremental and not easily detected. It's something like the street encounter between Horace Greeley's wife, Mary (who was rabidly opposed to any killing of animals for any reason) with the writer Margaret Fuller. Greeley touched Fuller's kid gloves and began to scream, 'Skin of a beast, skin of a beast!' Mrs. Greeley, however, was wearing silk and so Fuller began yelling, 'Entrails of a worm, entrails of a worm!'[2] We have little vision for our own hypocrisy unless the Spirit opens our eyes; it is very subtle.

If in verse 1 Jesus implies hypocrisy is subtle, in verses 2-3 He affirms it is *futile*. All the baggage hypocrisy uses— hiddenness, secrecy, darkness, whispering—will be uncovered, exposed, and told on the last day. How useless, then, the shelter of all our devious fig leaves. What an incentive to candor, openness, and—a much-abused political term—transparency.[3] Above all, however, we should ponder long and prayerfully over the subtle peril suggested in Jesus' words, 'the *leaven* of the Pharisees.' It has a way of working unnoticed in us.

Secondly, Jesus tells us that **we should be controlled by a supreme fear** (vv. 4-7). Jesus is still speaking to His disciples (He calls them 'my friends'), telling them not to be afraid of 'those who kill the body' (v. 4a). This is not a theoretical matter; Jesus had just spoken about those who killed the prophets (11:47-48). And the disciples could certainly smell 'killing' in the livid verbal pounding the theologians and Pharisees had dished out to Jesus (11:53-54). One reason not to fear those who kill the body is that they are really so helpless—after killing 'they don't have anything more they can do' (v. 4b). Jesus does not guarantee His servants immunity from being killed; rather, He tells them that the killers have no real 'clout.' Yet Jesus *does* want His disciples to be fearful: 'Fear

---

2. Cited in Marvin Olasky, *Prodigal Press* (Westchester, IL: Crossway, 1988), pp. 46.

3. Luke 12:2-3 are very like Matthew 10:26-27. There the disciples are to proclaim publicly what Jesus teaches them privately. But that does not seem to be the stress here in Luke, where verses 2-3 seem connected to the 'hypocrisy' theme of verse 1. Cf. 1 Corinthians 4:5, when the Lord comes, 'he will bring to light what is hidden in darkness and will expose the motives of men's hearts' (NIV).

the One who after he has killed has authority to throw into hell' (v. 5). God cannot only inflict death but, beyond death, has authority to inflict eternal misery as well. Apparently, Jesus didn't blink when He said that. He underscored His point: 'Yes, I tell you, fear *him* [emphatic]' (v. 5c). And yet disciples will not experience Him in His frightening authority but in His constant care. This God is the One who, when you swing a fine bargain for five sparrows (v. 6) always knows what will happen to sparrow No. 4. Indeed, He's done the math and knows your total hair count (v. 7). Nothing slips by Him. Awesome authority (v. 5) and miniscule care (vv. 6-7)—the perfect combination.

Jesus, then, presses a supreme fear upon us in order to allay all other fears. 'Christ therefore does not simply tell us not to fear, but rather to make sure we fear the things that ought to be feared the most; and fearing them will deliver us from lesser fears.'[4] Or, as the hymn has it:

> Fear him, ye saints, and you will then
> have nothing else to fear:
> make you his service your delight;
> he'll make your wants his care.[5]

Many of Jesus' servants have found His words to be their ballast. Back in the 1920s in the Soviet Union, Cornelius Martens was hauled into the office of the local Communist Party boss, who ordered two lackeys to strip Martens of his clothes. The Baptist preacher said, 'Don't trouble yourself—I shall undress. I don't fear to die, for I shall be going home to the Lord. If He has decided my hour hasn't come, you can't do me any harm here.' This drove the official into a livid rage.[6] Martens had imbibed Jesus' word in verse 4, and nothing maddens Christ-haters more than to be told they are

4. David Gooding, *According to Luke* (1987; reprint ed., Coleraine, N. Ireland: Myrtlefield Trust, 2013), p. 249.

5. 'Through All the Changing Scenes of Life,' based on Psalm 34, *Trinity Hymnal* (1990), No. 624, stanza 6.

6. See James and Marti Hefley, *By Their Blood*, 2nd ed. (Grand Rapids: Baker, 1996), pp. 233-34. The Commie boss aimed his revolver at Martens, tried to shoot three times, but his finger had frozen on the trigger. His body quivered as if he were close to a coronary. He sent Martens away, telling him to never return!

essentially powerless. Once we tremble before the One who has authority to throw into hell the muscle-men of this age appear worse than trivial.

Thirdly, Jesus tells His disciples that **they will have to face a social fear** (vv. 8-12). He speaks of those who may confess Him 'before men' (v. 8) and those who may deny Him 'before men' (v. 9). That 'before men' speaks of social pressure that might suppress confession of Jesus or motivate denial of Him. Then Jesus speaks of disciples being taken on to hostile turf—synagogues, rulers, and authorities (v. 11)—public venues where pressure is brought to neuter their confession of Jesus.

Jesus brings both clarity and comfort to His disciples in this situation. The clarity is in verses 8-9: the one who confesses Jesus before men, the Son of Man will also confess before the angels of God (v. 8); the one who denies Jesus before men shall be denied before the angels of God (v. 9). The 'denial' in verse 9 does not refer to what occurs under a temporary failure of nerve (e.g., Peter's denial) but to a definitive repudiation of Jesus. In this context, it seems equivalent to one who 'blasphemes against the Holy Spirit' (v. 10b).

Notice in verses 8 and 9 that everything revolves around Jesus' 'me'—everything hangs on confessing 'me' or denying 'me.' Jesus assumes that He Himself is that crucial and ultimate. He is presupposing His deity. He does not assert it as such; rather He assumes it, and sometimes that comes across as even more powerful.

But then Jesus also gives encouragement to His 'confessors' who will be dragged into hostile assemblies and courts. They needn't flinch at this pressure nor worry about how they can defend themselves or about what they will say, 'for the Holy Spirit will teach you in that very hour what you must say' (v. 12). Disciples needn't anguish over how they can answer hostile interrogators; the Holy Spirit will give them what they need to say. Jesus does not promise they will be released or acquitted—only provided with the witness they need to bear. And it goes without saying that verse 12 must always be taken with verse 11: it's an emergency ration not a flimsy excuse for would-be Bible expositors to be sloppy and lazy about preparing to teach or preach.

Martyn Lloyd-Jones has passed on a beautiful illustration of this verse-12-provision. He tells of a young girl in the days of the Covenanters in Scotland. She was going to attend a Covenanter communion service one Sunday afternoon, and, of course, such services were strictly prohibited by the 'authorities.' The king's soldiers were looking everywhere for any going to partake in such a service. As the girl turned a corner, perhaps with a gasp, she came face to face with a band of soldiers and she knew she was trapped. Momentarily nonplussed, she found herself answering their questions with: 'My Elder Brother has died and they are going to read His will this afternoon, and He has done something for me and has left something for me, and I want to hear them read the will.' And they allowed her to go on.[7] 'For the Holy Spirit will teach you in that very hour what you must say.'

---

7. D. Martyn Lloyd-Jones, *Spiritual Depression* (Grand Rapids: Eerdmans, 1965), pp. 104-5.

30

Fools, Rich and Poor
(Luke 12:13-34)

Wealth has its privileges. Peter Moore tells of an oil magnate whose will stipulated that he be buried upright behind the steering wheel of his gold-plated Rolls Royce. So large earth-moving equipment scooped out a huge hole. As the crane was lowering this unique coffin into the ground, one of the workers was overheard saying, 'Man, that's really living.'[1] Well, no, it's really dying. But wealth can pull off such shenanigans. Yet not all rich folks do. The prosperous farmer in Jesus' story doesn't go to that extreme; he does, however, engage in a precise calculation regarding the future he assumes he has. That too the wealthy seem to have the luxury of doing. But we're getting way ahead of ourselves. It was a question—or a request or a demand— from one of Jesus' hearers that led Jesus to tell this rich farmer story, so we need to back up and deal with this setting, then the parable itself (one that's a bit unusual in that God speaks in it, v. 20), and the follow-up teaching that flows from it.

First, we look at the setting of the parable in order to sense **the depth of need** Jesus exposes (vv. 13-15). A fellow in the crowd demands that Jesus tell his brother 'to divide the inheritance with me' (v. 13). He may have been a younger

---

1. *Disarming the Secular Gods* (Downers Grove, IL: InterVarsity, 1989), p. 175.

brother and conceivably the oldest son was delaying parceling out the inheritance of a deceased father (cf. Deut. 21:17). He doesn't ask Jesus to mediate the dispute but to take his side. He assumes he is in the right and Jesus should push his case. Jesus refuses—such work is not within the confines of his 'calling' (v. 14). Then in verse 15 Jesus highlights the real peril that can lurk behind concern (even behind what may be a just concern) over an inheritance:[2]

> Watch out and be on guard against every form of covetousness, because one's life does not consist of his possessions—not even when he has an abundance of them.

'Every form of covetousness.' Covetousness comes in many guises. It can even be the driving force behind getting one's inheritance (v. 13). An obvious concern for justice can mask the hidden motivation of greed. Covetousness lies in ambush behind a whole plethora of legitimate concerns. Paul seems to say that once coveting came on his radar, he found coveting popping up all over the place (Rom. 7:7-8).

During World War II both sides built a number of dummy airdromes that sported wooden planes. William Shirer tells of an informant in Holland who in 1940 told him that the Germans had recently completed a very large air installation near Amsterdam and had lined up on it more than a hundred dummy planes made of wood. They waited for the British to come bomb them. That they did. The next morning. They let loose a lot of bombs—bombs made of wood![3] The Brits were simply saying, 'Look, we know what's *really* there.' And that is Jesus' procedure here. He implies that we may dress our circumstances up in terms of justice and equity while covetousness and greed and idolatry are what is 'really there.'

I wonder about that fellow in the crowd (v. 13). He certainly wanted to *use* Jesus; I doubt he expected Jesus to search him. 'There are many people who want Jesus to solve their

---

2. Jesus speaks 'to them' (v. 15a), possibly His disciples (vv. 1, 22) but more likely the 'crowd' of verse 13.

3. William L. Shirer, *Berlin Diary 1934-1941* (New York: Barnes & Noble, 1997), p. 242.

problems but not to change their hearts.'[4] Does Jesus have to refuse us (cf. v. 14)? Does He have to say, 'Oh, *that's* not your *real* problem' (cf. v. 15).

Secondly, we must look at the parable itself to see what **the anatomy of folly** (vv. 16-21) looks like. To avert undue prejudice against Jesus' farmer, please note that all indications are that he came by his (increased) wealth quite honestly (v. 16).[5]

We don't realize this farmer is a fool until he talks— to himself (vv. 17-19). He has a false estimate of *blessing* (vv. 17-18) for he assumes that his primary purpose is only to 'collect' or 'store' new gifts.[6] He has a false estimate of *time*, for he assumes he is fixed for 'many years' (v. 19), whereas God terminates his life on 'this night' (v. 20).[7] He has a false sense of *purpose*, 'take it easy' (v. 19b) instead of being 'rich toward God' (v. 21). He has a false sense of *control*—notice how he says, '*You have* many good things' (v. 19), while God faces him with 'Whose will they be?' (v. 20). James 4:15 ought always to be our sincere mantra: 'Instead you ought to say, "If the Lord wills, we will live and do this or that."' And he had a false sense of *value*: his focus was wholly on 'many good things' (v. 19) with no apparent thought for his soul or life (v. 20).

When God dubs the farmer a 'fool' he does not, of course, mean that he is brainless but godless (cf. Isa. 32:5-6), if

---

4. Warren W. Wiersbe, *Meet Yourself in the Parables* (Wheaton: Victor, 1981), p. 114 (emphasis omitted).

5. Darrell L. Bock, *Luke 9:51–24:53*, BECNT (Grand Rapids: Baker, 1996), p. 1151; Kenneth Bailey points out that the man was already rich (v. 16) before the crop surplus (*Jesus Through Middle Eastern Eyes* [Downers Grove, IL: InterVarsity, 2008], p. 303).

6. Some point to the repeated use of 'I' and 'my' in verses 17-19 as underscoring the farmer's self-centeredness. But Klyne Snodgrass cautions against making too much of this since rhetorically verses 17-19 are a soliloquy and first person pronouns are typical in that case (*Stories with Intent* [Grand Rapids: Eerdmans, 2008], p. 398).

7. William Barclay tells of an old story of three apprentice devils who were coming from hell to earth for their term of service. Before they left they were telling Satan what they proposed to do. One said, 'I will tell them that there is no God.' Satan demurs, citing the fact that in their heart of hearts men know that there is. The second says he will tell folks there is no hell. Satan rejects that as a hopeless scheme since even in the present life people 'have experienced the remorse of hell.' The third said, 'I will tell them *that there is no hurry.*' Satan was satisfied: 'Go ... and you will ruin them by the million' (*And Jesus Said* [Philadelphia: Westminster, 1970], pp. 124-25).

not viciously yet essentially so. He asked the right initial question, 'What shall I do?,' but then went off the rails. The answer is James 5:13: 'Is anyone among you in trouble? Let him pray. Is anyone in good spirits? Let him sing praise.' That's not a pat answer—singing praise is an anti-idolatry serum that orients our minds to the Giver of good. Sadly, like the farmer, we slip into our 'deity outfit,' assume that 'my times are in my hands,' and make security our god.

I'm thinking of a friend of ours who'd been diagnosed with cancer and who had fought it for some time. She was a devoted mother of two teen-aged children, and, as well, an amateur musician, playing the guitar and sometimes writing her own songs. As the specter of cancer kept pressing down on her, she wrote and sang a new song, 'Just One More Christmas, Jesus.' It was really quite well done and a tear-producer. In the song she was asking the Lord to let her live and enjoy one more Christmas with the kids she loved. Carol was no fool. There's a world of difference between 'Just One More Christmas, Jesus' and 'You have many good things laid back for many years.'

Now in the teaching that follows Jesus marks out **the path to freedom** (vv. 22-34). Notice at verse 22 that Jesus speaks 'to his disciples'—what He now says has special relevance to them. But He is not letting the 'rich fool' drop out of sight. Notice His opening line: 'For this reason I tell you ...' (v. 22a). He is assuming that what He is about to say has a basis in and connection with the 'rich fool' teaching. There is a continuity of argument and application in verses 22-34. We might put it this way: Jesus will flesh out what 'rich in relation to God' (v. 21) means in verses 22-34; it means a life of dependent trust on the Father.

Let's approach this segment by looking at Jesus' assumption (v. 22) and then Jesus' arguments (vv. 23ff.). We start with verse 22 and Jesus' assumption: 'For this reason, I tell you, don't go being anxious about your life— what you'll eat, nor about your body—what you'll put on.' As noted, the words 'for this reason' connect what follows with what has preceded. The instruction for the disciples flows out of the story of the rich farmer. There is a *connection*. We might put it like this: Jesus assumes there are two kinds of fool. The one who worries over bigger barns and one who worries over skimpy pantries. One man is preoccupied over the abundance he has, another over the deficiency he fears. In either case, the focus is the same, but a poor man's covetousness may seem less obvious. Yet Jesus had insisted that we beware of 'every form of covetousness' (v. 15), even the poor-man variety. So worry over food and clothing is also saying that life consists in the abundance of one's possessions (v. 15). We don't usually see it that way. It's so easy to see blatant greed and to cut down the 'rich fool' for it. We may even elaborate: 'Why, he probably even commercialized Christmas by stringing Christmas lights around his silos and playing "Silver Bells" over the intercom in his dairy barn.' But Jesus brings us down to earth, as if to say, 'No, this may be *your* problem.' Jesus implies, 'Don't think rank secularism is limited to rich farmers—needy disciples can fall into it as well.'

Then Jesus presses certain arguments against disciples' being consumed with their life-support systems (vv. 23-34). His arguments center chiefly around the matters of value (vv. 23-28) and relationship (vv. 29-32). In the 'value' section Jesus places emphasis on *thinking* (*katanoeō*, to consider, set the mind down on, vv. 24, 27). This is the verb used in Hebrews 3:1, where the writer urges believers to 'consider Jesus.' There's a time to set your mind down on Jesus and a time to think about ravens: 'Consider the ravens' (v. 24a). Ravens (or crows) were technically 'unclean' (Lev. 11:15; Deut. 14:14) and so off-limits for the Israelites' menu. What then is there to consider about the ravens? 'How they do not sow nor harvest; they do not have storage room or barn, yet God [emphatic] feeds them; you are far more valuable than the birds!' (v. 24b). They don't plant or harvest or put up silos (though Jesus is not denying that they do 'work' to find food). Yet God feeds them—Jesus is simply saying what the Bible had said (Job 38:41; Ps. 147:9). When God feeds them it may be with armadillo road-kill. Next time you are driving along and see those shiny dark birds picking at a smashed-up skunk corpse on the asphalt, you should begin singing, 'Great Is Thy Faithfulness.' Set your mind on the crows. If He is the God who feeds dirty birds, won't He take thought for the likes of you?[8]

We are also to 'consider the lilies' (v. 27a). Jesus may be referring to various wild flowers that grace the Galilean countryside in the spring. What are we to consider? Well, 'How they grow! They don't work hard or spin thread. But I say to you, not even Solomon in all his glory was decked out like one of these' (v. 27b).[9] Now 'consider.' Why does God waste His creativity? Placing lavish splendor on such a momentary, fleeting, fragile item? Why invest in such beauty? I suppose, it's because God is not a pragmatist. He sends reams of rain on places where there are no humans to benefit from it—maybe just so that grass will grow (Job 38:25-27). These lilies don't spin thread or make cloth for their décor; God decks them out in all their glory—even if they will soon be collected along with the grass and serve as 'oven starter' for cooking dinner (v. 28).

Jesus says we need to think about dirty birds and delicate flowers. Jesus seems to assume that, with anxiety, a lot of the problem is in our *mind*. We don't *think* enough—or rightly.

Jesus' second major argument centers on relationship (vv. 29-32).[10] 'And you,' Jesus says, 'don't keep seeking what you are to eat and what you are to drink and don't be up in the air (over things)' (v. 29). Don't be so unsettled. And why not? Well, because you should be different—the pagans keep drooling over all these things; you shouldn't have a pagan appetite. Then comes the supreme reason: 'but *your Father* [emphatic] knows that you need them' (v. 30b). Everything rests on having a Father and having such a Father you can rest. Occasionally, my father would repeat a little ditty in one

---

8. Jesus adds a note on the powerlessness of anxiety (vv. 25-26). I take Jesus to be speaking of life-span rather than height. One might crank up one's anxiety to the max but for all that can't tack on a few inches to one's life-span (though perhaps it could *lessen* one's life-span). If anxiety is so useless in such a small matter, why mess with it in other matters? For some helpful notes about what Jesus does *not* mean to imply in his raven allusion, see David Gooding, *According to Luke* (1987; reprint ed., Coleraine, N. Ireland: Myrtlefield Trust, 2013), pp. 254-55.

9. Not that disciples act like lilies. Disciples do work. Jesus, remember, is not forbidding work but the anxiety and worry that pervade it.

10. I am not going to scour out the text of verses 29-34 here but only highlight the keynote.

of his sermons: 'Said the robin to the sparrow, "I should really like to know, why these anxious human beings rush about and worry so." Said the sparrow to the robin, "I think that it must be, that they have no heavenly Father such as cares for you and me."' You are a step up on crows and lilies—and you have a Father who knows all about it.

Can you find yourself in Jesus' parable and teaching? Maybe in the rich farmer, who only thought of bushels per acre? Or maybe among the crowd of disciples needing to think deeply about dirty birds and fragile lilies?

31

Kingdom: Did I Say 'Kingdom'?

(Luke 12:35-53)

Sometimes it is difficult to trace connections in Luke's gospel, or, in this case, in the record of Jesus' teaching Luke gives. I suggest that the 'kingdom of God' is the theme of 12:35-53 and that it follows on fairly smoothly from Jesus' 'kingdom' notes in verses 31-32. There He told His disciples to 'keep seeking' God's kingdom and not to have a pagan fixation on food, drink, and anxiety (vv. 29-30). They would not be bereft, for the Father delights to 'give' them the kingdom (v. 32). Which is why they are freed up to use any earthly resources they have for others (v. 33) and so show that their hearts treasure God's kingdom above all else (v. 34). Then in verses 35 and following the kingdom orientation continues, especially under the notion of expecting the Lord. And so in verses 35-40 Jesus speaks of **the expectancy of the kingdom.**

Jesus wants us prepared. The traditional 'Let your loins be girded' (v. 35) is analogous to our colloquial, 'Hitch up your pants,' 'Cinch up your belt,' or even 'Roll up your sleeves.' He depicts a scene at night—lamps are to be lit and disciples are to be like men who are expecting their master to get home from a wedding celebration. They should be so ready that as soon as he knocks, the door opens (v. 36). It could be a long while before his arrival—like the second or third 'watch' of the night (v. 38). If Jesus assumes the Jewish system of three 'watches' (6-10, 10-2, 2-6), then He implies it could be the wee hours of the morning before they hear His knock. But if He finds them awake and watching (vv. 37a, 38a), 'How blessed those fellows are!' (v. 38b). The long wait did not take the edge off their vigilance.

Jesus startles us as He depicts the master's exuberance on finding wide-awake servants: 'Indeed, I tell you, he will get ready and make them recline at table, and come serve them' (v. 37b). This completely upsets the 'proper' order of things (cf. 17:7-10). What UK citizen, dining out some evening, would expect to hear a somewhat elderly waitress say, 'Hello, my name's Elizabeth, and I'll be taking care of you this evening'? It's too outlandish to contemplate. But Jesus is trying to be outlandish in verse 37—He wants us to sense how delighted He is when His servants are fully focused on His coming. They must expect the unexpected (cf. v. 39).

'Daily Bread' once carried the story of a traveler who came upon a lovely but secluded estate on the shore of a tranquil lake in Switzerland. He knocked at the gate; an aged caretaker invited him in. The caretaker seemed delighted to see another human and eagerly escorted him through the well-tended grounds. The tourist asked, 'How long have you been here?' 'Twenty-four years.' 'How often has your master returned?' 'Four times.' 'When was the last?' 'Oh, about twelve years ago. I am almost always alone—it is very seldom that even a stranger visits me.' The visitor, eager to commend, said, 'Yet, you have the garden in such perfect order, and everything is flourishing as if you were expecting your master tomorrow!' 'No, Sir,' came the correction, 'I have it fixed as if he were coming *today*!' That is the attitude Jesus covets in His disciples.

Secondly, Jesus speaks of **the responsibility in the kingdom** (vv. 41-48). Peter listens carefully and asks whether Jesus meant His parable (vv. 35ff.) 'for us ... or also for all' (v. 41). Now we want to know what Peter meant. Did he mean for 'us in the inner circle of your disciples or for all your disciples,' or, 'for us disciples or for everyone at large'? I lean to the former option. Jesus' answer (v. 42) suggests He is speaking of servants who have special responsibilities for other servants; He implies He is speaking, first of all, especially to Peter and his associates.

Jesus mentions a 'house manager' whom the master has put in charge of the bevy of servants—he is to make sure that the latter receive their 'food allowance' when they need it (v. 42). There are doubtless other duties but this one gets primary attention. The house manager is a slave (*doulos*, v. 43) who has oversight and is responsible for providing for the other slaves who make up the household. Here Jesus depicts a 'faithful, sensible house manager' (v. 42) who fulfills the charge given him. 'How blessed that slave,' Jesus exclaims, 'who his master finds doing just that when he comes!' (v. 43). Such faithfulness can expect a 'promotion' (v. 44).

But then Jesus raises another option. What if that slave lets the delegated authority go to his head, tells himself that his master will not show up for a long time, abuses and beats both male and female servants, and simply parties and lives like a drunken sop? What then? The Lord will come when that rogue does not expect, hack him in two, and assign him a place with the unfaithful (v. 46). If the severance-language bothers you, you might mollify yourself by saying it's only a parable. But if so, he also ends up with the 'unfaithful'—which is precisely where he belongs because by attitude and behavior he has shown he is no servant of his master. If you wonder why he meets such severe treatment, verse 47 supplies the answer. He knew his master's will and refused to do it. That knowledge makes him all the more culpable, as opposed to someone who did not have his advantages (v. 48).

I think the 'ministers of the word' in the early church would have found Jesus' picture of the faithful house manager rather encouraging. There is a certain *simplicity* about it. He is to give other slaves their 'food allotment.' Then Jesus declares a blessing on that slave who is 'doing just that' when his master returns. That is, he is simply doing what Jesus called him to do. And it may hearten contemporary preachers and teachers. Here, for example, is a man who has been pastor of a church of perhaps one hundred members. It's in a small town where there are opportunities for personal evangelism but no likelihood of exploding church growth. He's been laboring there for eleven years now, diligently studying the word and giving his people their 'food allotment' every Lord's Day. His picture never appears on a brochure for a popular Bible conference; he'll never be an adjunct professor at the nearest seminary; he'll never be able to pursue an advanced degree beyond his basic seminary or theological college training; he'll never be a speaker on one of those cruises sponsored by a fine evangelical organization for their premier contributors. No, he simply gives his people their needed 'food allotment.' And Jesus seems delightfully satisfied with that.

Finally, in verses 49-53 Jesus underscores **the conflict of the kingdom.** He first speaks of 'fire' (v. 49) and then of 'baptism' (v. 50), both terms emphatic in the Greek text. The former is part of Jesus' 'mission statement': 'I have come to throw fire upon the earth.' It is something that Jesus does. The latter statement about baptism is something that happens to Jesus. I think 'fire' here (v. 49) likely symbolizes divine judgment (as it often does; see, e.g., Jer. 43:12; Hosea 8:14; Amos 1:4-2:5; Nahum 3:13), or at least some form of severity that Jesus will impose. The baptism Jesus is 'to be baptized with' is His death. In Mark 10:38 Jesus pairs His 'baptism' with drinking a 'cup.' The 'cup' in well-known OT use is the cup of Yahweh's wrath that sinful nations must drink (Isa. 51:17, 22-23; Jer. 25:15-29). So in His coming death Jesus will drink the 'cup' of God's wrath on human sin and, in a similar way, His 'baptism' refers to being inundated and overwhelmed by the catastrophe of God's judgment.[1] And Jesus feels a holy impatience about both the 'fire' and His 'baptism.' Of the fire He says, 'How I wish it were already set ablaze!' (v. 49b).[2] Of His 'baptism,' 'And what pressure I am under until it is accomplished' (v. 50b).

Jesus goes on to speak about *division* in verse 51: 'Do you suppose that I have come to give peace on the earth? No, I tell you, but rather division.' I suggest this verse interprets the 'fire' of verse 49; the 'fire' alludes to the severe discord Jesus brings.[3] And verses 52-53 depict what that discord will look

---

1. Cf. G. R. Beasley-Murray, *Baptism in the New Testament* (Grand Rapids: Eerdmans, 1962), pp. 72-76; Darrell L. Bock, *Luke 9:51-24:53*, BECNT (Grand Rapids: Baker, 1996), pp. 1193-94.

2. The text is difficult here; this is a common rendering.

3. NIDNTTE, 4:194. Cf. J. C. Ryle, *Expository Thoughts on the Gospels: St. Luke*, 2 vols. (New York: Baker & Taylor, 1858), 2:99. The two statements with their 'upon the earth' seem parallel. I have always thought verse 51 would make a splendid preaching text on the Sunday closest to Christmas!

like. It will invade and disturb the intimate confines of the family circle. Jesus may be taking this picture from Micah 7:6. There the prophet describes the danger the remnant believer in Judah (ca. 700 B.C.) was going to face; he dare not trust his closest friends or even his spouse; danger and opposition will arise from those in his own family circle.[4] That is the sort of conflict the disciples will face when they hold allegiance to Jesus. Holding on to Jesus will separate you from others— and not simply from any others, but from the others who matter most to you (v. 53). Love for Jesus may mean you will lose the love of those you love most. Coming to Jesus may be only the beginning of your problems.

And yet this kingdom conflict is not so surprising but perhaps almost expected. Agatha Christie has a fascinating note in her autobiography. She writes of life during the Second World War and says that after years of war, war-life (if one could call it that) didn't seem exceptional but almost normal. It was, she said, natural to expect that you might soon be killed, that loved ones might well be killed; you would hear of friends who had been casualties. Broken windows, bombs, rockets and so on were not extraordinary but a nearly natural part of life. Indeed, after three years of war, one couldn't exactly project a time when there would not be a war anymore.[5] I doubt she exaggerated. She was simply saying that these are the conditions you expect when there is war going on. So with Jesus' kingdom. It will willy-nilly involve conflict. Jesus brings division. You must then regard it as 'natural' if your friends reject you and your own kin stiff-arm you and detest you. If you turn to Jesus, others may turn away from you. Jesus may not bring you peace but trouble.

---

4. For discussion of the text in its context, see my *Study Commentary on Micah* (Darlington: Evangelical Press, 2010), pp. 140-49.

5. See Agatha Christie, *An Autobiography* (New York: Bantam, 1977), p. 475.

32

Seeing, and Not Perceiving

(Luke 12:54–13:21)

There's a turn in the narrative at 12:54. 'Now he said also to the crowds' (v. 54a). The 'also' tells us what follows is connected to what Jesus had already said in chapter 12, but 'to the crowds' clues us that the disciples (12:1, 22) are no longer His primary target. Hence I posit a new segment begins here. In fact, one could construe 12:54–14:24 as a major segment on 'the kingdom of God and the Jewish people.' One could even push back the beginning of that segment to 11:14, for chapter 11 deals largely with the unbelief of 'this generation.' We are, then, in the middle of almost four chapters that deal largely with the unbelief and resistance of the Jews to Jesus and His teaching. In our present section you may wonder what adverse weather and court cases and Pilate's brutality and fig trees and a doubled-up woman and a pile of bread dough have in common. It all centers on the unbelief and danger of Israel, a people Yahweh once described to Isaiah as seeing and yet not seeing (Isa. 6:9).

Here Jesus confronts the crowds with **the urgency they need to feel** (12:54-13:9). And first there is the urgency of *discernment* (12:54-59). Israel is not assessing things properly. Oh, if it's a matter of weather conditions, they do quite well. If they see a cloud rising to the west, they say, 'Rainstorm's coming'—and that's what happens (v. 54). Or when the south wind kicks up, someone says, 'It'll be a scorcher'—and so it is (v. 55). 'Hypocrites,' Jesus calls them (v. 56)—they can assess indicators in earth and sky, but how is it they do not know how to assess 'this time,' i.e., the presence of the very kingdom of God in Jesus and His work? Why don't they get it? Why don't you, Jesus says, figure out, 'judge,' discern, on your own what is right (v. 57)? He sketches a situation: you are on your way with an opponent to a magistrate; you must jump at that opportunity to cut a deal and settle out of court; otherwise, he may drag you before the judge, who will hand you over to the bailiff in charge of debts and debtors' prison— and that's where you'll end up (vv. 58-59). Sometimes we can squeeze Jesus' parables or analogies so hard we make them bleed. I doubt Jesus is wanting us to ask, at least here, whether the fellow will ever get out of debtors' prison nor who the 'opponent' may represent. He wants his hearers to catch the 'no brainer' element, to see the sheer urgency of those moments before the parties arrive at court, in short, to discern the window of opportunity. Jesus is, of course, speaking to the 'crowds' (v. 54), to Israel and Israelites, but when He 'applies' verses 57-58, He speaks to individual Israelites ('I say to you,' singular, v. 59a),[1] urging them, we might say, to step out of 'this generation' (see Luke 11) while there is time, to repent and acknowledge Jesus for who His words and works proclaim Him to be.

Next, the comments of some of the crowd lead Jesus to speak of the urgency of *repentance* (13:1-5). On that very occasion some spoke up and told Jesus of 'the Galileans whose blood Pilate had mixed with their sacrifices' (v. 1). This atrocity likely occurred at some Passover time. Although we have no outside collaboration of the event, it would not be out of character for what we know of Pilate.[2]

---

1. Alfred Plummer, *A Critical and Exegetical Commentary on the Gospel According to St. Luke*, ICC (New York: Charles Scribner's Sons, 1902), p. 336.

2. On Pontius Pilate, see D. H. Wheaton, NBD, 3rd ed., 929-30; also DJG, 2nd ed., 679-80. On the basis of verse 1, J. C. Ryle observes *how much more ready people are to talk of the deaths of others than their own*. He adds: 'It is the same in the present day. A murder,—a sudden death,—a shipwreck, or a railway accident, will completely occupy the minds of a neighborhood, and be in the mouth of every one you meet. And yet these very persons dislike talking of their own deaths, and their own prospects in the world beyond the grave' (*Expository Thoughts on the Gospels: St. Luke*, 2 vols. [New York: Baker & Taylor, 1858], 2:108).

Why would they bring up this moral atrocity? We might think from Jesus' response in verse 2 that they were raising a 'problem of evil' conundrum. But verse 2 may simply be Jesus' way of high-jacking their concern in order to turn it round to the point *He* wants to make. I don't think we can be sure, but there is likely much to be said for Kenneth Bailey's view. His point is that in the Middle East reports like this are intended to stir an outburst of indignation and rage in the hearers and to elicit a denunciation of the perpetrators, as if to say, 'Now what do you think of *that?*' It may well be, then, that they told of Pilate's bloody work so that Jesus would exclaim, 'He did *what?*'[3]

Whatever the case, Jesus didn't take the bait; He moves in another direction, to a different consideration: 'Do you think that these Galileans were worse sinners than all Galileans because they have suffered these things?' (v. 2). Note the import of Jesus' retort; He implies that *human tragedy is no index of immense human sinfulness*. Note He doesn't say that the sufferers were sinless or innocent; only that disaster is no gauge of the degree of sinfulness. But then He adds to the case-load of His hearers with an anecdote of His own: 'Or those eighteen on whom the tower in Siloam fell and killed them ...' (v. 4). Was that an indication they were more guilty than the rest of Jerusalem's residents?[4] Jesus inserts a 'jab' in each case (vv. 3, 5): 'No, I tell you, but unless you repent you will all perish as well.' In short, *earthly disasters are eternal caution lights*. The 'perishing' Jesus notes is not some future Roman devastation in A.D. 70 but the kind He spoke of in 12:4-5.[5] We may get our juices up over human injustice or

---

3. Kenneth E. Bailey, *Poet & Peasant* and *Through Peasant Eyes*, combined ed. (Grand Rapids: Eerdmans, 1983), pp. 75-77.

4. The instances cited in verses 1 and 4 carry an unspoken assumption: how prevalent tragedies are in the course of human life (in a fallen world). How often we must speak of the sheer sadness of human life. A husband and father receives a diagnosis of pancreatic cancer and is dead within two months. A family is driving home one night from a sporting event, hit by a drunk driver, and three of them killed instantly. A much-loved wife, mother, and grandmother in only late middle age contracts Lou Gehrig's disease (ALS) and dies within weeks. A terrorist blows himself up in a shopping venue and takes fifteen other lives. One can rail about the 'unfairness' of it all, but we should at least acknowledge how good and honest the Bible is—it has told us life will be this way.

5. Cf. Bock, *Luke 9:51-24:53*, BECNT (Grand Rapids: Baker, 1996), pp. 1206-7.

over the problem of suffering and our most horrible examples of it, but it's small stuff when you put it beside 'perishing.'

'Unless you repent,' Jesus had said. But now, in a parable (vv. 6-9), Jesus goes on to say the time for repentance may be fleeting. He presses home the urgency of *opportunity:*

> Then he added this parable: 'A certain fellow had a fig tree (that was) planted in his vineyard, and he came seeking fruit from it and did not find any. And he said to the vineyard worker, "Look, for three years I've been coming seeking fruit from this fig tree and I don't find any; so whack it down. Why should it also use up the ground?"' (13:6-7).

It goes almost without saying that this was a mature fig tree, one from which the owner could expect fruit—it was not subject to the limitations of Leviticus 19:23-25. He was ready to whack it down. But his hired man asked for a stay in the execution. He would dig round it and fertilize it with manure and maybe it'd be different next year. If not, the axe is ready.

The fig tree represents Israel, and the point is that opportunity for Israel is fading quickly—they are on 'extended time.' Luke lets us see just how seemingly hopeless Israel is, for there are thirty-eight sections in Luke 9:51–19:28 and in twenty-two of them Jesus faces rejection or resistance or hostility of Jewish people to Him. The covenant people need to repent. The trouble is not Galileans' blood nor falling towers but their own blindness to their own need—and the time for repentance is running out.

There's an urgency that should drive Israel. Sometimes, however, urgency loses a bit of its urgency. In 1864 Confederate general Robert E. Lee directed his crusty subordinate, Jubal Early, to take his 15,000 men and make a lightning strike on the northern capital, on Washington. Early couldn't hope to occupy the city, but he could strike strategic targets and scare the liver and politics out of the place. But as Early and his troops came to Frederick, Maryland, on their dash to Washington, Early decided to demand a ransom for not burning that city. He demanded $200,000; city leaders said it'd take them forty-eight hours to raise it; Early gave them half that. He got his gold but the day's delay gave General

Grant time to hustle adequate reserves into Washington and Early's surprise turned into a tepid threat and return. All because he did not keep urgency urgent. Nor is Israel the only audience who needs to hear this call. Perhaps something similar could be said to the residents of my own land: Do you think that those who died in the 9/11 attacks were greater sinners than all Americans? Unless you repent you will all perish as well.

Secondly, by His Sabbath work Jesus shows His opponents **the freedom they ought to celebrate** (13:10-17). Now when you read verse 10 ('Now he was teaching in one of the synagogues on the Sabbath') you may be tempted to think that Luke has merely tacked on another incident about Jesus' miraculous work. But that is not it at all. There is nothing helter-skelter about the arrangement. He means to provide in the synagogue ruler (v. 14) a living color example of Israel's inability to discern 'this time' (12:54-59) and Exhibit A of the fruitlessness of Israel (13:6-9). So time and precise location may be omitted but the episode is thematically connected with what precedes, the denseness and opposition of Israel. There is a new setting but the same theme.

Look at what we find in 'church.' 'And there was a woman having for eighteen years a malady brought on by a spirit, and she was bent over double and not able to straighten up at all' (v. 11). Jesus says in verse 16 that Satan had 'bound' her. Her condition is a bit of a mystery but, drawing simply on verse 11, Ellis seems right that her condition was 'a purely physical effect caused by demonic power and not "demon possession" of the personality.'[6] There's mystery in that too, but it seems to properly construe the text. How pitiful and miserable she was. And—though myriad voices may tell us not to 'moralize'—we shouldn't miss the fact that for all her wretchedness she had 'shuffled her way to the synagogue to hear the word of God.'[7] She had a tremendous problem—and she was in public worship. She 'says' a lot merely by the fact that she was *there*.

---

6. E. Earle Ellis, *The Gospel of Luke*, NCB, rev. ed. (London: Oliphants, 1974), p. 186.

7. David Goodling, *According to Luke* (1987; reprint ed., Coleraine, N. Ireland: Myrtlefield Trust, 2013), p. 266.

'Jesus saw her' (v. 12a). Simple words yet they are vintage Jesus. He always seems to have an eye for individual need. And notice that His gift to her comes on His own initiative—there is no mention of any faith on her part or of any appeal that she makes. Jesus calls her over, describes His gift in terms of freedom ('Woman, you are freed from your malady,' v. 12b), placed His hands on her 'and immediately she was made straight and began to glorify God' (v. 13). This freedom is obviously very physical (cf. Rom. 8:23) but also very spiritual, for it is over a spirit (v. 11), over Satan (v. 16; cf. Eph. 1:20b-21).

Jesus' deed drives the local synagogue ruler through the roof. Such a healing was 'work'; work is forbidden on the Sabbath; and so, as the voice of orthodoxy, he makes his announcement: schedule your healings on other days so you don't desecrate the Sabbath (v. 14). This woman, he held, did not need to be healed that day; she may be bent over like a human pretzel but her case could've been put off a day or two. But Jesus calls him down. Actually, Luke says 'the Lord answered him' (v. 15a), perhaps intending 'Lord' to pack a virile note of authority. Jesus not only answers the synagogue ruler but others of the same ilk: He uses the plural, 'Hypocrites!' Jesus continues His rebuke and argument:

> Doesn't each of you on the Sabbath free his ox or his donkey from the feeding trough and lead (it) off to drink? And must not this woman, daughter of Abraham that she is, whom Satan has bound, why, for eighteen years—must she not be freed from this bondage on the Sabbath day? (vv. 15-16).

These men made a merciful exception for livestock on the Sabbath—they had to have water. They believed in animal rights but didn't mind imposing the minutiae of misery on humans, like this woman. Jesus, as it were, stacks up His case even as He describes her. He stresses her *humanity* ('this woman,' who, unlike your ox or donkey, has dragged herself to synagogue), her *privilege* ('daughter of Abraham that she is,' belonging to God's covenant people), her *tragedy* ('whom Satan has bound'), and her *misery* ('why, for eighteen years'—think of the tedium and despair of that). Then Jesus declares what we could almost call His verdict: 'Must she not be freed from this bondage on the Sabbath day?' Note: Jesus is not arguing from propriety but from necessity; He is not saying, 'It is fitting,' but, 'It is necessary.' She 'must' —it is a divine imperative. Jesus' 'must' trumps the synagogue ruler's 'must' in verse 14 ('six days in which one must work'). It was God's will that this woman be set free from her bondage on the Sabbath day, the day of freedom.[8] This passage indicates that there was, to a significant degree, something wrong in first-century Judaism. If this was what covenant religion had come to be, it wasn't working right. It reminds me of a report our church secretary once passed on to me. One summer on a lake about an hour east of Bakersfield, California, some folks who were novices at boating were having problems. No matter what they did, they couldn't get their new 22-foot boat going. It was sluggish in every maneuver, no matter how much power they applied. After an hour of frustration, they floated into a nearby marina to get help. A topside check revealed everything working perfectly. Engine ran fine, outboard drive went up and down, propeller was correct size and pitch. So one of the marina employees jumped into the water to check underneath. He came up choking on water because he was laughing so hard. Under the boat, still strapped securely in place, was the trailer! That seems to have been the case with the first-century synagogue. Covenant religion was not functioning as it should because it was tied down in scores of legalistic minutiae. But our text gives us a freedom to celebrate—Jesus not only gives liberty from Satan's power but also from unbiblical religious oppression.

Finally, Jesus speaks of **the secrecy they need to understand** (vv. 18-21). Do not miss the connecting words in verse 18a: 'He said *therefore*.'[9] Jesus intends a link between

---

8. The idea of 'setting free' appears in our passage in verses 12 (*apoluō*, 'to set free'), v. 15 (*luō*, 'to loose, free') and v. 16 (also *luō*, in the passive). We should also bear in mind the broad OT background of the Sabbath as the *day of freedom*. When the Israelites were slaves in Egypt, they never had a Sabbath. Slaves don't get Sabbaths. Only after Yahweh sets them free from bondage do they get to enjoy Sabbaths. Sabbaths are the privilege of a free people and so a sense of freedom should always mark them.

9. The NIV obscures the logical connection by translating 'Then Jesus asked ....' But without the 'therefore' (*oun*) translated as such the English reader can miss the

the parables in verses 18-21 and the healing and uproar in the synagogue in verses 11-17. The implication is that the synagogue episode had something to do with the 'kingdom of God.' If the parables in 18-21 highlight the initial obscurity and hiddenness of the kingdom of God, then we could take 10-17 as being an illustration of that. But we're getting ahead of things.

We've the mustard seed and leaven parables here, and we must get at the main point of them. There is no explicit stress on the smallness of the mustard seed in Luke's account (vv. 18-19), but then that was proverbial, taken for granted. The stress is not on growth but contrast, not on some developmental process but on the end result of such a minute beginning. The mustard plant would usually achieve seven or eight feet in height, or even twelve.[10] An obscure beginning but a significant final product. Then there is that woman and her leaven (vv. 20-21). The leaven is a hunk of sourdough left over from a previous baking. But three measures of flour! This woman is into serious bread! That's something like a bushel of flour. 'That's 128 cups! That's sixteen five-pound bags! And when you get done putting in the forty-two or so cups of water you need to make it come together, you've got a little over 101 pounds of dough on your hands.'[11] Perhaps she was stirring up a community batch. In any case, she slips that sourdough into the dough and, quietly and secretly, it works through the whole batch. What is comparatively meagre produces such a pervasive result.

What connection, then, do these parables (vv. 18-21) have with that synagogue service (vv. 10-17)? They make you stop and think. Because you might look on verses 10-17 in an entirely wrong way. You might say, 'That's all very nice, and I'm glad that woman was restored, but it really doesn't amount to much; it's only a synagogue service in the provincial backwater of the Roman empire, so will anybody really give a

---

logical link. This seems to be vintage NIV. It is a very readable and, on the whole, commendable translation, but it has an aggravating tendency to obscure or omit textual connections.

10. Cf. William Barclay, *And Jesus Said* (Philadelphia: Westminster, 1970), p. 52.

11. Robert Farrar Capon, *The Parables of the Kingdom* (Grand Rapids: Eerdmans, 1985), pp. 118.

rip about it?' But remember 18c—'He said *therefore* ....' There is a connection. The parables explain the synagogue miracle and the synagogue miracle is a picture of what the parables teach. In short, Jesus so much as says: When you see the kingdom of God in your midst (= vv. 10-17), it never seems to amount to much (= vv. 18-21)—it always seems like mustard seed and leaven-level stuff; but don't miss the presence of the kingdom in the small stuff. So then we ought to respond something like this:

> God of mustard seed and leaven,
> give us eyes to see and faith to enjoy
> the rather mundane evidence
> that Jesus already reigns.

33

From Curiosity to Anguish
(Luke 13:22-35)

Our passage begins and ends with Jerusalem. Luke reminds us that Jerusalem is the object of Jesus' journey (v. 22) but shows us it is also the subject of Jesus' lament (vv. 34-35; cf. 33b).[1]

First, we notice **the shock Jesus gives about the kingdom of God** (vv. 22-30). It all begins with someone's question, 'Lord, are the saved going to be few?' (v. 23).[2] Jesus refuses to allow this to be a matter of curiosity but makes it a matter of urgency. Note that He does not merely answer the individual question but 'them' (v. 23b), i.e., others in the crowd who heard the inquiry. So the following imperative verb is also plural: 'Make every effort to enter through the narrow door ...' (v. 24a). There *is* a door, there is opportunity, but there is also

---

1. Some hold that our passage is the very center of a 'chiastic' structure of 9:51-19:48. See Kenneth E. Bailey, *Poet & Peasant* and *Through Peasant Eyes*, combined ed. (Grand Rapids: Eerdmans, 1983), pp. 79-85. I don't find the argument convincing; some of the material does not easily fit or seems to require some gerrymandering to make it do so. In our present passage, note how Jesus' teaching includes a sobering word (vv. 22-30), a settling word (vv. 31-33), and a sad word (vv. 34-35).

2. This matter was a lively issue in Judaism. The Mishnah, citing Isaiah 60:21, held that 'all Israelites have a share in the world to come'—although it goes on to cite a significant number of exceptions (*Sanhedrin*, 10.1-3; Danby's edition, pp. 397-98). On the other hand, in 4 Ezra 8:1-3 (ca. A.D. 100) 'Ezra' is told that 'the Most High made this world for the sake of many, but the world to come for the sake of few .... Many have been created, but few will be saved' (see J. H. Charlesworth, ed., *The Old Testament Pseudepigrapha*, 1:542).

urgency, for the door is narrow—and there will be 'many' (cf. the contrast with the 'few' in the original question) who will seek to enter and won't be able. Matters about salvation, about entering the kingdom of God can never be academic with Jesus. He will not allow you to deal with them as fodder for interesting theological discussions.

Jesus then intensifies His warning by oozing into a semi-parable meant to teach that *salvation is more than familiarity with Jesus* (vv. 25-28). He tells of the master of a house having shut the door and his hearers as among those begging entrance. The master of the house asserts, 'I do not know you—where you are from' (v. 25b; cf. v. 27a). They so much as say, 'Sure, you do,' or in the words of the text, 'We ate and drank in your presence, and you taught in our streets' (v. 26). Don't you remember—we shared meals with you and we were in the audience when you came through our town teaching.

Their words assume they have an 'in' with Jesus, a certain claim on Him. During the American 'Civil War,' journalists and newspapers criticized President Lincoln because his oldest son, Robert, was safely studying at Harvard rather than serving with the other less favored masses in the military. Lincoln felt the sting of such criticism though he also had to deal with the hysteria of his wife—the Lincolns had already lost two young sons in death and Mrs. Lincoln was frantic over Robert's dying in combat. So Lincoln wrote to General Grant, asking if Robert (without embarrassment to Grant) might serve in some way on Grant's headquarters' staff. Robert then entered the army in February 1865 as a captain in Grant's entourage and served in a non-combat role.[3] Lincoln could engineer this because he had an 'in' with Grant. Although he wasn't pushy in the matter, he still had a claim on Grant, for he had adamantly supported Grant in previous months when critics had demanded Grant's dismissal over alleged alcohol abuse. And so Robert Lincoln held a privileged place. But Jesus denies that His contemporaries have an 'in' with Him or any claim on Him because they had shared meals with Him or listened to His sermons. That does not give them 'leverage.' Familiarity with Jesus is not the same

---

3. Webb Garrison, *A Treasury of Civil War Tales* (Nashville: Rutledge Hill, 1988), pp. 220-23.

as having a place in the kingdom of God. This should have been a scary word for Jesus' Jewish hearers—and also for multitudes of church members in our own day.

Jesus goes on to underscore the theme of *reversal* (vv. 28-30). He pictures a division within Israel. He depicts the anguish of His hearers when they see Abraham, Isaac, Jacob and all the prophets in the kingdom of God, 'but you yourselves being thrown out' (v. 28). Yet there will be a 'full house' for kingdom festivities, for 'they will come' from the four compass points to take their place at the kingdom table (v. 29). This is an allusion to the inclusion of gentile believers in the kingdom (cf., e.g., Isa. 2:2-3; 25:6-8; 49:1, 6, 12; 66:19-20). Who would ever think (except for folks who read the OT carefully) that such unwashed masses would be hobnobbing with patriarchs and prophets? Hence, Jesus concludes, 'There are last ones who will be first and there are first ones who will be last' (v. 30). Jesus does not intend verse 30 as an iron-clad, all encompassing rule; He rather implies it will be a general pattern or trend. There are gentiles ('last ones') who will have a place at the kingdom table, and there are Israelites ('first ones') who will not. We could say, then, that the answer to the question in verse 23 is: Fewer than one would expect, more than one would imagine. All this simply reinforces Jesus' original plea to His present audience: 'Make every effort to enter through the narrow door' (v. 24a). There is a door, but it is narrow, and the time is limited (cf. v. 25a).

Secondly, our passage stresses **the freedom Jesus has in the plan of God** (vv. 31-33). I don't think one can be sure of whether the Pharisees who warn Jesus to 'get out' (v. 31) are friendly (so Stein) or hostile (so Arndt). Not all Pharisees were malicious. However, we needn't determine Pharisaic disposition in order to see the main thrust of this segment.

Jesus gives them a reply to take back to Herod Antipas. Jesus calls him a fox, which can connote being sly or clever but also being insignificant and of little account.[4] Jesus' word for Herod is: 'Look, I cast out demons and perform healings today and tomorrow and on the third day I reach my goal' (v. 32). By the 'third day' I think Jesus is alluding—as is usual in Luke's

---

4. W. L. Liefeld and D. W. Pao, 'Luke,' EBC, rev. ed., 13 vols. (Grand Rapids: Zondervan, 2007), 10:239.

gospel (9:22; 18:33; 24:7, 46)—to the day of His resurrection. Not that Herod would grasp that, but Jesus' disciples would—later. It's as if Jesus is saying He is going about His work right now and nothing—not even Herod—is going to stop that nor His reaching His triumphant goal in His resurrection. Then in verse 33 Jesus gives a more 'general' statement with not so grand a conclusion: 'But I must go on today and tomorrow and the next day, because it is not possible for a prophet to perish outside of Jerusalem.' If nothing will hinder His ministry and triumph (v. 32), it will not hinder His ministry and suffering either (v. 33). It is God's plan and decree that it will be this way, that Jesus will go on in His works and into His suffering, and there is no scheme of Herod, real or concocted, that can change that. Can you sense the liberty Jesus feels as He stands within the unfailing sovereign plan of God? Of course, Jesus' words here relate to His own ministry, suffering, and resurrection, but there is some overflow as well for Jesus' people. Think of the settledness Jesus' perspective must have given Him. 'My times are in your hand' (Ps. 31:15a). And until the time God has determined for my life to end, I go my way 'today and tomorrow' with what He has given me to do. As George Whitefield said, 'We are immortal till our work is done.'[5] Yes, Yahweh's book contains 'the days that were formed for me' (Ps. 139:16) and, until they come to an end, I can go on today and tomorrow in peace.

With the mention of Jerusalem in verse 33 Jesus erupts in a lament over the city in verses 34-35:

> Jerusalem, Jerusalem,
> who kills the prophets
>   and stones those sent to her,
> how often I wanted to gather your children
>   like a bird (gathers) her brood under her wings
> —and you were not willing.
> See! Your house is (left) abandoned to you.
> I tell you, you will never see me until you say,
>   'Blessed is the One who comes in the name of the Lord.'

---

5. Arnold A. Dallimore, *George Whitefield*, 2 vols. (Westchester, IL: Crossway, 1979), 2:285.

Here, then, is **the anguish Jesus shows over the city of God** (vv. 34-35).

'Jerusalem' here is the bastion of unbelief and represents Israel in her ongoing rejection of God's corrective revelation. We should pay special attention to 'How often I wanted to gather your children.' I do not think the scope of this statement can be limited merely to the earthly ministry of Jesus. I think it rather clearly hints of His pre-existence and of His repeated efforts throughout Israel's mostly apostasizing history to recall them to Himself.[6] All this met with Israel's stubborn recalcitrance. Hence, He says, 'Your house is abandoned' — judgment is now on its way.

His final word, doom that it is, yet contains a hint of hope: 'You will never see me again, until you say, "Blessed is the One who comes in the name of the Lord."' Israel's hope is never finally extinguished. The 'Blessed' quote comes from Psalm 118:26. There are various 'voices' who speak in Psalm 118. One speaks in the first person, 'I' (vv. 5-7, 10-14, 17-19, 21). He is evidently the king in distress, yet Yahweh helps him and so he either has—or will—cut off 'all nations' who surround him. Yahweh has brought him through his desperate trial victoriously, and he approaches the temple gate in the wake of his victory. There other 'voices' speak, welcoming him ('Blessed is he who comes in the name of Yahweh,' v. 26a) and those who accompany him ('we bless you [plural] from the house of Yahweh,' v. 26b). The words of Psalm 118:26a cited in verse 35 express the ecstatic welcome that Israel (or, in the psalm, her representatives) gives her victorious, conquering king. Jesus implies that the day will yet come when Jerusalem will make this right response to Him.

That may be then, but it is not now. Now is the time of Jesus' lament and anguish. There is something, if I may use tautology, so Christ-like about Jesus' lament. He is, after all, speaking judgment (v. 35a), and yet He does so with such distress and anguish of soul. Surely that is how it should be done. Once when Andrew Bonar and Robert Murray M'Cheyne were conversing, M'Cheyne asked Bonar what his

6. So Calvin on Matthew 23:37. Cf. also Dale Bruner: 'What prophet would say this of himself? Jesus speaks here as if he were God looking back over Israel's long apostate history' (*Matthew: A Commentary*, 2 vols. [Dallas: Word, 1990], 2:833).

text had been on the previous Lord's Day. Bonar said, '"The wicked shall be turned into hell"' (Ps. 9:17a, AV/KJV). Bonar said that on 'hearing this awful text,' M'Cheyne asked, 'Were you able to preach it *with tenderness?*'[7] So here we see Jesus in all His perfection, for He doesn't shy from speaking judgment but does so with tears and, Yahweh-like, has no pleasure in the death of the wicked (Ezek. 18:23). Can you want to rebuff a Savior like this?

---

7. Andrew Bonar, *Robert Murray M'Cheyne* (1844; reprint ed., London: Banner of Truth, 1962), 53. In this regard, cf. the words of George Whitefield: 'You blame me for weeping, but how can I help it when you will not weep for yourselves, though your immortal souls are on the verge of destruction, and for aught you know, you are hearing your last sermon, and may never more have an opportunity to have Christ offered to you' (see Dallimore, *George Whitefield*, 2:483).

Subject Index

Page numbers with the suffix 'n' (e.g. 34n) refer to information found only in the footnotes. Abbreviations from page 7 and 8 have been used.

Scripture Index

Christian Focus Publications

Our mission statement —

STAYING FAITHFUL

In dependence upon God we seek to impact the world through literature faithful to His infallible Word, the Bible. Our aim is to ensure that the Lord Jesus Christ is presented as the only hope to obtain forgiveness of sin, live a useful life and look forward to heaven with Him.

Our books are published in four imprints:

CHRISTIAN
FOCUS

Popular works including biographies, commentaries, basic doctrine and Christian living.

CHRISTIAN
HERITAGE

Books representing some of the best material from the rich heritage of the church.

MENTOR

CF4•K

Books written at a level suitable for Bible College and seminary students, pastors, and other serious readers. The imprint includes commentaries, doctrinal studies, examination of current issues and church history.

Children's books for quality Bible teaching and for all age groups: Sunday school curriculum, puzzle and activity books; personal and family devotional titles, biographies and inspirational stories — because you are never too young to know Jesus!

Christian Focus Publications Ltd,
Geanies House, Fearn, Ross-shire,
IV20 1TW, Scotland, United Kingdom.
www.christianfocus.com
blog.christianfocus.com